Understanding the Web:

**Social,
Political,
and
Economic
Dimensions
of the
Internet**

Understanding the Web:

Edited by

Alan B. Albarran
Southern
Methodist University

David H. Goff
University of
Southern Mississippi

**Social,
Political,
and
Economic
Dimensions
of the
Internet**

Iowa State Press
A Blackwell Publishing Company

Alan B. Albarran is Associate Dean and Professor of Electronic Media and Film in the Meadows School of the Arts, Southern Methodist University, Dallas, Texas. Dr. Albarran's research focuses on the management and economics of the communication industries. He is the author of three other books and numerous scholarly articles. He also serves as the editor of the *Journal of Media Economics*.

David H. Goff is a Professor of Radio, Television, and Film in the School of Communication at the University of Southern Mississippi, Hattiesburg. Dr. Goff's research interests include the convergence of telecommunications technologies and industries, media economics, and the Internet as a medium, particularly in the United States and Western Europe.

Iowa State Press
A Blackwell Publishing Company
2121 State Avenue, Ames, Iowa 50014

Orders: 1-800-862-6657
Office: 1-515-292-0140
Fax: 1-515-292-3348
Web site: www.iowastatepress.com

♾ Printed on acid-free paper in the United States of America

First edition, 2000
First paperback edition, 2003

The Library of Congress has cataloged the hardcover edition of this book as follows:

Understanding the Wed: social, political, and economic dimensions of the Internet / edited by Alan B. Albarran, David H. Goff — 1st ed.
    p.cm.
  Includes index.
  ISBN 0-8138-2527-X
    1. World Wide Web—Social Aspects. 2. Internet (Computer network)—Social aspects. 3. Information society. I. Albarran, Alan B. II. Goff, David H.

HM851.U53 2000
303.48′33—dc21
                                                                                    99-087114

The last digit is the print number: 9 8 7 6 5 4 3 2 1

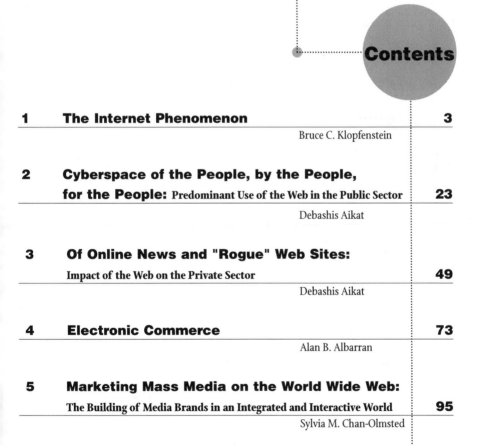

Contents

Contributing 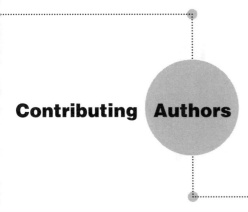 Authors

Debashis "Deb" Aikat (Ph.D., Ohio University) is an assistant professor and media futurist in the School of Journalism and Mass Communication at the University of North Carolina at Chapel Hill, USA. An expert on people, products and perspectives that are shaping the digital revolution, Aikat is an award-winning teacher and researcher on the impact of communication technologies, social aspects of new media, interactive media, and other futuristic aspects of mass communication.

Alan B. Albarran (Ph.D., The Ohio State University) is co-editor of *Understanding the Web*. Albarran's research focuses on the management and economics of the communication industries. He is the author of three other books and numerous scholarly articles in the *Journal of Broadcasting & Electronic Media*, the *Journal of Media Economics, Mass Communication & Society, Convergence,* and the *Southwestern Mass Communication Journal*. Albarran also serves as the editor of *The Journal of Media Economics*.

Sylvia M. Chan-Olmsted (Ph.D., Michigan State University). Sylvia conducts research in the areas of media economics, telecommunication management and marketing, strategic competition, and brand management. She has published articles in the *Journal of Broadcasting & Electronic Media*, *Journal of Radio Studies*, *Journal of Media Planning*, and the *Journal of Media Economics*. She is co-editor of the book *Global Media Economics* (Ames: Iowa State University Press, 1998).

David H. Goff (Ph.D., The University of Massachusetts) is co-editor of *Understanding the Web*. David is a Professor of Radio, Television, and Film in the School of Communication at the University of Southern Mississippi. His scholarly interests are focused on the social, economic, and policy dimensions of the convergence of media technologies and industries in the United States and in Western Europe.

Bruce C. Klopfenstein (Ph.D., The Ohio State University, 1985) is professor of telecommunications at Bowling Green State University where his teaching and research interests focus on new media technologies. He is currently co-principal investigator for a $1.8 million U.S. Department of Education project to develop a web-based system to introduce innovative teaching practices. Klopfenstein is co-author of *The Whole Internet: Academic Edition* (O' Reilly, 1996), is co-editor of *Cyberpath to Development: Issues and Challenges in South Asia* (Greenwood Press, c. 2000), and has published articles related to new technologies in the *Journal of Broadcasting and Electronic Media, Convergence: The Journal of Research into New Media Technologies*, the *Journal of Media Economics*, and the *Journal of the American Society for Information Science*. The most recent book chapters appear in *Handbook of Communications Technologies: The Next Decade* (CRC Press, 2000).

Laurie Thomas Lee (Ph.D., Michigan State University, 1993) is an Assistant Professor in the Department of Broadcasting, College of Journalism and Mass Communication, at the University of Nebraska-Lincoln. Her primary research interests include the law and economics of new technologies such as the Internet, cable and telephony, with a specialization in privacy law. She has published in such journals as *The Information Society: An International Journal, Journal of Broadcasting & Electronic Media, The Journal of Media Economics, The New Jersey Journal of Communication, John Marshall Law Review, California Western Law Review*, and *Telematics and Informatics*.

Under a grant from the National Association of Broadcasters, Lee has also authored a report titled Internet Users and Content Providers: Predictors of Success for Broadcast Stations.

John V. Pavlik (Ph.D., Mass Communication, University of Minnesota, 1983) is Executive Director of The Center for New Media, The Graduate School of Journalism, Columbia University, where he is also a Professor. Pavlik's primary research interests include the impact of new media on journalism and society. He has published widely on this topic, including articles in *New Media & Society, Media Ethics, Television Quarterly*, the *Media Studies Journal*, the *Columbia Journalism Review*, and *Nieman Reports*. He is the author of *New Media Technology: Cultural and Commercial Perspectives* (Needham Heights, MA: Allyn & Bacon, Second Edition, 1998). Pavlik is also co-editor (with Frederick Williams) of *The People's Right to Know: Media, Democracy and the Information Highway* (Mahwah, NJ: Lawrence Erlbaum Associates, 1994) and (with Everette E. Dennis) *Media Technology: A Freedom Forum Center Reader* (Mountain View, CA: Mayfield Publishing, 1993).

Steven S. Ross (M.S., Columbia University) is Associate Professor of Professional Practice at Columbia University's Graduate School of Journalism where he specializes in new media and computer-assisted reporting. Since 1994, Ross has, with the aid of Don Middleberg, been conducting the nation's largest surveys of journalists' use of on line services including (but not limited to) the World Wide Web. Latest results can be seen at *[http://www.mediasource.com]*. His published work includes books on multimedia, the Internet, statistics, data exchange, product safety, and toxic substances. His software models of magazine and newspaper economics are considered industry standards. In February 1998 he was listed among the nation's top 50 names to know in new media, by *Online Journalism Review*.

Ardyth Broadrick Sohn (Ph.D., Southern Illinois University) has research interests in media management and media ethics. She has published in several journals including *Journalism & Mass Communication Quarterly, Newspaper Research Journal, Journalism Educator*, and *Social Science Journal*. Books include Sohn, Wicks, Lacy, and Sylvie, *Media Management: A Case Book Approach* (Mahwah, NJ: Lawrence Erlbaum Associates, 1999); Sohn and Giles, *Readings in Media Management* (Columbia, SC: AEJMC Publications, 1992); and Sohn, Ogan and Polich, *Newspaper Leadership* (Englewood Cliffs, NJ: Prentice-Hall, 1986).

Barry Vacker (Ph.D., The University of Texas at Austin). Vacker's research interests include aesthetics, technology, and cultural theory, about which he recently completed a book entitled *Chaos at the Edge of Utopia*. He has also published articles in *Psychology & Marketing* (special edition on the pursuit of beauty) and the *International Journal of Advertising*.

Rita Kirk Whillock (Ph.D., University of Missouri) writes about political communication. She is the author of *Political Empiricism: Communication Strategies in State and Local Elections* and the co-editor of two books, *Hate Speech* (Thousand Oaks, CA: Sage, 1995) and *Soundbite Culture: The Death of Discourse in a Wired World* (Thousand Oaks, CA: Sage, 1999). Her articles have appeared in journals such as *Political Communication, Presidential Studies Quarterly*, and the *World Communication Journal*.

Preface

The planning for this book began at the Dynasty Chinese restaurant in New York City. We were attending the 1997 Faculty–Industry Seminar sponsored by the International Radio and Television Society, and after a day of panels and sessions examining the role of the Internet in media industries, four of us ventured out of the hotel for dinner.

Over a meal that happened to coincide with the beginning of the Chinese New Year, our group began to talk about the Internet and how we were using the latest communication technology in our classrooms and research. Needless to say, we were all fascinated with the Internet, and we discussed how the Web was changing everything. Dave Goff is credited for saying the prophetic words "we should do a book on the Internet!"

None of these ideas made their way to a napkin (the restaurant used cloth napkins and probably would not have appreciated us writing on them), but we did continue to discuss the topic via e-mails for the next few months. We both agreed that there already existed plenty of books on the Internet, especially in the "how to do a web page" area. We wanted to produce a book that critically and systematically examined the Web and its impact on our lives.

Taking a macroscopic perspective, we concluded that three broad dimensions deserved discussion: social, political, and economic. On the social side, it was obvious that the Web was impacting human interaction and culture in multiple ways. In terms of politics, the Web had proven to be an important tool in both the 1996 and 1997 election years and was increasingly employed in promoting issues and political perspectives. Regarding the economic dimension, it was clear that Internet commerce offered incredible potential and would change the ways in which businesses traded with each other and people shopped for goods and services.

But where were these changes taking place and whom did they impact? That question led us to expand our approach and examine the topic of the Internet at four distinct levels: the individual, group, nation/state, and global levels. By adopting this framework as a guide, we could be assured of approaching the subject in a detailed, systematic manner, using both macro and micro perspectives. The next step was to identify individual authors whose areas of expertise would complement our own efforts.

The process of finding contributors took several more months, but by the spring of 1998 we had a proposal for this book ready to submit to publishers. Largely because of Alan's relationship with Iowa State University Press, we gave Acquisitions Editor Judi Brown the first look at the proposal. Judi was intrigued by the topic, and quickly commissioned reviews (which were very favorable toward publication). A contract soon emerged, and you hold the finished product in your hands.

Alan B. Albarran
David H. Goff

Acknowledgments

We are grateful to Acquisitions Editor Judi Brown, Managing Editor Janet Hronek, and the rest of the staff at Iowa State University Press for their support and assistance in the publication of this work. Likewise, we appreciate the comments of the anonymous reviewers who provided helpful comments on the proposal for the book.

We especially appreciate each of the contributors for their hard work, their efforts to meet deadlines, their response to constructive criticism, and their belief in the value of this collaborative volume. We thank each of them for their work.

We are eternally grateful to our families for their support, love, and especially their patience with us through the preparation of this book.

Introduction

Understanding the Web: Social, Political, and Economic Dimensions of the Internet is designed for two audiences. First, we see this book as a text for use in college and university classrooms where courses related to information technology and its impact and effects on society are taught. While the book springs from the perspective of academicians engaged in the study of communication, the selected topics cut across a number of different fields and should offer something of value to readers from a variety of disciplines.

Second, we believe that this book presents a broad-based analysis of the Internet. From that standpoint, we feel the book will be of interest to individuals who want to better understand how the Web affects different aspects of our daily lives. We trust that other researchers studying the Internet will also find this book to be a useful reference source, and we anticipate many libraries will acquire this book as part of their holdings.

The book is organized in the following manner. The first three chapters provide an orientation to the Internet. In Chapter 1, Bruce Klopfenstein provides an overview of the Internet phenomenon from a historical/diffusion perspective. As a scholar who has studied new communication technologies and written on the Internet, Klopfenstein brings a unique perspective in the opening chapter of the book.

Chapters 2 and 3, written by Debashis Aikat, deal with the uses of the Internet in the public and private sectors, respectively. Chapter 2 examines the predominant uses of the World Wide Web (WWW) by individuals, the educational community, and governments. Chapter 3 takes a similar approach in considering how businesses and other organizations utilize the Internet.

The next set of three chapters covers significant commercial applications of the Internet. In Chapter 4, Alan Albarran examines the role of electronic commerce by focusing on emerging models of electronic commerce, barriers to electronic commerce growth and development, and impact on business and economics. In Chapter 5, Sylvia Chan-Olmsted assesses the marketing significance of the Internet and outlines strategic uses of the Internet for media firms paying particular attention to the role of the Web in brand management. Chapter 6, by John Pavlik and Steven Ross, examines the impact of the Internet on newsgathering and other journalistic processes and considers issues of journalistic ethics.

The next five chapters provide coverage of broad-based social, political, and economic dimensions of the Internet phenomenon. In Chapter 7, Laurie Thomas Lee addresses the issues of Internet privacy, online security, and the protection of intellectual property. Rita Whillock, in Chapter 8, examines the effects of the Internet on the political process. A political communications expert and consultant to political candidates, Whillock argues the Web has further devalued and isolated the individual voter. In Chapter 9, Ardyth Sohn presents the issues associated with Internet content, particularly problematic content. Sohn discusses the difficulties of protecting the interests of some while maintaining access to objectionable but legal forms of content assured by the First Amendment. Chapter 10, by Barry Vacker, examines the impact of the Web on culture by drawing parallels to the significance of the printing press and the television industry. Vacker takes a philosophical look at the topic and draws a number of fascinating conclusions. David Goff, in Chapter 11, looks at the social, political, and economic issues associated with the ongoing development of the infrastructure of the global network of networks that comprises the Internet.

Chapter 12, by co-editors David Goff and Alan Albarran, provides an assessment of the state of our understanding of the social, political, and economic significance of the Internet.

Understanding the Web:

**Social,
Political,
and
Economic
Dimensions
of the
Internet**

Connecting

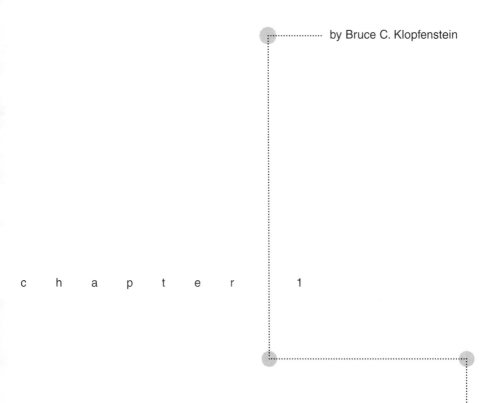

by Bruce C. Klopfenstein

c   h   a   p   t   e   r   1

The Internet Phenomenon

Introduction

Electronic media of communication are by definition products of technology. Recent generations have seen the introduction of at least one new medium since the emergence of the telephone in the last century. Motion pictures arrived early in the century and were followed by radio broadcasting in the 1920s, television in the 1950s, and satellite-delivered cable television in the 1980s. Whether these new media reflected a revolution in communication is still the subject of debate. The telephone replaced the telegraph. The motion picture had its roots in both photography and live theater. Radio took talent from vaudeville. Television promoted radio stars. Cable television borrowed previously existing content from television and movie studios. The impacts of each of these unique communication media on society are, of course, substantial.

From the perspective of the world in the 1960s and 1970s, a futuristic nirvana of a world in which various communication functions would be available via wired technologies was envisioned. This vision was realized in the 1970s and 1980s as millions of dollars were invested in commercial electronic text services. As students of media technology are well aware, these broadcast teletext and online videotex services were generally tremendous failures. A market for text- and graphics-based communication systems could not be dictated using a top-down approach.

Meanwhile, computer networks were established in the 1960s to allow researchers (especially those in the defense department and their academic colleagues in the civilian world) to share precious computing capabilities. Messaging systems were added without fanfare, and scientists began to send "electronic mail" to one another via the mainframe messaging utilities. From these humble, noncommercial beginnings emerged the closest thing our generation has seen to a media revolution: the Internet and the World Wide Web (Krol and Klopfenstein, 1996).

As of this writing, approximately 80 million Americans had been on the Internet at some point (Ziff-Davis, 1998). The number of Internet users globally in 1998 easily may have exceeded 100 million (Woods, 1998). More than one-fourth of American adults had an e-mail address by the start of 1998. In fact, a major commercial research report indicated that more than half of all Americans and Canadians between the ages of 16 and 34 were Internet users as of mid-1998 (Bridis, 1998). One authoritative source estimated that users totaled over 150 million in 1999 (How Many Online?, 1999). Other estimates take the U.S. user population, add 30-35 percent to it, and use that as an estimate of the number of global users. The emphasis of this chapter is on the Internet and web phenomenon in the United States, where a recent survey suggested as many as 84 percent of global Internet users reside. The Internet's rapid spread around the world is the exception, not the rule, in communication technology diffusion (Klopfenstein, 1997).

The purpose of this chapter is to review the Internet phenomenon as it has emerged at the end of the century. The subject is a fluid one, and it is not possible to predict with great accuracy one path by which this communication medium will proceed into the future. The author is an expert on the history of media technologies in general and the Internet in particular (Krol and Klopfenstein, 1996). It is hoped this chapter will serve as a starting point, especially for those who have only experienced the Internet phenomenon in recent years.

Brief History of the Internet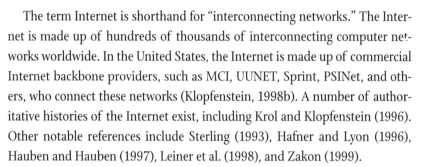

The term Internet is shorthand for "interconnecting networks." The Internet is made up of hundreds of thousands of interconnecting computer networks worldwide. In the United States, the Internet is made up of commercial Internet backbone providers, such as MCI, UUNET, Sprint, PSINet, and others, who connect these networks (Klopfenstein, 1998b). A number of authoritative histories of the Internet exist, including Krol and Klopfenstein (1996). Other notable references include Sterling (1993), Hafner and Lyon (1996), Hauben and Hauben (1997), Leiner et al. (1998), and Zakon (1999).

The Internet was born of a need to develop a reliable communication network that was literally able to withstand a nuclear attack (Krol and Klopfenstein, 1996). The process for its development is not unlike that of the Apollo space program with the Advanced Research Projects Agency (ARPA) taking the role of NASA (ARPA was renamed Defense Advanced Research Projects Agency, or DARPA, in 1972). The global Internet's progenitor was the Advanced Research Projects Agency Network (ARPANET), created to enable widely dispersed teams of engineers working on the same government projects to share their information and computing resources. This same goal would describe the creation of the World Wide Web two decades later. The first ARPANET e-mail message was sent in 1972, and Usenet was established in 1979. E-mail took on an unanticipated life of its own as researchers quickly adapted it for applications beyond professional collaboration.

Unlike standard corporate computer networks, the rapidly growing, decentralized ARPANET could accommodate many different kinds of machines. As long as individual machines could speak the language of the new network, their brand names, their content, their ownership, and their location were irrelevant. With the introduction of the Transmission Control Protocol/Internet Protocol (TCP/IP) in 1983, the Internet was in operation. It would remain in the domain of commercial, government, and university researchers until the invention of the Web. The ARPANET evolved into a series of regional sub-networks at college campuses, research organizations, and government agencies, all linked up to a backbone network run by the National Science Foundation (NSF). IBM funded BITNET in the 1980s, but it was displaced by the eventually more popular Internet and shut down on January 1, 1997.

The coalescence around one network standard made connecting more computers an attractive task. Researchers such as those at the European Laboratory for Particle Physics (CERN) knew that text-based e-mail over the Internet was one thing, but sharing scientific documents over computer networks was another. By 1990, Tim Berners-Lee (Brody, 1998) developed a hypertext system, first envisioned by Vannevar Bush (1945), that allowed for linking documents in multiple windows. The system for sharing documents over a network (e.g., the Internet) was publicly demonstrated in 1991, and Berners-Lee named the system the World Wide Web (Cailliau, 1995). The National Center for Supercomputing Applications (NCSA) at the University of Illinois released their "browser" called Mosaic in early 1993, with Macintosh and Windows versions introduced shortly thereafter. The original goal of creating the World Wide Web (WWW) to allow sharing of documents regardless of original format set the stage for the Web to evolve into the multimedia file delivery and display system that we know today (Klopfenstein, 1997). The WWW uses the Internet to transmit web documents from server (web site) to client (end user). As seen in Figure 1.1, the introduction of the Web had a dramatic impact on Internet growth as defined by the number of linked computer hosts. A summary of key events in the history of the Web as authored by web pioneer Robert Cailliau appears as Table 1.1.

Early web sites included many scientific sites, some of which were of interest to the average person. In 1993, for example, a server with pictures from a dinosaur exhibition in Honolulu became a showcase for the WWW (Cailliau, 1995). College students quickly learned about the Web and installed the workstation browser software that was made available freely on the Internet. Usenet discussion groups were filled with enthusiastic postings about the new medium (Hauben and Hauben, 1997). The growth of Internet hosts is displayed in Figure 1.1 and reflects the impact of the WWW from 1993 to 1999 (although not all Internet hosts are web hosts). Note that the method for counting hosts was corrected in 1998 to reflect previously hidden servers [see Network Wizards (1999) for a complete explanation].

Figure 1.1.   Internet host growth, 1993–1999.

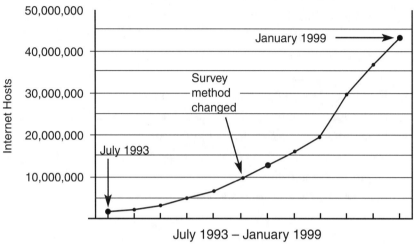

Source: Network Wizards (1999).

Table 1.1.   Milestones of web history.

1995	*San Jose Mercury News* tells readers how to write a web page.
1994	The Internet becomes a household word, largely due to the ease-of-use of Mosaic:
	Commercial sites start appearing on the Internet
	Discussion of Internet commerce becomes common
	Web browsers are available for almost all computer platforms
	CommerceNet founded
	W30 founded—CERN gives up the WWW to MIT
	Netscape Navigator released
	White House Web
1993	Marc Andreessen and Eric Bina at NCSA write Mosaic in three months.
1992	Physicists from around the world start running web servers. Only line-oriented text versions are available.
1991	The WWW library of Common code is worked on with portability in mind.
1990	The first version is made available on the NeXTStep OS. It's called the World Wide Web.
1989	Tim Berners-Lee and Robert Cailliau at CERN start work on a project to link hypertext in the High-Energy Physics department.

Source: Adapted from Cailliau (1995).

Media historians will note that the Web was responsible for the dramatic change from text-based, online information to graphics-oriented content. Also worth noting historically is that in the consumer marketplace, primitive video-tex systems other than France's Minitel generally failed to find a widespread audience in the 1980s. Bulletin board services (BBS) served a limited number of online zealots who were willing to do whatever it took to get hooked up (Rheingold, 1993). CompuServe found profitability in a select group of heavy, metered users among its several hundred thousand mainly dormant subscribers (Klopfenstein and Sedman, 1987). Prodigy survived on the elusive promise of profitability, while America Online (AOL) pushed the limits of available home computer technologies. American Online had the advantage of being at the right place at the right time. As shocking as it may seem, it was only a few years ago that CompuServe was among those commercial online providers who initially denied e-mail exchanges between their members and those who had Internet-only addresses.

Directly related to the growth of the WWW was the diffusion of an enabling technology: relatively inexpensive home computers (Lin, 1998). Approximately 50 percent of U.S. households had personal computers as of this writing, and Intellicast estimated in late 1997 that 61 percent of computer owners were also online (see [http://www.intelliquest.com/products/mbt/wwits. html]). In the 1990s, modems became standard features for these computers and many came with online access software preinstalled (e.g., America Online, CompuServe, and/or Prodigy). This set the stage for the impending Internet explosion. The ease with which online services could be tested by consumers without committing to one is directly related to their probability of adoption; this demonstrates the innovation attribute trialability, the degree to which an innovation may be experimented with on a limited basis (Rogers, 1986; 1995).

Figure 1.2 displays the growth of personal computer (PC) penetration in the United States, but what is not clear from these data is the number of households that were buying replacement computers. In other words, both first-adopting households and replacement households were purchasing new, more powerful computers. It is also true that penetration of PCs in households that have children is far higher than in those without (Lin, 1998; U.S. NTIA, 1999), and there is evidence that the children themselves influence the decision to adopt (McNeal,

1998). At least 70 percent of all households with home computers also had a modem as of the end of 1997 (U.S. NTIA, 1999). Research shows that there is a very strong relationship between household income and computer and modem penetration rates, and education exerts an influence independent of income (Clemente, 1998). Age has had important effects that are independent of income, and its influence will continue to be felt as the age distribution of the population changes in the future. Household composition also plays a role. Households in urban areas tend to be better equipped than households in rural areas (U.S. NTIA, 1999). A phenomenon reminiscent of radio, television, and VCRs is also occurring as households are adopting second and third operating personal computers (Net Market Size, 1999).

Figure 1.2.   Penetration of personal computers in U.S. households, 1994–2000.

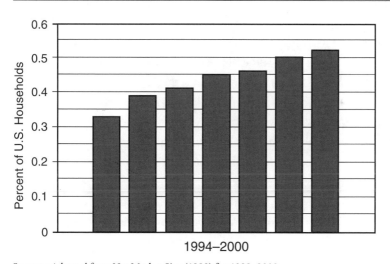

Sources: Adapted from Net Market Size (1999) for 1998–2000.

▶ Browser Wars

When the VCR was introduced into the marketplace in the late 1970s, many observers believed that the incompatible VHS and Beta formats would cripple the new home video business. What ensued instead was a dramatic battle between the two formats that led directly to product innovations such as longer recording times and lower prices (Klopfenstein, 1989). The lesson repeated here with the Internet phenomenon is that the emergence of two major players in the WWW browser market led to rapid product innovation as well as some incompatibilities.

The first well-known browser was called Mosaic, and it was introduced at the National Center for Supercomputing Applications (NCSA) at the University of Illinois. It was made available free on the Internet, and that is key to the rapidity with which it spread throughout the Internet user community. At that time, Internet users were largely both male and computer literate. Use of graphics files on the Internet around 1990 was very limited. The appearance of images, especially color images, on a computer screen that had been largely text-based was a dramatic change. Beyond the display of images, the World Wide Web itself made computer operating platforms (e.g., Unix, Mac or Windows) virtually irrelevant; files were easily shared on any system (Krol and Klopfenstein, 1996).

Netscape was founded in 1994 by James Clark, former head of Silicon Graphics (SGI) and Marc Andreessen who, along with Eric Bina, created the Mosaic browser while at the University of Illinois (Gilder, 1995). Netscape was made available free to academic users (the vast majority of Internet users at the time), but other users were asked to buy it. While there were actually many versions of other browsers available, as the commercial successors to Mosaic, Netscape quickly became the browser of choice.

The unprecedented growth of Netscape as a software firm did not go unnoticed by software giant Microsoft. Critics attacked Microsoft for being slow to react to the emergence of the Internet. Netscape, meanwhile, began to talk about replacing Windows as the desktop environment for everyday tasks. As if the stakes hadn't already been high enough, Microsoft was publicly made aware of the challenge before it.

Microsoft's response was to introduce what appeared to be a copycat browser called Internet Explorer, and the company quickly matched its version number to that of Netscape. Microsoft gave the browser away free and quickly bundled it with Windows 95 shipments. Microsoft further integrated the web browser into its next operating system release, Windows 98. Citing a memo between Microsoft and hardware vendors, the Department of Justice sued Microsoft for requiring systems manufacturers to distribute Explorer as a condition for selling Windows 95, a possible violation of the Sherman Antitrust Act. The case began in 1998. As of late 1998, all new Macintoshes and Windows 98 PCs came with Internet Explorer preinstalled. Netscape announced it would make its browser available free of charge in January 1998.

Fair or unfair, Internet Explorer has continued to erode Netscape's top position in the browser market. Incompatible utilities between the two browsers have impacted the design of web sites, while each company continues to develop new multimedia utilities. America Online, which was using a version of Internet Explorer itself, was the third most popular vehicle for accessing the Internet when, late in 1998, it announced an agreement to purchase Netscape. While this purchase might ensure a browser competitor to Internet Explorer in the near future, it is also possible that AOL was at least as interested in the number of users who use the Netscape web portal. Netscape itself seemed to be putting more effort into developing that content site than into marketing its browser.

▶ Internet Portals

By 1999, the topic of Internet portals became the hottest one since the push technologies of about 18 months earlier. As an indication of how the Internet was becoming like other mainstream, commercial media in the United States in terms of a number of gathering users (i.e., an audience), prominent web sites tried to be literally one-stop shopping centers for web surfers. Mergers and acquisitions of Internet portals were two of the most closely watched categories on Wall Street and two of the hottest strategies for online businesses. Examples include the proposed acquisition of Lycos by USA Networks (Andrews, 1999), @Home Corp.'s purchase of Excite (Piller, 1999), NBC's investment in CNET, and even AOL's purchase of Netscape. Portals are among the most heavily visited sites on the Internet. An estimated 47.3 percent of all Internet surfers visited Yahoo.com at least once in the past month according to Media Metrix (Machlis, 1999). Disney and Infoseek created the "Go Network" in an attempt to complement other media holdings like ABC and ESPN. The strategy is easy to understand: businesses need to decide whether to dream up a scheme to attract web surfers or invest in one that is already established. From a historical perspective, it appears established media companies will have dominant portals on the Web.

Structure of the Internet

The structure of the Internet is complex and, by nature, fluid. Who are the providers of the conduits? Telephone companies, Internet service providers (ISPs), rural electric companies, cable television companies, and even newspapers, among others. Although there have been around 5,000 ISPs in the United States, most experts expect this number to peak and then decline through industry consolidation (Klopfenstein, 1998a, 1998b).

Internet content providers are even more diverse than conduit providers. The amount of information on the WWW has been growing exponentially. As of August 1998, one source reported that available public web content was three terabytes (3 million megabytes), the Web was doubling in size every eight months, and there were approximately 20 million web content areas (i.e., top-level pages of sites, individual home pages, and significant subsections of corporate web sites). Ninety percent of all web traffic was spread over 100,000 different host machines and 50 percent of all traffic went to the top 900 web sites currently available (Web Spawns, 1998).

The Web has been organizing itself into what is looking more and more like mainstream media. While the WWW before 1996 was the domain of web pioneers and had the frontier atmosphere of the wild, wild West, the Web (for better or worse) is moving further and further away from its unique start and melding into the existing commercial media industry structure. Users can recognize established media names like CNN as well as new ones like Yahoo!

Dreams of Internet commerce (sales and/or advertising/promotion of products) guide many web investors today. Evidence of the parallel structure of the Internet is seen in such commonalities as the role of TV ratings firm Nielsen in measuring Internet use (Tedesco, 1998) and the establishment in 1996 of the Internet Advertising Bureau. The IAB became "the first global association devoted exclusively to maximizing the use and effectiveness of advertising on the Internet" (see [http://www.iab.net]). This organization fits right in with its preceding industry counterparts: the Radio Advertising Bureau, the Television Advertising Bureau and the Cable Advertising Bureau.

As noted at the outset of this chapter, there's no denying that the Web has been driven by U.S. organizations [Graphics, Visualization, and Usability

(GVU) Center's 9th WWW User Survey (1998)]. This is critical for under-standing the current web structure because of the unique case of media history in the United States. Media content historically has been subsidized by adver-tising. While web content providers such as *USA Today* tried to sell subscrip-tions to their services, many subscription-only web services turned instead to advertiser support. One of the oldest and most used web sites, Yahoo!, has never been subscription-based. Yahoo! was well on its way to generating $200 million in advertising revenues by the end of 1998 (Web ad, 1998).

While advertising supports web content providers, there is another large segment of the industry: Internet service providers (ISPs). The rev-enues of the ISP industry are already approaching those of the cable televi-sion industry, with annual revenues approaching $10 billion (Klopfenstein, 1998b) and with $20 billion in sight by 2000 (Walker, 1999). This means the ISP industry is already generating about as much revenue as the entire network television industry (ABC, CBS, NBC, and Fox) (Walker, 1999). In-dustry analyst Paul Kagan predicted that "internet/interactive" media rev-enues would double those of radio broadcasting and be about two-thirds those of television by 2007 as seen in data posted publicly on the Web by his company (see *[http://www.pkbaseline.com]*). Also worth noting from these projections is the more optimistic tone Kagan sounded for newer me-dia when compared to more established media (e.g., publishing and tradi-tional broadcasting).

The Future of the Internet

Forecasting the future of new media technologies is more of an art than it is a science (Klopfenstein, 1985). There are always unpredictable events that will impact the future of the Internet and its applications. Each event may cause a discontinuance in the path of media evolution. History is a guide, a teacher, and a source of context. Before getting to these levels of analyses, key variables that will affect the future of the Internet are noted. The chapter is concluded in keeping with the layout of this book, as the future of the Internet is discussed from four levels of analysis: individual, group, national, and global.

▶ Bandwidth Paradox

As more powerful multimedia computers with faster modems are introduced to the marketplace, an estimated 50,000 new Internet users are added every day (see [http://www.iconoclast.com]). As web site developers introduce bandwidth intensive applications such as audio and video, it is reasonable to ask if the network bandwidth demand will exceed the supply. At the same time, the ISP and the telecommunication industries continue to develop and deploy new technologies that allow far greater bandwidth. Despite dire predictions that the Internet would come to a crashing halt (and AOL's much publicized difficulties in early 1998 as reported in Klopfenstein, 1998b), a reasonable balance between available bandwidth and bandwidth demand has been established.

Table 1.2.   Data connection speeds.

Connection	Approximate Data Rate[a]	Bandwidth	Time/100K
14.4 modem	1.8 KB/sec	14.4 kbps	55 seconds
28.8 modem	3.6 KB/sec	28.8 kbps	27 seconds
33.6 modem	4.2 KB/sec	33.6 kbps	23 seconds
ISDN	7–16 KB/sec	56–128 kbps	14–6 seconds
Frame Relay	7–64 KB/sec	56–512 kbps	14–1.5 seconds
T1	32–193 KB/sec	256–512 kbps	3.1–0.5 seconds
1X CD	150 KB/sec	1.2 mbps	.66 second
Digital Subscriber Line	188–375 KB/sec	1.5–3 mbps	0.53 second
2X CD	200 KB/sec	1.6 mbps	0.5 second
4X CD	450 KB/sec	3.6 mbps	0.02 second
10X CD	1.2 MB/sec	9.6 mbps	0.08 second
Fast Ethernet	1.25 MB/sec	10 mbps	0.08 second
1X DVD	1.35 MB/sec	12 mbps	0.07 second
16X CD	2.4 MB/sec	19.2 mbps	0.04 second
24X CD	3.6 MB/sec	28.8 mbps	0.02 second
T3	5.5 MB/sec	44 mbps	0.018 second
Asynchronous DSL	10 MB/sec	80 mbps	0.01 second
Universal Serial Bus	12 MB/sec	96 mbps	0.0083 second

[a]Data Rates: KB/sec is kilobytes per second (1 byte = 8 bits); kbps = 1,000 bits per second; MB/sec is megabytes per second (1 megabyte = 1,000,000 bytes); mbps is megabits per second.

Source: Compiled from various resources available on the Internet.

Table 1.2 lists various data technologies and their transfer speeds including storage technologies for the purposes of comparison. The most promising high bandwidth technologies appear to be cable modems and digital sub-scriber lines (DSL). The integrated services digital network (ISDN) has been available for a decade, but telephone companies failed to introduce ISDN in a timely and reasonably priced fashion. It now appears other technologies will leapfrog ISDN (Greiner, 1997). Regardless of the technology involved, higher bandwidths will be available for home users in the future. The combination of increasing bandwidth and improving data compression techniques strongly suggests that audio and video applications will be more readily available to the home in the relatively near future.

▶ Limitless Access

Although the Internet in the United States in 1999 seems fairly ubiquitous, there is room for growth. In some ways, the Internet is already more prevalent than the telephone. More school classrooms have Internet connections than tele-phones, for example. The telephone suggests the model for access that the Inter-net may follow in the short run. The telephone was a wire-based system in the United States until the last decade. An economic point has now been reached at which individuals like college students may opt for a portable telephone over a standard wired service. Wireless Internet access technologies are in the pipeline, and the day is coming when (for better or worse) we can all have direct, wireless Internet access (Johnson, 1998; Moore, Johnson and Kippola, 1999). As was the case with telephone use before 1990, Internet access has been limited to comput-ers wired either by telephone or a wired network. Internet pioneer Vint Cerf be-lieves that the days of dial-up Internet access are numbered (Brody, 1998).

▶ Convergence

An unanswered question regarding Internet access from the home remains. Will access be realized via a computer or be merged with the television set? WebTV and digital broadcasting are two avenues that allow this. The televi-sion set is used as the web display device with WebTV. Digital broadcasting will allow simultaneous transmission of any kind of information, whether program-related or not.

▶ The Individual and the Future of the Internet

In the United States, individual Internet access rapidly became a fact of life for most college students and graduates in the late 1990s. Individual household access also grew dramatically in the same period. Inexpensive Internet access meant that many people could try out the Internet, and the quality of available information from known existing media outlets such as *USA Today*, ESPN, and *TV Guide* added substance to previously unknown sites such as Yahoo! and Infoseek. The Internet seems well on its way to becoming an indispensable media tool. Existing media adapt to the presence of new media, and that has already happened. Broadcasters, print media, and Hollywood have already found ways to promote existing products while often producing original content for the net. It may well be that access to educational materials will eventually have the most dramatic impact on the individual as the need for continuing education through distance learning is met on the Internet.

▶ The Social Future of the Internet

Electronic mail was added as a utility to computer mainframes without much thought being given to its eventual widespread application. In perhaps a similar way, social networks are springing up on the Internet. Whether via discussion boards or chat rooms, more social gatherings are taking place virtually than ever before, and this phenomenon was not particularly anticipated. A study released in 1998 reported that 35 percent of all Internet users have used the Internet to chat while 50 percent of those who are 18–24 have done so (Ziff-Davis, 1998). At one extreme, "Internet addiction" became the latest malady to reach pop psychology proportions in the late 1990s (Swartz, 1997; Kraut et al., 1998). At the other extreme, bereaved widows could find support in online communities (Bedell, 1998). Widely available anonymous or semi-anonymous Internet communication has opened up new avenues for the establishment of any number of online communities. An Internet messaging application (instant messages, chats, and direct file transfer between individual users) that bears watching is ICQ ("I seek you"). This latest Internet start-up (acquired by AOL in 1998) seems to be pushing its way into the mainstream as of this writing (Holmes, 1998).

▶ The Future of the Internet at the National Level

The implications of increasing Internet access at the national level are mind boggling. The implications for social, economic, and political impacts are great. Because social and economic aspects of the Internet have already been discussed, we can take a moment to examine the political implications of the Internet at the national level.

Dramatic events in 1998 pointed to the potential for the Internet to play a role in the nation's political life. This potential was highlighted by the American scandal involving President Bill Clinton and White House intern Monica Lewinsky. Self-appointed Internet "journalist"/gossip monger Matt Drudge has demonstrated the positive and negative political potentials of the Internet (anyone can publish on the Internet regardless of credentials). The Internet was used to distribute government documents about the investigation of the President with the immediate demand slowing some web services to a crawl and even crashing some online servers.

Evidence about the Internet's impact on the electoral process is being collected. It is reasonable to assume that the Internet has often been used to reinforce previously existing political beliefs. An Internet presence is becoming the norm as campaigns can easily place as much information as they choose on a web site. This is in direct contrast to old media such as direct mail where increases in the amount of content (i.e., paper) and users (postage) are directly related to increased costs.

Net.Capitol released a study of the 1998 political campaign with reasonable findings. The existence of some kind of Internet presence (e-mail, web, or both) was apparently independent of money. Minor parties were indistinguishable from the major parties in their pattern of having or not having Internet addresses. There was no statistical difference in the overall pattern of Internet usage between Republicans and Democrats. Competition fueled the drive to have a web page but not the drive to use e-mail; the Web was favored by better-funded campaigns, while the opposite was true of e-mail. Major parties favored the Web while minor parties favored e-mail; within the major parties, statewide campaigns favored the Web while House campaigns favored e-mail; and within House campaigns, incumbents favored the Web while their major party challengers favored e-mail (Loeb, 1998).

It is not unreasonable to speculate about the possibilities of voting online. As has been the case in electronic shopping, perceptions may be more of a barrier than technology. As long as voters and politicians are not comfortable with the Internet as being safe from fraud, we will continue to trek to the voting booth. The implications for political participation via online balloting are also dramatic. A new generation of voters might easily be brought into the political system via online balloting. Because this would challenge existing ways of electing public servants who are, by definition, well served by the existing electoral systems, one would not expect a stampede from those now in office to champion online voting. Worth noting is that the recent Graphics, Visualization, and Usability (GVU) Center's 10th study found that 83 percent of online users are also registered voters (Georgia Tech Research Corporation, 1999).

▶ Global Internet Access

The rest of the world is beginning to catch up with the United States in Internet access if not use (Net Geography, 1998). In fact, Finland, Norway, and Iceland already have more Internet users per capita than the United States (Nolan, 1998). One forecast predicted that the number of worldwide Internet users is expected to double to 300 million by 2005, with the greatest growth in Asia and South America (Study: Net Population, 1999). The online population was expected to rise 61 percent to 95 million in the United States, more than double to 88 million in Europe, and quadruple to 118 million in the rest of the world. Internet use is expected to grow as the cost of access drops dramatically. Companies such as Gateway, British Telecom, and Dixons Group (the United Kingdom's largest electronics retailer) offer free Internet access to their customers. This author finds the forecast for 300 million global Internet users in 2005 to be very conservative.

Internet traffic has been increasing 1,000 percent each year due to the increased use of audio and video applications such as telephone calls, playing of music, and videoconferencing, which were expected to triple to 6 percent of overall traffic by 2003. Global revenue worldwide was expected to more than double to $19 billion in 2002 as the cost of transferring data falls and demand rises. The cost of transferring one terabyte of data, the equivalent of 25,000 music CDs, will fall to less than $300 by 2003 compared to $80,000 in 1998.

Conclusion

The Internet phenomenon is one that truly compares to any media revolution in our lifetime. The notion of a truly interconnected world that had already begun with broadcasting and telephone technologies appears likely to blossom via the Internet. The opportunities for global commerce and communication will be limited more by individual choices and language differences than by technology. The U.S. model of commercially supported content is not necessarily the one the rest of the world will follow. The United States historically has supported its media through advertising, so that path was actually predictable. While the developed world may choose to model itself after the American commercial model, the remainder of the world may choose another path.

The Internet phenomenon in the United States is now characterized as much by consolidation as it is by innovation. Whether the Internet begins to look more like television or vice versa may be the key question as we progress in the new millennium. Will Internet technologies free us from the shackles of our late 20th century hectic lifestyles? Perhaps the diffusion of computing technology holds a clue. While it was easy to believe that the computer would free us of many mundane tasks and even be largely responsible for what was assumed to be the achievable goal of a shorter work week, that has simply not been the case. It does not seem unreasonable to suggest that the increased ubiquity of the Internet will offer us more opportunities than ever for communication and information access. There has never been a better time to apply our expertise in the field of communication.

References

http://www.pkbaseline.com
http://www.iab.net
http://www.iconoclast.com

www.intelliquest.com/products/mbt/wwits.html

Andrews, W. 1999, February 15. In Every Way, Lycos/USA Is a Big Deal. *Internet World.* [Online] Retrieved from the World Wide Web: *http://www.internetworld.com/print/1999/02/15/ news/19990215-every.html*

Bedell, D. 1998, November 24. Hi! It's Atlas: Life in the Chat Lane Is Anonymous, Adventurous and Now Animated with 3-D Alter Egos, *The Dallas Morning News,* p. 1F.

Bridis, T. 1998, August 25. New Study Shows One-Third of Americans on the Internet. AP [Online]. Available: *http://www.apwire.org.* [Accessed via *www.elibrary.com* [November 12, 1999].

Brody, H. 1998, May/June. Net Cerfing: Q&A with Vint Cerf, One of the Internet's Founding Fathers. *Technology Review,* 101(3): 72–75.

Brody H. 1998, July. The Web Maestro: An Interview with Tom Berners-Lee. *Technology Review,* 1999, pp. 33–42.

Bush, V. 1945. As We May Think. *Atlantic Monthly,* 176(1): 101–08.

Cailliau, R. 1995, November 2. A Short History of the Web. Presentation to the launching of the European branch of the W3 Consortium, Paris, France [Online]. Retrieved March 3, 1999, from the World Wide Web: *http://www.inria.fr/Actualites/Cailliau-fra.html*

Clemente, P.C. 1998. *The State of the Net: The New Frontier.* New York: McGraw-Hill.

Georgia Tech Research Corporation. 1999. *GVU's 10th WWW User Survey* [Online]. Retrieved March 9, 1999, from the World Wide Web: *http://www.gvu.gatech.edu/user_surveys/ survey-1998-10/*

Georgia Tech University Graphics, Visualization and Usability Center, GVU's 9th WWW User Survey. 1998, April. [Online]. Available: *http://www.gvu.gatech.edu/user_surveys/survey-1998-04/* [12 November 1998].

Gilder, G. 1995, August. The coming software shift. *Forbes ASAP* [Online]. Retrieved February 22, 1999, from the World Wide Web: *http://www.forbes.com/asap/gilder/telecosm14a.htm*

Greiner, L. 1997, November 28. Battle of the Bandwidth: Networking Technologies Square Off in a Struggle for Market Dominance. *Computer Dealer News,* 13:33–34.

Hafner, K., and Lyon, M. 1996. Where Wizards Stay Up late: The Origins of the Internet. New York: Simon and Schuster.

Hauben, M., and Hauben, R. 1997. *Netizens: On the History and Impact of Usenet and the Internet.* Los Alamitos, CA: IEEE Computer Society Press.

Holmes, T.E. 1998, August 19. Seeking Friends with ICQ: Getting Parts as Good as New. *USA Today,* p.D4.

How Many Online? 1999, February. Nua Internet Surveys [Online]. Retrieved from the World Wide Web: *http://www.nua.ie/surveys/how_many_online/index.html*

Johnson, D. 1998, August-September. Who's on the Internet and Why. *The Futurist,* 32(6): 11–12.

Klopfenstein, B.C. 1985. *Forecasting the Market for Home Video Players: A Retrospective Analysis.* Dissertation Abstracts International, 46-03, 0546A (University Microfilms No. AAI8510588).

————. 1989. The Diffusion of the Videocassette Recorder in the United States. In Mark Levy, ed., *The VCR Age: Home Video and Mass Communication*, 21–39. Newbury Park, CA: Sage Publications.

————. 1997. New Technology and the Future of the Media. In Alan Wells and Ernest A. Hakanen, eds., *Mass Media and Society*, 19–49. Greenwich, CT: Ablex.

————. 1998a. Internet Economics: An Annotated Bibliography. *Journal of Media Economics*, 11(1): 33–48.

————. 1998b. Internet Economics: Pricing Internet Access. *Convergence: The Journal of Research into New Media Technologies*, 4(1): 10–20.

Klopfenstein, B.C., and Sedman, D. 1987, June. Research on the Videotex User: What We've Learned and Where We're Going. Paper presented at the American Society for Information Sciences Mid-Year Meeting, Cincinnati, OH.

Kraut, R.; Patterson, M.; Lundmark, V.; Kiesler, S; Mukophadhyay,T.; and Scherlis, W. 1998. Internet Paradox: A Social Technology That Reduces Social Involvement and Psychological Well Being? *American Psychologist*, 53(9): 1017–31.

Krol, E., and Klopfenstein, B.C. 1996. The Whole Internet: User's Guide and Catalog, Academic Edition. Belmont, CA: Wadsworth Publishing and O'Reilly and Associates.

Leiner, B.M.; Cerf, V.G.; Clark, D.D.; Kahn, R.E.; Kleinrock, L.; Lynch, D.C.; Postel, J.; Roberts, L.G.; and Wolff, S. 1998, February 20. A Brief History of the Internet [Online]. Retrieved from the World Wide Web: *http://www.isoc.org/internet-history/brief.html*

Lin, CA. 1998. Exploring Personal Computer Adoption Dynamics. *Journal of Broadcasting & Electronic Media*, 42(1):95–112.

Loeb, E. 1998. Summary Statistics of Internet Usage in Campaign '98. Net.Capitol, Inc. [Online] Retrieved March 9, 1998, from the World Wide Web: *http://www.capweb.net/ classic/epl 1998.morph*

Machlis, S. 1999, March 1. Should My Company Care About Portals? *Computerworld*, p. 4.

McNeal, J.V. 1998, April. Tapping the Three Kids' Markets. *American Demographics* 20(4): 86.

Moore, G.; Johnson, P.; and Kippola, T. 1999, February 22. The Next Network. *Forbes ASAP*. [Online] Retrieved from the World Wide Web: *http://www.forbes.com/asap/99/0222/ 093.htm*

Net Geography. 1998. [Online]. Retrieved March 9, 1998, from the World Wide Web: *http://www.emarketer.com/estats/net_geography_exp.html*

Net Market Size and Growth: PC Growth. 1999. [Online] Retrieved February 26, 1999, from the World Wide Web: *http://www.emarketer.com/estats/nmsg_pc_growth.htm*

Network Wizards. 1999. Internet Domain Survey, January 1999. [Online] Retrieved March 3, 1999, from the World Wide Web: *www.isc.org/ds/www-9901/report.htm*

Nolan, S. 1998, July 15. Counting Heads Internationally: What's the Magic Number? [Online] Retrieved from the World Wide Web: *http://searchz.com/wmo/071598.shtml*

Piller, C. 1999, January 20. @Home to Buy Excite as Portal Stakes Rise. *Los Angeles Times,* p. C-1.

Rheingold, H. 1993. *The Virtual Community: Homesteading on the Electronic Frontier.* Reading, MA: Addison-Wesley.

Rogers, E. 1995. Diffusion of Innovation. New York: Free Press.

Rogers, E. 1986. *Communication Technology: The New Media in Society.* New York: Free Press.

Sterling, B. 1993, February. A Short History of the Internet. *The Magazine of Fantasy and Science Fiction.* [Online] Available at various URLs. Retrieved August 15, 1998, from the World Wide Web: *http://www.aces.uiuc.edu/AIM/scale/nethistory*

Study: Net Population to Double by 2005. 1999. *[Online] Retrieved March 1, 1999, from the World Wide Web: *http://www.news.com/News/Item/0,4,33031,00.html?st.ne.lh..ni*

Swartz, J. 1997. Cyber Addiction Is Called a Real Malady. *San Francisco Chronicle.* [Online] Retrieved March 9, 1999, from *http://www.sfgate.com/chronicle/archive/1997/08/15/ MN42255.DTL*

Tedesco, R. 1998. New Yardstick for a New Medium. *Broadcasting & Cable,* 128(6): 54.

United States Department of Commerce. National Telecommunications and Information Administration. 1999. Falling Through the Net: Defining the Digital Divide. Available: http://www.ntia.doc.gov/ntiahome/fttn99/ [12 November 1999].

Walker, L. 1999, June 10. U.S. Internet Reserve Put at $301 Billion. The Washington Post, p. E7.

Web Spawns 1.5 Million Pages Daily According to Findings from Alexa Internet. 1998, August 31. [Online]. Retrieved from the WWW November 12, 1999: *http://www.alexa.com/ company/inthenews/webfacts.html*

Woods, B. 1998, July 21. Five portals to the tops by 2000. November News Network. [Online]. Retrieved from the WWW. November 4, 1999: *http://www.newsbytes.com/*

Zakon, R. H. 1999. Hobbes' Internet Timeline v4.0. [Online] Retrieved March 3, 1999, from the World Wide Web: *http://info.isoc.org/guest/zakon/Internet/History/HIT.html*

Ziff-Davis 1998. The Web Explored: The Ziff-Davis/Roper Starch, Quarterly Update, Second Quarter 1998. [Online] Retrieved March 8, 1999, from the World Wide Web: *http://www.ziffdavis.com/marketresearch/IT2Q.htm*

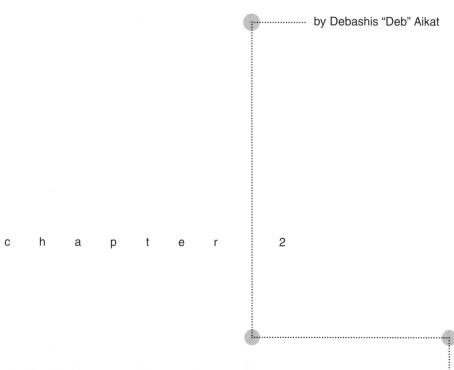

by Debashis "Deb" Aikat

c   h   a   p   t   e   r   2

Cyberspace of the People, by the People, for the People:
Predominant Use of the Web in the Public Sector

Writing on an antiquated manual typewriter, science fiction writer William Gibson coined the term *cyberspace* in his 1984 novel *Neuromancer* to describe the real and cultural dynamics of people and machines working within the confines of computer-based networks. An expatriate American living in Canada, Gibson used cyberspace as the setting for his early novels and short stories. In his fiction, cyberspace is a computer-generated landscape where characters enter by "jacking in" or plugging electrodes directly into sockets implanted in the brain. What they see when they get there is a three-dimensional representation of the information—great warehouses and skyscrapers of data (Gibson, 1987). Today, Gibson's imaginary world has been invoked in myriad ways on the World Wide Web. As the steam engine and automobile started changing the way we lived and worked by the late 19th century, information technologies of the late 20th century are not only changing our lives, but are transforming society and the way public sector units like universities, libraries, and the government function.

A major theme of this chapter is the examination of the predominant uses of the Web by individuals, the public education community, and government entities from a social, political, and economic perspective. The chapter also explores major concentrations of "noncommercial" online activity and the myriad ways people use the Web. Specifically, the chapter considers how individuals use the Web; innovative applications of the Web in public education, such as distance education and online learning; and how federal, state, and local governments are using the Web. The analysis considers the impact of the Web along four dimensions—individual, group, national, and global.

The Digital Divide: Technology Haves and Have-nots

There is little doubt that Americans of all ages, races, and backgrounds are becoming increasingly aware of the Internet. However, despite significant growth in Internet usage and computer ownership, certain underprivileged groups like minorities and low-income households are still far less likely to have personal computers or online access to the Internet than white or more affluent households. The chasm between information technology haves and have-nots has widened in three years, from 1994 to 1997, according to a United States Commerce Department report. The have-nots comprise low-income groups, minorities, and the young, particularly in rural areas and central cities. Between 1994 and 1997, the digital divide between households of different races and income levels also widened (NTIA, 1998).

Although 50 percent more Americans owned computers in 1997 than in 1994, and families using e-mail quadrupled during the same period, the digital divide widened between the upper- and lower-income segments of society. The disparity among racial groups has also grown. African Americans and Hispanic households lag behind the national average for telephone, computer, and online access when compared to whites. The gaps in ownership levels between whites and African Americans and between whites and Hispanics were far greater in 1997 than they were in 1994. White households were more than twice as likely than African American and Hispanic homes to own a computer. Lagging significantly behind the national average, single-parent, female households are less likely to have computers than dual-parent households, 25 percent versus 57.2 percent (USIS, 1998).

Web Pages Empower People as Communicators

The Web has empowered common people with the potential for disseminating information and ideas to the millions of people that comprise the population of the Internet. This can be done at little or no cost when compared to the expensive resources traditional media require to reach a mass audience. According to Hawn (1996), the personal web page is a low-cost technological opportunity for people to exercise their First Amendment rights. Kevin Kelly (1994), publisher of the digital trend magazine *Wired*, equates the Web with a new political structure. By elevating the communication capabilities of individuals, the Internet promotes heterogeneity and a new kind of pure democracy where we can be equal players in the global information game. Innovators like Sage Weil have explored this new communication role for the individual with the creation of webrings as a way to navigate the Web and unite web sites into an online community. Today the Webring is a free service that allows web sites to form "rings" based on similar interests, giving web users a fast and efficient way to find content and providing a great way for sites to build traffic and gain exposure. A quick review of RingWorld *[http://www.webring.org/]*, the subject-oriented online directory of the Webring system with links to related webrings, indicates that there are over 5,000 active rings and each webring may contain anywhere from a dozen to a few hundred pages. If a webring does not already exist to suit one's needs, a person can create a new one as well.

While the Webring has united thousands of home pages based on shared interests, personal web pages have enriched the diversity of Internet content. Dvorak described the personal web page phenomenon as irresistible, because toying with HTML, the basic language for writing web pages, "gives one a feeling of control and empowerment that reminds [one] of the era in which personal computing was in its infancy" (Dvorak, 1997).

The Internet as a Social Technology ▄

The role and impact of the Internet as a social technology is highly debated in popular and academic circles. Relationships created through Internet discussion groups (newsgroups), web-based or otherwise, have been classified under two conflicting visions. One perspective asserts that online interactions liberate interpersonal relations from the confines of physical locality and create opportunities for new, but genuine, personal relationships and communities. In contrast, others find that online relationships are shallow, impersonal, or hostile. These points are explained below.

The empowering role of the Internet is illustrated by how online interactions enrich interpersonal relations through the development of social relationships and by community building. Parks and Floyd (1996) interviewed 176 members of Internet newsgroups and their contributors. A majority (61 percent) reported forming a new personal relationship via a newsgroup. Whether an individual formed such a relationship depended primarily on the frequency and length of newsgroup participation. Online relationships often reached high levels of relational development and broadened to include interaction in other channels and settings. Internet newsgroups allow individuals to interact with others in a relatively anonymous fashion and even to conceal their identities. Thus, membership in these groups should become an important part of identity. McKenna and Bargh (1998) found that members of newsgroups dealing with marginalized concealable identities modified their newsgroup behavior according to the reactions of other members, unlike members of marginalized conspicuous or mainstream newsgroups. This increase in identity importance from newsgroup participation in both marginalized sexual identities and marginalized ideological identities not only generates greater self-acceptance, but also reveals the secret identity to family and friends. Results supported the view that Internet groups obey general principles of social group functioning and have real-life consequences for individuals.

However, in sharp contrast to the socially gratifying aspects of newsgroup communication, online relationships can have unpleasant consequences, as illustrated by two events, Matt Mihaly's suicide note and Jake Baker's story in the newsgroup alt.sex.stories. In a fit of despair one night in March 1994, Cornell University student Matt Mihaly posted a note to the newsgroup alt.drugs stating that he was going to kill himself and sought advice. Suicide notes are common on the Internet and are generally ignored, but Mihaly's note prompted a newsgroup reader to get in touch with Cornell's computer services department, which immediately alerted a crisis management team. Although his note was not sincere and he did not intend to kill himself, Mihaly was taken to a local mental hospital (Neely, 1995). In January 1995, University of Michigan student Jake Baker posted a newsgroup story that gained international media attention. Baker's story, posted to the newsgroup alt.sex.stories, graphically depicted the rape, torture, and murder of a female schoolmate. What made this story different is that Baker used the real name of the fellow student. University of Michigan president James Duderstad suspended Baker on the grounds that he was an immediate threat to another student. One week later, the FBI arrested Baker, charging him with five counts of transporting threatening material across state lines in connection with his e-mail, to which charge he pled not guilty. A U.S. district judge dismissed the charges, citing the government's lack of evidence that Baker planned to act on his writings (SAFE, 1995).

Psychological studies indicate two paradoxical functions of Internet usage. One, the Internet enables users to amplify their individual selves and thus provides a more solid anchorage in daily life. Two, the Internet enables individuals to distance themselves from daily life, the self, and others. Uchoa (1996) asserts that the dehumanizing tendencies of the everyday world have caused the Internet to become a haven for people deprived of human qualities such as individuality, compassion, or civility. This explains why the Web is home to porn merchants, pedophiles, and corrupt individuals who take advantage of gullible users. The Internet provides the same opportunities for crime that the real world offers. Electronic mail messages lend a perceived credibility to fraudulent claims for money. Pyramid schemes, false offshore investment companies, and fraudulent medical firms are abundant on the Web. The most common crimes committed on the Internet are electronic variants of time-tested, real-world scams, thefts, and cons, primarily forgery, assault, fraud, and robbery. Consumer protection agencies search for dubious activity to protect people against common online crimes although their presence on the Net is insignificant compared to the vast number of criminals on the Internet. The next section will analyze the role of the Web in public education, examining how educational institutions are using the Web in general and in innovative applications like distance education and online learning.

The Web Revolutionizes Public Education ▬

Various Internet applications including the Web are altering teaching strategies from the elementary school to institutes of higher education. The Web has revolutionized public education in eight major ways. First, the web provides unparalleled opportunities for hypertext-based learning. The Web is based on the principle of hypertext, which enables coherent organization and association of information through "links." Second, the pedagogical core of the Web is arguably an essential part of any learning activity because the vast body of information available on the Internet is almost limitless. Third, the Web has revolutionized classroom instruction. Lectures can now be posted as web pages complete with illustrations, text, and links to additional Internet resources. Fourth, web use is asynchronous and not place-bound. Material on the Web can be accessed without the traditional limitations of time or geography. A student with web access can read course materials 24 hours a day, seven days a week, anyplace, anywhere, even on vacation. Creating web-based resources also saves paper and counteracts the common tendency to make redundant copies of class material. Fifth, the Web fosters the creation of educational communities. Several web-based applications such as discussion forums and chat areas can help unite students into a community. The Internet is now second only to the telephone as a powerful medium for connecting people and resources. Several interactive web applications can facilitate teamwork in a class. Students can interact online or work collectively on projects in password-protected discussion areas, read case studies, and exchange ideas. Sixth, with its extraordinary visual power, the Web has now made it easier for any teacher to enhance class presentations by incorporating multimedia features like audio and video on the Web which students can keep referring to as often as they wish. Students also can learn from examining images at other sites. Seventh, the virtual capabilities of the Web have helped recreate the concept of education with the unlimited possibilities of virtual or electronic classroom resources that are accessible around the clock. These electronic resources include such online materials as course schedules, class lectures, images, links to additional information resources, self-paced testing sources, and examinations with automated grading mechanisms. Finally, the Web encourages self-paced self-learning through features like frequently asked questions (FAQs), keyword searching, resource discovery, and access to vast resource archives of knowledge. The Web gives students and teachers alike the ability to roam as far as their curiosity and quest for knowledge will take them.

With computers becoming standard equipment, most college students now have access to e-mail and the Internet. Some assert that the day is not far when every student from kindergarten through high school and beyond will have access to the Internet. However, such rapid growth creates a pedagogical challenge for teachers who have to learn the technology well enough to use it. This is especially true for teachers who were educated and trained before technological advances led to the proliferation of computers in classrooms, workplaces, and homes. The next section will analyze the challenges of introducing new technologies on the campus.

▶ Weaving Technology into the Campus

While emerging technologies like the Web are a bridge to the 21st century, one of the challenges of educators worldwide is to make technology work for education. In some institutions such challenges have been initiated with ambitious campus-wide projects. In July 1997, the University of California–Los Angeles (UCLA) College of Letters and Science launched an effort to build a web page for every undergraduate course offered by the college. The course web pages contained links for "virtual office hours" to supplement face-to-face contact between students and teachers. This effort was launched as part of UCLA's three-year Instructional Enhancement Initiative (IEI), which was designed to both enhance instruction and provide its 23,000 undergraduate students with improved electronic access to course information. The university also began investing $4.1 million per year in infrastructure to support the IEI, hired about 80 technology consultants, added more than 700 new computers and other new equipment, and provided new online connections to faculty, lecturers, and teaching assistants (Lebo, 1997).

UCLA's web-page initiative led to some unexpected innovations. The most prominent example has been "my.ucla" *[http://My.UCLA.edu]*, a web-based service that automatically makes a private web page for each of the 30,000 registered students. The pages guide students to web sites for the courses they are taking, as well as to sites for other campus resources. This focus on web pages has led other parts of the university to offer their services online. Student reaction to the initiative has ranged from praise to picketing. Some students oppose the mandatory student fees of more than $100 a year for this service. Many students are aware of the fees and are quick to complain when a particular course page does not seem worth its price tag (Young, 1998). A survey of 4,000 UCLA students conducted by the university in the fall of 1998 found that over 60 percent felt that the web pages had increased their interaction with professors. The real value of the web sites was their effectiveness in helping students select courses for the next quarter. The web sites often give more information than the traditional course listings published by the university (Young, 1998).

Despite widespread advantages, such mandatory initiatives have been described as high-handed. There are institutions where the faculty has opposed such high-tech initiatives. In spring 1997, the full-time faculty of Canada's third largest university, York University in Toronto, went on a historic two-month strike against the administration's efforts to implement instructional technology. The most upsetting of these efforts was an official solicitation to private corporations to place their logos on university course web pages in return for a $10,000 contribution to the courseware development budget. The strike ended after the faculty secured a formal contractual item protecting against similar administrative endeavors (Noble, 1998). York students also joined the fray. In fall 1998, the York Federation of Students handbook, distributed annually to all students, contained an explicit warning about the dangers of online education (Noble, 1998).

The University of California–Los Angeles (UCLA) and York only reflect the two extremes of the spectrum. A review of the adoption of Internet technologies in institutions around the world indicates that the Web is being adopted in myriad ways and for diverse functions in academe. The advent of the Web has been so widespread that of the 3,500 colleges and universities in the United States, between 75 and 80 percent have already begun using the Web for marketing purposes by putting admissions applications and catalogs online. A smaller number have put core business processes, such as paying bills and financial aid applications, online. Course registration will be a mainstream application in the education sector by 2000. The next section will analyze the role of the Web in spearheading the growth of distance education.

▶ Distance Education: Study Wherever You Are

The growth of the Web has created an immense potential for distance education. Distance education involves linking teachers and students in different geographic locations using technology that enables interaction. (Assessment, 1989). Distance education is becoming more and more common in diverse fields ranging from archeology to management studies. With a few clicks of the mouse, thousands of people across the country are attending classes on the Internet, linking into colleges and universities in pursuit of advanced degrees and training certificates. The *Peterson's 1998 Guide to Distance Learning Programs* lists more than 700 accredited institutions in United States and Canada, up from 93 listed institutions just five years ago in the guide's 1993 version (Peterson's Guides, 1993). More than 700 colleges and universities in the United States and Canada now offer more than 2,000 degree and certificate programs including 237 associate, 285 baccalaureate, 422 master's, and 33 doctoral programs, as well as 168 undergraduate and 69 graduate certificate programs (Peterson's Guides, 1998). Although these offerings come through a combination of media (television, videocassette, audiocassette, computer, book, and mail), the Internet has spearheaded the rapid growth of distance learning.

Spurred by fierce competition for students, colleges and universities are plunging headlong into the rapidly evolving world of online education, a world that barely existed, even in 1993, before the advent of the Web. The University of Phoenix *[http://www.uophx.edu/]*, a for-profit institution that has officials at many traditional universities scared because of its rapid spread online, had nearly 5,000 students in its online program in fall 1998, more than double the number in 1996 (Arenson, 1998). The Western Governors University *[http://www.wgu.edu/]* is an online college sponsored by 17 states and Guam.

Started in fall of 1998 to improve access to college education for adults and to help accommodate an expected rush of students without building classrooms, the university offers associate's degrees in liberal arts and applied science.

The California Virtual University *[http://www.california.edu/]*, a consortium of nearly 100 California universities and colleges, opened in fall 1998 with more than 1,600 online courses. The California Virtual University does not grant degrees or certificates, but helps people find out about distance education courses and certificate or degree programs offered by California's leading institutions of higher education.

Oxford University *[http://www.ox.ac.uk]*, Britain's oldest university, has decided to offer degree courses over the Internet. Their online venture has been part of a policy to deliver "individualized courses for each student" and the opportunity of an Oxford education to students who might not have to step inside its hallowed portals (University of Oxford, 1998). The online courses were initially funded by a $500,000 grant from the Paul G. Allen Virtual Education Foundation, named for Paul Allen, a U.S. entrepreneur and co-founder of Microsoft. Oxford's first online degrees have been designed for postgraduate students in medicine, computing, and software engineering. The university's elite undergraduate degrees may eventually be delivered on the Internet, although there is resistance from traditionalists who think Oxford's collegiate experience must remain an essential part of any course. Oxford tutors will supervise studies using e-mail, Internet discussions, and voice-based conferencing.

In March 1999, The Open University *[http://www.open.ac.uk]*, Britain's pioneer in distance education, launched its first online course—"You, Your Computer and the Net"—for those who feel uncertain and uninformed about new communications technologies. The course, designed for students with little or no technical knowledge, evoked tremendous response. The 2,000 students who enrolled used a dedicated web site and e-mail access to communicate with individual tutors. In fall 1998, Stanford University *[http://www.stanford.edu]* began its first completely online degree program (a master's in electrical engineering) and the first online master's degree offered by a major research university in the United States. Students accepted into this degree program compete for graduate admission on the same terms as those who intend to complete their graduate work on campus. The start-up costs of the 30 courses required for the online program are being supported by a $450,000 grant from the Alfred P. Sloan Foundation, which covers the incremental costs for the first two years of the program. By the third year, participants expect it to be self-supporting. The new web-based offerings will be priced similarly to existing remotely delivered courses, which are considerably more expensive than normal tuition.

Who is taking distance education courses? According to Peterson's, most students who enroll in distance education courses are over 25 years old, are employed, and have previous college experience. Over half are female. As a group, distance education students are highly motivated. Their course completion rate exceeds that of students enrolled in traditional, on-campus courses. The most successful distance education students are committed individuals who have the discipline to establish a regular study schedule each week and adhere to it without having to be reminded by an instructor or classmates to meet deadlines. A wide range of employers—businesses, hospitals, government offices, military installations—which find it difficult to release employees for on-campus study, are discovering that it is a good investment to bring the classroom to their work sites. According to a survey conducted by the International Foundation of Employee Benefits Plans, employees rank continuing education as more important than childcare, flextime, and family leave. Distance education offers several advantages, including flexibility, accessibility, and convenience. The cost and time savings are significant—there are no travel costs, and the actual time devoted to classes averages about 50 percent less than on-campus education or training (Peterson's Guides, 1998). Groups served by distance education include

- The geographically isolated,
- Professionals who cannot attend classes on traditional campuses,
- Students who cannot attend on-campus classes due to family, job, or other commitments,
- Physically handicapped individuals,
- People affected by socioeconomic factors that make distance education not just an alternative, but rather their only choice for access to quality education, and
- Nontraditional students such as housewives.

Governments Adopt the Web in Myriad Ways ▬

The Web has emerged as the most reliable and easy-to-use online medium for accessing government information. For over 200 years, the cornerstone of information policy in the United States has been the principle of universal access to government information. The growth of government information on the Internet has been dramatic, leading to new government roles in the emerging information infrastructure (Cerf, 1995). The Internet has revolutionized public participation and access to government information (Evans, 1998). Everybody with access to the Web can obtain copies of primary-source government documents through the Internet. In September 1998, the U.S. Congress' decision to release Independent Counsel Kenneth Starr's report *[http://thomas.loc.gov/icreport/]* over the Internet was "seen as a defining moment for the Web, a test of both its technical infrastructure and its ability to play a critical role in the political process" (Harmon, 1998). In many ways, the ad hoc experiment in electronic democracy was a success. The extraordinary run on government and news sites—by one count, 20 million Americans had read parts of the report online within 48 hours of its release—reflected a public thirst for instant, unfiltered information driven in part by the technology itself (Harmon, 1998).

In 1993, Congress took steps to improve access to federal electronic information by passing the Government Printing Office Electronic Information Access Enhancement Act . This Act directed the U.S. Government Printing Office (GPO) and the Office of Superintendent of Documents to

- Maintain an electronic directory of federal electronic information,
- Provide a system of online access to appropriate government publications as determined and distributed by the Superintendent of Documents, and
- Operate an electronic storage facility for federal electronic information.

As mandated by the Act, GPO Access was created in 1993 to provide access to various electronic publications including the Congressional Record, the Federal Register, bills, and the U.S. Code. Initially, GPO Access sold subscriptions, based upon incremental costs, but depository libraries were provided with no-fee access. In November 1994, soon after the Republican-controlled House of Representatives swept into office, Speaker-Elect Newt Gingrich (R, GA), in his first major speech, called for the need to make the transition from a Second Wave mechanical bureaucratic society to a Third Wave information society based on Alvin Toffler's model (Gingrich, 1994).

The policy of the Gingrich-led Congress to make federal government information freely available on the Internet revolutionized the way citizens of the United States relate to the government. For instance, by the time the 104th Congress convened in January 1995, the House Information System was up and running on a seven-day, 24-hour schedule, its Sun workstations serving incoming online queries at a rate of some 200,000 a week. In December 1995, GPO Access eliminated access fees and has since emerged as an example to other government agencies in providing free access to electronic government information. This led every government unit in the United States, from Agriculture to Transportation, and all federal agencies to post their activities, information, and databases on the Web. The new electronic environment also changed traditional methods by which government information is delivered to and accessed by the public.

To keep up with the emerging popularity of the Web as an information source, the Government Printing Office introduced widespread measures to transform its 1,400 federal depository libraries throughout the United States and its territories. In less than three years, from 1996 to 1998, federal depository libraries, which are congressionally designated public, academic, law, and federal libraries for the general public, changed from a primarily print-based system to a predominantly electronic environment.

▶ Of Web Access and Cybermobiles: Impact of the Web on Libraries

While older federal documents are available in traditional formats like paper, microfiche, diskette, and CD-ROM, some of the newer publications are only available on the Web. This has led to new roles and responsibilities for the depository libraries, which now provide free web access and other Internet services to their patrons. In addition to upgraded technical capabilities in the depository libraries, librarians are now required to possess a basic level of technical expertise to retrieve electronic information.

The role played by libraries in providing access to information via the Web has attained creative dimensions. To increase computer literacy among the general population, librarians have come up with innovative projects to target specific audiences that do not have access to personal computers but would like to have the opportunity to learn. In 1996, the Muncie Public Library in Indiana started planning for a "cybermobile" that would be similar to a bookmobile, but instead of books the vehicle would have Internet-connected computers which patrons can learn to use. The Cybermobile [http://www.munpl.org/Main_Pages/Cybermobile.htm] began serving the Muncie community in August 1998. Designed with widely available off-the-shelf components, the Cybermobile offers complete access to the Internet from six user stations that are connected in a typical LAN topology that includes an on-board file server and a supervisor's station. The Cybermobile also offers a book collection to supplement its teaching role to target audiences (Drumm and Groom, 1998). The Cybermobile is a wonderful example of how libraries are reaching out to their communities to take new technology to the elderly and the disadvantaged. Other libraries such as the Public Library of Charlotte and Mecklenburg County in North Carolina have adopted the program.

▶ The Cornucopia of Federal Information

The United States government is among the best and most useful sources of information on the Internet (Evans, 1998). Regarded as the single largest publisher in the world, GPO Access [http://www.gpo.gov/], the government's on-line information service, hosts millions of documents published by the federal government, from transcripts of speeches to how-to manuals to legal records. Although some U.S. documents are classified as "top secret," the vast majority are available online free to the public. Useful government resources enable people not only in the United States but also around the world to access vital information by, for example,

- Getting flight data on the next NASA launch [http://www.nasa.gov/],
- Looking at the FBI's Ten Most Wanted Fugitives List [http://www.fbi.gov/],
- Dissecting a "virtual frog" at the U.S. Energy Department's Lawrence Berkeley National Laboratory [http://www-itg.lbl.gov/ITG.hm.pg.docs/dissect/],

- Contacting Congress members by electronic mail [http://thomas.loc.gov/],
- Downloading tax forms [http://www.irs.gov/],
- Searching the Federal Research Division's Vietnam-era prisoner-of-war/ missing-in-action database [http://lcweb2.loc.gov/pow/powhome.html],
- Researching online resources of the Library of Congress [http://www.loc.gov/],
- Seeing the latest pictures of the Jet Propulsion Laboratory's robotic exploration of the solar system [http://www.jpl.nasa.gov/],
- Looking up latest reports from the United States National Institutes of Health on Cancer and AIDS [http://www.nih.gov/], or
- Getting financial facts on saving and investing wisely from the United States Securities and Exchange Commission [http://www.sec.gov/].

Online access to government information has also led to the growth of information databases such as the Transactional Records Access Clearinghouse (TRAC), which is a data gathering, data research, and data distribution organization associated with Syracuse University. The purpose of TRAC [http.//trac.syr.edu/] is to provide the American people—and institutions of oversight such as the Congress, news organizations, public interest groups, businesses, scholars, and lawyers—with comprehensive information about the activities of federal enforcement and regulatory agencies, and the communities in which they take place.

The U.S. Census Bureau [http://www.census.gov] is using the Web as a dominant information source. After the 2000 census has been collected and tabulated, the U.S. Census Bureau will post the bulk of the data on its web site, rendering paperbound copies of the nation's statistical profile relics of 20th century record-keeping. According to Fulwood (1998), the transition of the census to the Web caps a nearly decade-long effort by the Census Bureau to wean the public and media from relying on government demographers to crunch the numbers and divide the bottom line from a mass of raw data. The idea is to put this new system in place and allow people to do the sophisticated number crunching themselves, online. This would enable anyone with access to the Web to sort through the volumes of census data on file, create special categories, and download detailed demographic or population information. So complete is the Census Bureau's transition from paper to pixels that most of its survey results (about 90 percent) are published electronically on the Web. This is significant when compared to 1992–93 when most census reports were about 90 percent on paper (Fulwood, 1998).

▶ Innovative Approaches by State Governments

State governments in the United States are finding new ways to provide free access to information. The enormous increase in public use of the Internet has provided an opportunity for all state governments to adopt online databases, the Internet, computer bulletin boards, CD-ROMs, and multimedia public kiosks to make information quickly and easily available. California was the first state to pass legislation (in 1993) requiring public access to legislative information through the Internet, in order to make the legislature more open to the public (Bourquard and Greenberg, 1996).

Many lawmakers believe that state government information on the Web has contributed to restoring the faith of a public that has arguably become apathetic to the democratic process. Alaska *[http://www.legis.state.ak.us/]*, Illinois *[http://www.state.il.us/legis/]*, Florida *[http://www.leg.state.fl.us/]*, and Virginia *[http://legis.state.va.us/]* were among the first state legislatures to provide dial-up access to their legislative computer systems. In the 1970s, business firms, lobbyists, and some private citizens searched legislative systems via computers equipped with modems, primarily to obtain information on the status of bills. By 1985, 11 state legislatures offered dial-up access to the general public (Bourquard and Greenberg, 1996). In those days, some legislatures provided information through gopher, an early Internet program that organized information into text and menus. The advent of the Web enabled these sites to incorporate text, graphics, sound, or video. Other innovations like TVW's *[http://www.tvw.org/]* live coverage of proceedings of the state government via the Internet and cable television are becoming vital communication modes. A private nonprofit organization founded in 1993 and located in Olympia, Washington, TVW's sole purpose is to provide unedited coverage of state government deliberations and public policy events of statewide significance. The network is often referred to as the state-level counterpart to C-SPAN. The TVW network was the first state-level public affairs network to provide live audio coverage of all state legislative deliberations (up to 11 simultaneous streams) and state Supreme Court oral arguments over the Internet. According to Rose (1998) the Internet affords many advantages over television due to its adaptability to the flexible scheduling of legislative sessions. Other states, such as Louisiana and California, are planning to provide similar services. Meanwhile, audio coverage of legislative sessions is already being provided on web sites in such states as Wisconsin, Nevada, Texas, Missouri, Georgia, and Florida (Rose, 1998).

The Web has demonstrated strong interest in obtaining legislative information via the Internet. The California Assembly *[http://www. assembly.ca.gov/]* opened its web site in November 1995. During the first five weeks of operation, more than 23,000 searches were performed, and more than 80,000 documents were retrieved. Minnesota's gopher site averaged 50,000 hits per month (Bourquard and Greenberg, 1996). Texas and California are among the leading states when it comes to putting government information online, according to Maxwell (1995). The California Home Page *[http://www.ca.gov/]* has more government Internet sites than any other state home page in the country. It links to various web servers operated by a range of institutions, from the Air Resources Board to the University of California (Maxwell, 1995). The State of Texas Government World Wide Web *[http://info.texas.gov/]* links to information sources relating to job openings in the state government, state maps, tourist information, lottery results, detailed legislative information (including the full text of bills introduced in the legislature), the Texas Constitution, U.S. Census Bureau information about Texas House and Senate districts, and election results. It also links to city and county Internet sites. The Texas Department of Economic Development's Texas-One web site *[http://www.texas-one.org]* provides extensive information about doing business in Texas. It has links to business and hub directories, a market exchange where companies can post announcements about items they are seeking to buy or sell, and government procurement opportunities. It also has links to other resources including international trade leads, a directory of more than 14,000 Texas businesses owned by minorities or women, and a searchable directory of the 500 largest Texas businesses (Maxwell, 1995).

Throughout the United States, state governments have taken innovative approaches to match the public's enthusiasm to government information. For instance, the web site of the Florida Legislature is called Online Sunshine and was developed in 1995 by the Legislative Data Center to make it easy for people to learn about the legislative process, specific legislation, and individual legislators. Online Sunshine contains basic information, including the text of bills, state statutes, calendars, and lobbyists. According to Bourquard and Greenberg (1996), the Florida Legislature has taken a three-way approach to providing better access to legislative information. In addition to an Internet web site, the legislature has developed a touchscreen multimedia kiosk and a computer bulletin board. The kiosk, which looks like an automated teller machine, provides an easy way for individuals who are not computer literate to find biographical information about legislators, legislative schedules, and bill status. The first kiosk became available in the Capitol in 1994, and in 1995 two more were placed, in Fort Lauderdale and Hillsborough. The legislature unveiled its new bulletin board in the spring of 1995, featuring proposed legislation, legislative calendars, House and Senate rules, the Florida statutes and Constitution, and information on members and lobbyists (Bourquard and Greenberg, 1996).

A growing number of state government agencies are setting up online information services to provide the ever-increasing number of computer savvy citizens with the latest legislative news and developments. The range of information offered has expanded from legislative developments to include information about the state administration, history, business, and tourism. This change is illustrated by the StateSearch web site *[http://www.nasire.org/stateSearch/]*. StateSearch is designed to serve as a topical clearinghouse for state government information on the Internet. StateSearch arranges information by subject (e.g., criminal justice, information technology, state homepages, disability agencies, judicial). StateSearch is a service of National Association of State Information Resource Executives (NASIRE), which represents state chief information officers and information resource executives and managers from the 50 states, six U.S. territories, and the District of Columbia.

▶ City Web Sites Provide Convenience to the Consumer

Local governments throughout the United States have used the Web innovatively to make public information available electronically. Eventually, local government web pages may offer free or fee-based web sites for citizens or government-sponsored initiatives that will allow sponsors to gauge public opinion, recruit fundraisers, and hold discussion groups. *The Indianapolis Star* reported that the entire city government in Franklin, Indiana, was available for contact through the Internet (Bird, 1998). Mayor Herschel Cook, an inexperienced computer user, initiated Franklin's new web site *[http://www.ci. franklin.in.us/]* to boost government access. To complain, to praise, or simply stay in touch, residents could contact officials directly, including the mayor, by electronic mail.

Maricopa County, in Arizona, found significant advantages in providing online access to public records. By linking imaging and Internet technologies, county government streamlined its documentation capabilities and put them on the Web. In doing so, it has become the first U.S. county to publish public records online (Bowser, 1998). With a population of more than 2.3 million people, Maricopa County is one of the largest and fastest growing counties in the United States. Between 3,000 and 8,000 new documents are recorded daily in the County Recorder's Office, and since 1992 document imaging has made the process more manageable (Bowser, 1998). The county's imaging system converts paper documents into electronic images that are then stored on optical disks. Internally, the technology provides staffers with immediate access to data, eliminating lost paperwork and boosting productivity; externally, software links the images to the Internet, allowing computer users nationwide to search and view Maricopa County's public documents. Since incorporating its document-imaging solution, the county has experienced a number of benefits. The volume of recording transactions doubled with no increase in staff. The Web has enabled widespread sharing of recorder's information with other county offices (including the assessor, treasurer, and county transportation department) as well as better control and management of recording transactions, allowing the county recorder to be immediately responsive to the public. Another benefit is the reduced staff time for signature verification of election petitions and early voter ballots. Automated processing of recording documents reduces administrative costs and allows parallel processing of documents in less time. According to the county recorder, public reaction has been overwhelming—the new system recorded between 350 and 450 hits per day (Bowser, 1998).

Information, however, is not the only thing the public accessed over the Web. The interactive features of the Web enable Seattle citizens to pay parking tickets and both traffic and nontraffic fines levied by the Municipal Court of Seattle *[http://www.pan.ci.seattle.wa.us/courts/]*. The court acknowledges receipt of a fine by e-mail and regular mail. The court plans to eliminate paper receipts if electronic payments go up significantly. As the parking ticket operations gain widespread acceptance, the city anticipates that citizens will be able to use the Web to pay utility bills and taxes, as well as fees for permits, licenses, and facility reservations (Bowser, 1998).

Various other city government web sites also provide convenience to the consumer. For example, the Houston Department of Public Works and Engineering operates an OnlinePermits! Houston web site *[http://houston.online permits.com/]* to provide building permit information and access to application forms. Applications may be completed and submitted to the appropriate department online, and permit status may be checked electronically at any time. The service allows contractors, architects, and engineers to apply for permits, check on the inspection status of a building, or locate approved permits. The free online system is accessible at the public library for those who do not have computers. Also, area Builders' Square retailers provide free workstations for contractors. Before the advent of such web services, applying for a permit could take several hours. Now, it can take fewer than 10 minutes. Since the system has been in place, more than $13.2 billion worth of permits have been issued; 85 percent of those were approved within a day (Bowser, 1998).

"Click here to extend the Due Date for your Traffic Ticket On-Line" is one of the first things that you notice on the home page of the Los Angeles Municipal Court *[http://www.lamuni.org/]*, which enables citizens to pay for speeding tickets electronically. Additionally, users can avoid embarrassment and save a few hours by registering for online traffic school. Nearly 12 branches of the Los Angeles Judicial District are participating in the program, which allows people to complete traffic school online in the comfort of their homes or offices (Bowser, 1998).

Created at the request of the city council, the City of San Diego Homepage *[http://www.sannet.gov/]* offers citizens a convenient way to interact with their local government by providing information about council members and the city's departments. For instance, through the mayor's page citizens can offer their views. If there is a problem with recycling or trash pick-up, users can fill out a form online and get quick results. One of San Diego's most popular sites, the San Diego Police Homepage *[http://www.sannet.gov/police/]* offers crime statistics, crime facts and figures *[http://www.sannet.gov/police/crime-facts/]* that are updated monthly, as well as information on police department careers and auctions.

Web access has made communication between local government and citizens much easier nationwide. Public records access, personnel postings, permitting, and legislative updates are now available online in dozens of cities and counties. A comprehensive list of city web sites can be accessed from USA CityLink *[http://www.usacitylink.com/]*, which provides information for all states and cities in the United States. Founded in 1994, the USA CityLink Project has offered links to the best city web sites, which are selected to match stringent project criteria.

▶ International Governments Disseminate Information

While the U.S. federal government is one of the most prolific publishers among world governments, other international governments are also using the Web to disseminate information. For instance, the British Monarchy web site *[http://www.royal.gov.uk/]* provides details of the royal collection and history of the monarchy. Visitors to the 10 Downing Street web site *[http://www.number-10.gov.uk/index.html]* can tour the official residence of the British Prime Minister and access information similar to that available at the U.S. White House web site *[http://www.whitehouse.gov/]*. Other sources of British government information include the Central Office of Information *[http://www.coi.gov.uk/coi/]*, House of Commons *[http://www.parliament.uk/commons/HSECOM.HTM]* and House of Lords *[http://www.parliament.the-stationery-office.co.uk/pa/ld/ldhome.htm]*, and profiles of Members of Parliament *[http://www.the-commons.com/]*.

Government sites of other countries and international organizations can be seen at the Governments on the WWW web site *[http://www.gksoft.com/govt/]*. Maintained by Gunnar Anzinger and available in both German and English, this web site is a comprehensive database of governmental institutions on the World Wide Web: parliaments, ministries, offices, law courts, embassies, city councils, public broadcasting corporations, central banks, and multinational organizations.

The U.S. Central Intelligence Agency (CIA) World Factbook *[http://www.cia.gov/cia/publications/factbook/]* is one of the most comprehensive resources of facts and statistics on more than 250 countries and other entities. The CIA's Directorate of Intelligence produces the CIA Factbook.

The Northwestern University Library's list of International Organizations web site *[http://www.library.nwu.edu/govpub/resource/internat/igo.html]* provides a single-page, alphabetical list of international organizations.

Cyberspace of the People, by the People, for the People

This chapter started with how the word *cyberspace* was coined by William Gibson, in his popular science fiction novel *Neuromancer*, to describe computer-generated landscapes or meeting places. This section summarizes the impact of the Web using four dimensions—individual, group, national, and global. We think these dimensions are important because they provide a relevant framework for analyzing and understanding the growth of the Web.

At the individual level, the Web has empowered anyone with Web access with the potential of disseminating information and ideas to the thousands of people that comprise the mass audience of the Internet. Such dissemination can be accomplished at little or no cost when compared to the expensive resources traditional media have needed to reach a mass audience. Apart from the advantages of empowerment, individuals can also benefit from the opportunities for distance education which bring hitherto unavailable educational opportunities to the home or office computer. The Web is so vital that some think not knowing how to use it or not having access to it will soon be as problematic as illiteracy. Today, the question is not whether to use this technology, but how to use it effectively.

On the group dimension, web-based electronic communities in the public sector have united people with shared interests. Various groups of people far and wide can now use the Web to access information on everything from government resources to the latest Hollywood release. In the less than 10 years since its inception, the Web has emerged as a collection of millions of distinct sites containing text, pictures, and even music and video clips, all linked together and accessible via the global computer network comprising the Internet. The Web is one of the main reasons for the exponential growth of the Internet: it is a revolutionary communications system requiring minimal technical understanding. Suddenly, it seems, the Web has attained an enviable ubiquity and potential for uniting groups, unrivalled by any other communication medium. Web services like Yahoo! offer free web-based e-mail and travel information; personal web pages have given new meaning to the right of free expression in mass media; thousands use the Web to do everything from shopping to dating; children communicate with Santa Claus online; and everyone from the British monarch to jail inmates has a home page. The Web has given each group a new identity.

At the national level, the Web has emerged as a countrywide phenomenon in developed nations such as the United States, Canada, Australia, England, Germany, France, just to name a few. The Web has also helped the Internet to emerge as a social technology that has bonded these nations in myriad ways. For instance, the Web has revolutionized delivery of government information. In sharp contrast to a century-old practice of providing federal documents on paper, federal information is now available in electronic format. That way government information is available to every citizen in the country at the same time that it is available to the highest paid Washington lobbyist. This has radically enhanced the flow of government information and the entire quality of knowledge in the United States. Web access has made communication between local government and citizens much easier nationwide. Public records access, personnel postings, permitting, and legislative updates are now available online in dozens of cities and counties. However, new computer technologies like the Web have further widened the gap between the poor and the well off. When compared with other regions of the world, the technology-fueled "new economy" in the United States has contributed to the highest number of Internet users. Although many more Americans now own computers and technology job opportunities are expanding, access to the Internet is still beyond the reach of a significant number of Americans.

At the global level, the Web in the public sector has tremendous potential. But outside the developed world, it may take decades before the benefits of the Web impact the world population. The Web is being adopted in myriad ways and for various functions in academe around the world. Pennsylvania State University, for example, set up a "World Campus" *[http://www.world campus.psu.edu/]* in February 1998 for students around the world to delve into the expertise of Penn State's renowned faculty, its learner support, and its resources; all thanks to a cyberspace journey of just a few seconds.

Summary and Conclusion

William Gibson's vision of cyberspace has become a reality, especially with the Web's utilization of powerful computers, data storage devices, interactive communications networks, and computer-generated multimedia. Less than five years ago, in spring 1995, *Time* magazine observed that the word *cyberspace* was being used to "describe not some science-fiction fantasy but today's increasingly interconnected computer systems—especially the millions of computers jacked into the Internet" (Elmer-DeWitt, 1995). Today, the Web has become the most exciting delineation of that "interconnected computer system" of the Internet. As the fastest growing segment of the Internet, the Web is fast emerging as an information universe. It is so much so that an increasing number of Americans believe that a working knowledge of computer technology in general and Internet applications like the Web in particular is essential for success in business, educational, and personal spheres.

The present chapter examined, from social, political, and economic perspectives, the predominant uses of the Web by individuals, its uses in public education, and it uses by government entities. This chapter identified major concentrations of "noncommercial" web activity in all facets of public life. Considering the myriad ways people use the Web—through personal pages, online learning, and in every function of federal, state, and local governments worldwide, the Web is fast emerging as a dominant information source in every sphere of life. The next chapter will explore the impact of the Web in the private sector.

References

Arenson, K.W. 1998, November 2. More Colleges Plunging into Uncharted Waters of Online Courses. *The New York Times on the Web.* [Online] Retrieved March 2, 1999, from the World Wide Web: *http:// www.nytimes.com/library/tech/98/11/biztech/articles/02online-education.html*

Assessment. 1989. Linking for Learning: A New Course for Education (OTA-SET-430). Washington, DC: U.S. Government Printing Office.

Bird, P. 1998. October 1. City's New Web Site Designed to Boost Government Access; To Complain, To Praise or Simply Stay in Touch, Residents May Contact Officials Directly by E-mail. *The Indianapolis Star,* p. 1.

Bourquard, J.A., and Greenberg, P. 1996, March 3. Savvy Citizens. *State Legislatures,* 2:28.

Bowser, B. 1998, January. Opening the Window to On-line Democracy: *http://www.localgovern ment. com. American City & County,* 113:32–38.

Cerf, V.G. 1995. Some Possible Government Roles in Information Infrastructure. *Serials Review,* 21(1): 11.

Drumm, J., and Groom, F. 1998, November. The Cybermobile Rolls onto Capitol Hill. *Computers in Libraries,* 18: 18–19

Dvorak, J.C. 1997, March. This Time It's Personal. *PC/Computing,* 10:63.

Elmer-DeWitt, P. 1995, Spring. Welcome to Cyberspace: What Is It? Where Is It? And How Do We Get There? *Time,* 145:4–11.

Evans, J H. 1998. *Government on the Net,* 1st ed. Berkeley, CA: Nolo Press.

Fulwood, S. III. 1998, November 15. U.S. Counting on Web To Be Census Source. *Los Angeles Times,* p. A-28.

Gibson, W. 1984. *Neuromancer.* New York: Ace Books.

———. 1987. *Burning Chrome.* New York: Ace Books.

Gingrich, N.L. 1994, March 11. Post-Election Speech to Washington Research Group. *The Washington Weekly.* [Online] Retrieved February 5, 1999, from the World Wide Web: *http://www.federal.com/Gingrich/11.11.94*

Harmon, A. 1998, September 20. Access to Clinton Data Abets E Pluribus Unum, '90s Style. *The New York Times on the Web.* [Online] Retrieved February 5, 1999, from the World Wide Web: *http://www.nytimes.com/library/politics/092098clinton-internet.html*

Hawn, M. 1996, August. Song of Myself: Personal Publishing on the Net. *Macworld,* 13: 131.

Kelly, K. 1994. *Out of Control.* London: Fourth Estate.

Lebo, H. 1997. Instructional Enhancement Initiative at UCLA Will Expand Computing and Internet Access for Undergraduates. *UCLA News and Information.* [Online] Retrieved March 1, 1999, from the World Wide Web: *http://www.uclanews.ucla.edu/Docs/hlsw319.html*

McKenna, K.Y.A., and Bargh, J.A. 1998, September. Coming Out in the Age of the Internet: Identity "Demarginalization" through Virtual Group Participation. *Journal of Personality & Social Psychology,* 75(3): 681–94.

Maxwell, B. 1995. Gateways to State and Local Government Information on the Internet. *Database,* 18:24.

Neely, K. 1995, January 6. Suicide on the Net. *The Guardian,* pp. 2, 10.

Noble, D. 1998 February. Digital Diploma Mills: The Automation of Higher Education. [Online] Retrieved March 20, 1999 from the World Wide Web: *http://www.firstmonday.dk/issues/issue3-3/noble/index.html*

NTIA. 1998. *Falling through the Net II: New Data on the Digital Divide.* Washington D.C.: Commerce Department's National Telecommunications and Information Administration.

Parks, M.R., and Floyd, K. 1996. Making Friends in Cyberspace. *Journal of Communication,* 46(1): 80–97.

Peterson's Guides. 1993. *The Electronic University: A Guide to Distance Learning.* Princeton, NJ: Peterson's Guides.

———. 1998. *Peterson's Guide to Distance Learning Programs,* 2nd ed. Princeton, NJ: Peterson's Guides.

Rose, G. 1998. Legislatures Live via the Web. *State Legislatures,* 24(5): 30.

SAFE (MIT Student Association for Freedom of Expression). 1995, August 27. Jake Baker Case Archive. [Online] Retrieved from the World Wide Web: *http://www.mit.edu:8001/activities/safe/safe/cases/umich-baker-story/*

Uchoa, A.R. 1996. Faces Paradoxais da Rede (Paradoxical Faces of the Net). *Percurso: Revista de Psicanalise,* 8(16)[1]: 91–97.

University of Oxford. 1998, May 29. Paul G. Allen Virtual Foundation Provides $500,000 for a Radical New Approach to Online Education at Oxford University (Press Release). [Online] Retrieved March 1, 1999, from the World Wide Web: *http://www.admin.ox.ac.uk/po/980529.htm*

USIS. 1998. *Gore Calls for Solutions to Correct "Digital Divide."* Washington D.C.: U.S. Information Service.

Young, J.R. 1998, May 15. A Year of Web Pages for Every Course: UCLA Debates Their Value. *The Chronicle of Higher Education.* [Online] Retrieved March 1, 1999, from the World Wide Web: *http://chronicle.com/free/v44/i36/36a02901.htm*

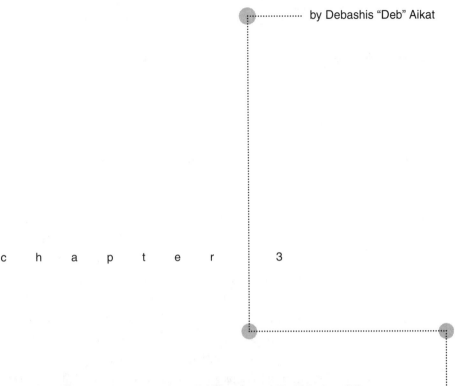

by Debashis "Deb" Aikat

c   h   a   p   t   e   r   3

Of Online News and "Rogue" Web Sites:
Impact of the Web on the Private Sector

This chapter provides an overview of major concentrations of web activity in the private sector. Special emphasis is given to: (1) how the Web is transforming the private sector, (2) the role of Internet technologies in unifying activists worldwide including the new phenomenon of "rogue" web sites for online protest, (3) the proliferation of online media, and (4) the growth of online news readership. The chapter considers the social, political, and economic significance of these developments and examines the impact of private sector Internet use at the individual, group, national, and global levels of analysis. In the conclusion section, we identify the key elements that contribute toward successful applications of the Web in the private sector and how the Web is transforming global business and society.

The Web Is Transforming the Private Sector

The Web is transforming global business and society, and has already emerged as a significant source of income for many individuals and private sector units. According to a 1998 Internet compensation survey by the American Electronics Association, salaries for Internet- and web-related jobs range from $39,500 to $120,100 a year, substantially outpacing the private sector wage average of $28,582 (DeBare, 1998).

Technology companies in the private sector account for a third of the annual economic growth in the United States (Gore, 1998). The widespread adoption of the Web in the private sector is evident from the record number of new Internet domain names registered in 1998. Most private sector companies register with Network Solutions, the designated registrar of domain names, which reported a record 621,000 new Internet domain names in the fourth quarter of 1998, up 137 percent from the fourth quarter of 1997. Almost 10,000 new names were registered each working day. The cumulative total of Internet domain registrations grew 118 percent, from 1.5 million by December 31, 1997, to nearly 3.4 million through December 31, 1998 (Richtel, 1999).

The Web brought business and profits to King's Restaurant in Kinston, North Carolina after it started delivering electronic orders from the Carolina Oink Express *[http://www.kingsbbq.com/]*. In 1997 the restaurant emerged as one of the region's biggest exporters after it started selling eastern North Carolina barbecue "shipped overnight anywhere in the United States." The Web is now changing the face of the music industry with its ability to offer a huge music selection, for free in most cases. With near-CD quality sound at high compression ratios, MP3 technology *[http://www.mp3.com/]* enables anyone with web access to download and distribute music with the help of an MP3 player or software for replaying MP3-compressed audio files.

Companies in the travel industry have embraced the Web. The SABRE Group, a world leader in travel-related information, offers free online travel reservations through Travelocity *[http://www.travelocity.com/]* and easySABRE *[http://www.easySabre.com/]*. Launched in February 1996, MapQuest *[http://www.mapquest.com/]* is another top-rated travel site where web users explore millions of towns and cities worldwide. Users can display addresses on a map, view nearby businesses, get driving directions, and plan a trip with lodging, restaurant, and city information. The American Airlines web site [http://www.AA.com/], unveiled in May 1995 and redesigned in June 1998, has been rated the most popular airline site on the Internet, drawing about 1.5 million visits per week. This site sends a weekly e-mail detailing last-minute, low-fare deals to 2.1 million subscribers (Imperato, 1999).

American Airlines also used its web site to report flight cancellations in February 1999 when pilots began calling in sick to protest consequences of a merger with Reno Air. Within hours of a September 1998 air crash off Nova Scotia, Canada, Swissair used its web site [http://www.swissair.com/] to disseminate information about help-line numbers for relatives. Later updates included a book of condolences, a transcript of flight SR111's communications with air traffic control, and new information on the crash, as it became available.

Corporate web sites offer a variety of information. Fannie Mae, the largest source of home mortgage funds in the United States, provides free online home-buying and refinancing information from its web site [http://www.home path.com/]. A plethora of online investing firms such as E*TRADE [http://www.etrade.com/] enable consumers to trade stocks online 24 hours a day, seven days a week. Procter & Gamble has dedicated its Tide ClothesLine web site [http://www.clothesline.com/] to keeping "clothes looking their best," with features like personalized solutions to tough laundry stains from "The Tide Stain Detective."

The advent of the web in the private sector has led to several legal ramifications. The search for user-friendly domain names has created a cottage industry of "cybersquatting" in which a new breed of electronic brokers called domain name sellers registers domain names relating to popular trademark names (Maloney, 1997). Until they are paid a high price, these brokers prevent companies from registering electronic addresses identifiable with their name, product, or service. In 1993 MTV video jockey Adam Curry registered mtv.com when MTV had no interest in the Internet. But in 1994, when Curry's mtv.com web site started to get a lot of press and numerous hits from web users, MTV sued Curry for trademark infringement, unfair competition, and deceptive trade practices. Curry and MTV ultimately settled out of court, and MTV is now listed as the official registrant for "mtv.com". Common keyword-based domain names such as pimples.com (registered by Procter & Gamble), eat.com (registered by Meyer Foods for Lipton), weather.com (registered by The Weather Channel), and news.com (registered by CNET, the computer network) have generated high traffic. In some cases, common keyword-based domain names like computer.com are up for sale for a "minimum cash bid" of $500,000. The initial registrant for this domain name was Van Clair Company—a firm based in San Carlos, California.

Not all is well with the growth of the private sector on the Web. Almost half of all unsolicited commercial e-mail ("spam") in 1998 consisted of phony offers designed to defraud consumers, according to a major report by the Center for Democracy and Technology (CDT) *[http://www.cdt.org/]*, a civil-liberties organization. According to the CDT report, spam diminishes the reputation and utility of e-mail and contributes to system crashes, lost messages, and general delays (Scoblionkov, 1998b). Spam has attracted the wrath of the Federal Trade Commission (FTC) which has compiled a list of "The Dirty Dozen Spam Scams," listing the most common fraudulent offers made in mass e-mails. The primary spam scams involve chain letters, "make money fast" promises, health scams, and bogus investment opportunities. The FTC also created an online tipsheet: "Cybersmarts: Tips for Protecting Yourself When Shopping Online" (Scoblionkov, 1998a).

The Web Empowers Activists, Groups Worldwide

Internet technologies such as e-mail and the Web are now being used as grassroots weapons of democracy. The Internet has bonded groups worldwide into virtual communities by generating greater dialogue between like-minded groups and individuals, encouraging a consensus of views. People are more aware of what others are doing: non-governmental organizations, citizens' groups, trade unions, worker's parties, consumer activists, and development and environmental groups are using the Internet. They not only exchange information among themselves to coordinate opposition or plan protests, but they also use e-mail and the Web to alert their diverse publics, including politicians, the media, and civil servants.

"Rogue" Web Sites: A New Phenomenon of Online Protest

The fabric of a modern society has always been influenced by protest, and "rogue" web sites illustrate how the Internet has changed the paradigm of protest in unprecedented ways. In the past, those who protested against a company or organization were essentially restricted to street demonstrations and pamphlets. But with the advent of the Web, protesters have gained an inexpensive, far-reaching, and influential public medium to voice their complaints. Various activists have set up rogue web sites to disseminate everything from flaws in cars and computer chips to closely guarded trade secrets of companies. Disgruntled employees as well as technically savvy individuals can generate controversy or destroy the reputation of a company. Apart from adversely influencing thousands of web users, rogue web sites have developed into an influential forum for consumer scorn. On the other hand, a growing number of companies have discovered that the Web gives them an equally powerful opportunity to fight back. The following four cases illustrate how the Internet is rapidly becoming a very fertile ground for the disgruntled in the form of rogue web sites.

The Kmart Sux web site *[http://www.glr.com/kstory.html]* was created by a Brandeis University student who worked at a Kmart store. His web site contained several pages of text blasting Kmart's operations, and it displayed Kmart's trademarked red K logo. Under pressure from Kmart, the student changed the K to an X and the color from red to blue. Despite repeated efforts by Kmart and its representatives to close down the Kmart Sux web site, it remains an icon of protest on the Internet. In another case, the Intel Secrets web site *[http://www.x86.org/secrets/intelsecrets.htm]* listed "deficiencies in Intel products." According to the webmaster of the Intel Secrets site, Intel responded to his site by investigating him for possible trademark infringement, revealing trade secrets, and violating a nondisclosure agreement he said he never signed. Despite his proclaimed innocence, he said he changed the logo he originally created for the site to avoid a trademark dispute and substituted one he felt was a clear parody. In another case, Intel's stock prices dropped in 1994 after computer experts and users published in newsgroups reports of flaws in its Pentium processors. Investors in the stock market and consumers alike began to doubt Intel's commitment to quality after it failed to immediately address the issue.

In April 1996, after yielding to public pressure and several class action lawsuits, Ford announced the recall of 8.7 million cars and trucks. The decision to recall was reached after a group called the "Association of Flaming Ford Owners" published a web site [http://www.flamingfords.com/] dedicated to focusing public attention on the problem—a faulty ignition switch that caused spontaneous vehicle fires in certain models. The web site generated an enormous amount of media attention, attracting coverage from *The New York Times*, CNN Interactive, and National Public Radio. A spokesperson for Ford told *The New York Times* that news articles on the fires provoked a spurt of complaints that helped the company isolate the problem. In fact, it was the online coalition that initially spurred much of the media coverage.

The McDonald's McSpotlight case also led to interesting consequences. In 1994, two United Kingdom environmentalists from North London distributed a leaflet accusing McDonald's, the fast food chain, of promoting an unhealthy diet, paying workers low wages, plotting against trade unions, and exploiting animals—among other evils. McDonald's sued the pair, and stumbled into what became the longest libel trial in British history, a David-and-Goliath battle that saw McDonald's demonized as a corporate monster in the press. The consequences of the "McLibel" trial were taken online. In what was publicized as an effort to combat corporate bullying tactics, a team of 60-plus volunteers across the globe formed an organization called the McInformation Network. On February 16, 1996, they launched the "McSpotlight" web site [http://www.mcspotlight.org/] dedicated to coverage of the trial and exposure of related information. McSpotlight essentially put McDonald's on continuous trial, allowing for public scrutiny of more than 21,000 files, 24 hours a day, including internal corporate memos, scientific reports, company publications, nearly 90 McLibel witness statements, and newspaper coverage. The site generated 1.7 million hits in a 12-week period, as well as coverage by *The New York Times, USA Today, The Chicago Tribune,* and NBC News.

Each of the four cases relating to rogue web sites illustrates two major issues. One, how activists have successfully used the potential of the Web against corporate giants, and two, while most companies are aggressively trying to reap the benefits of the Internet, they seem oblivious of how the Internet may have counterproductive effects. The rogue web sites have affected the targeted companies with such catastrophic consequences as marred credibility, lost revenues, lower market share, steep slumps in stock prices, adverse public opinion, significant drops in sales, and depletion of corporate marketing budgets as companies attempted to reverse the damage. On the other hand, some rogue web sites like Kmart Sux and Intel Secrets raise significant questions about the free speech rights of the publishers of rogue web sites versus the right of companies to protect their brand or property. According to First Amendment interpretations, speech that is strictly opinion and presentations that are clearly parody are protected. But whether or not publishers of rogue web sites are acting within their rights, the mere threat of a long and costly court fight with a company may be enough to intimidate some. Usually, the publishers of rogue web sites do not have the legal or financial prowess to fight a company suing them.

Media Web Sites Are Proliferating

Media web sites are proliferating on the Internet. The online media have transformed journalism with features like interactive, on-demand, customizable content, and the creative combinations of text, graphics, moving images, and sound. The Web also fosters the creation of "e-communities" based on shared interests and concerns, and offers unlimited space to achieve levels of reportorial depth, texture, and context that are impossible in any traditional medium. Online journalism also affords greater interactivity through two-way links where the editor is also the facilitator of communications, as well as unlimited access to a worldwide online audience.

One of the most comprehensive resources for online publications, the Editor and Publisher's online media directory, listed 11,157 online media-related web sites comprising 3,394 newspapers, 2,035 radio stations, 1,253 television sites, 3,861 magazines, 291 online city guides, 164 syndicated/news services, and 159 media associations. As of February 1999, when this directory was last updated, United States-based media constitute a majority of the radio, television, magazine, and newspaper web sites. For instance, United States-based media comprise 2,083 (61.3 percent) of the 3,394 online newspapers, 2,611 (67.6 percent) of the 3,861 e-zines, 881 (70.3 percent) of the 1,253 television sites, and 1,325 (65.1 percent) of the 2,035 radio stations on the Internet (*Media INFO Links,* 1999).

In sharp contrast to their traditional counterparts, the leaders in online news reflect a convergence of media pedigrees. They include cable television entities like CNN *[http://www.cnn.com/]* and ESPN *[http://www.espn.com/]*; conglomerates of computer companies like ZDNet *[http://www.zdnet.com/]* and CNet *[http://www.cnet.com*; and MSNBC *[http://www.msnbc.com/]*, a joint venture of the software giant Microsoft and the television network NBC. Also present are traditional media giants like Time Warner's Pathfinder *[http://www.pathfinder.com/]*, The Washington Post *[http://www.washington post.com/]*, The New York Times *[http://www.nytimes.com/]*, Condé Nast *[http://www.condenet.com/]*, the *Los Angeles Times [http://www.latimes.com/]*, and the *Wall Street Journal [http://www.wsj.com/]*. With the exception of the *Wall Street Journal,* most of these web sites offer free access and nearly 90 percent of web users go online to get news and information (Maddox, 1997).

On the Internet, where publications do not have to invest in expensive printing presses and distribution systems, the online media are vying for the attention of the reader. Consider the following changes and challenges. Most of the media web sites offer their information free, and this has led to questions about the profitability of media web sites. Time Warner has spent nearly $100 million and lost $30 million from 1994 through 1999 on Pathfinder, which has yet to earn a profit (Lyons, 1999). Time Warner launched Pathfinder *[http://www.pathfinder.com/]* on October 24, 1994, as a megasite incorporating its popular magazines—*Time, People, Fortune, Money,* and *Entertainment Weekly.* Five years later, in 1999, Pathfinder was generating only a fraction of the traffic seen at sites like Yahoo! and Lycos, and Time Warner elected to shut down this pioneering Internet gateway (Stone, 1999). In May 1998, *Mercury Center [http://www.mercurycenter.com/]*, the first full-content online newspaper in the United States and a voice of Silicon Valley with useful technology information and other news, turned five years old. At that time it declared itself a "free site" for all articles from the *San Jose Mercury News,* breaking news and updates of significant local stories. Until then, *Mercury Center* was a fee-based subscription service.

Although the lack of profitability of media web sites is troubling to media firms, that has not stopped other companies from developing innovations like "push" technology, also called webcasting, the delivery of information services directly to computer users' desktops via the Internet. Webcasting is growing rapidly, but it could provoke a backlash if it is seen as too intrusive or as consuming too many computing resources (Cortese, 1997). Users download special software and specify what information they want to receive, thus creating a profile stored in the webcast service's database. The users' client software can run either on an individual machine, dialing a modem to download updates at specified intervals, or on a corporate server where the data is downloaded automatically and delivered to employees to reduce network traffic. Webcasting has created many business opportunities for start-ups such as PointCast Network *[http://www.pointcast.com/]*, Marimba *[http://www.marimba.com/]*, and NewsEdge *[http://www.newsedge.com/]*. Push technology has the potential to change the way business information is delivered over the Internet by bringing order and relevance to the boundless data available on the Web, repackaging information from newspapers, magazines, television, and wire services and delivering it to computer users based on their interests. Webcasting provides a way to cope with information overload by "narrowcasting" data, including rich multimedia content, to specific users. Both Microsoft and Netscape are working to add push support to their market-leading products.

In contrast to push technology, local content providers like CitySearch *[http://www.citysearch.com/]* have developed a working model as leading providers of local city guides, local advertising and live event ticketing on the Internet. Their method of operation involves entering markets, hiring local talent, and using local media partners to provide content. CitySearch CEO Charles Conn believes these local partnerships are the secret to helping CitySearch fight off better funded competitors (AT&T, Microsoft) that may come into the market and try to take over. CitySearch has grown over the past two-and-a-half years to include markets in Canada, Australia, and Scandinavia. Recent successes include launching sites in Stockholm, Los Angeles, and San Diego. CitySearch partnered with Ticketmaster online *[http://www.ticketmaster.com/]* in 1998 to offer consumers up-to-date information on live entertainment events and a convenient means of purchasing tickets and related merchandise in 42 states, Canada, and the United Kingdom.

Weather information is another frequently accessed commodity on the Web. AccuWeather *[http://www.accuweather.com/]*, a weather forecasting service based in State College, Pennsylvania, recently introduced a service that enables newspaper web sites to offer readers personalized forecasts. The service allows readers to enter a ZIP code at their local newspaper's web site and receive a customized weather forecast. The weather service also provides a travel-forecast feature, giving users weather news about their current location and their destination. The Weather Channel *[http://www.weather.com]* extends its cable television presence via the Web, providing local forecasts, travel-related forecasts, and a variety of other types of weather information.

The Growth of Web Portals

Touted as solutions to information overload, web portals, in today's terms, are primary web sites or online services that function as a consumer's everyday first stop on the Internet. The first web portals were online services such as America Online and search engines like Yahoo!, but by 1998 most of the traditional search engines transformed themselves into web portals to attract a larger audience, and analysts expect portals to evolve into central databases for web users' data. Thus far, Yahoo! and America Online have captured the first and second spots, respectively, according to RelevantKnowledge, Inc. Industry estimates attribute more than half of the web portal traffic to these two sites (Briones, 1998).

Major portal sites like Excite, Lycos, and Infoseek began as search engines with features that allowed users to scour the net for information. However, several of these sites have moved into original content, news, and games in order to keep surfers at their site longer. The idea behind this strategy is to present unlimited access to information and thus become a content-rich site that people want to explore. In doing so, the site becomes lucrative to advertisers, and consequently profitable to investors. Web portals can achieve a high level of consumer loyalty, often due to customization. Most portals allow users to enter profiles of their likes and dislikes. The site then automatically changes and updates according to users' preferences whenever they log on (Briones, 1998). All web portals partner with content providers like AccuWeather *[http://www.accuweather.com/]* for meteorological data and Zip2 *[http://www.zip2.com/]* for directory listings or with news organizations like the Associated Press *[http://www.ap.org/]* or Reuters *[http://www.reuters.com/]*. In 1999, web portals partnered with an average of 20 such companies; by 2002, the web portals expect partnerships with hundreds of companies. The next section covers the history of the online media.

Online Media: From BBS to the Web

In the early 1980s, a few newspapers tried online services and abandoned them after initial setbacks. During the mid-1980s, Knight Ridder lost $50 million on Viewtron, an electronic news venture (Piirto, 1993), and that prompted industry leaders to take a cautious approach to investing in new electronic businesses (DeGeorge and Byrd, 1994). While some industry leaders declared electronic news services dead as a mass medium, others considered them a threat to the traditional media (Cameron et al., 1996). However, by 1994,with the emergence of the Web in the American mainstream, electronic news services began proliferating and receiving much media attention. By 1993 many publications like the *Palo Alto Weekly [http://www.service.com/paw/]*, which delivered electronic news via online service providers like America Online (AOL), started experimenting with the Web. *The San Jose Mercury News* led the trend by launching Mercury Center on the Web *[http://www.sjmercury.com/]* in May 1993, and it was also available to nearly 3 million AOL subscribers (until September 1995). Mercury Center was arguably the first online venture to offer a wide range of electronic information services (including a newspaper library from 1985 to present), the daily newspaper itself, communication with newspaper editors and staff, and other means to access personalized information. The potential of web-based newspapers was demonstrated in November 1994 during a newspaper strike in San Francisco. While eight unions at the *San Francisco Examiner* and *San Francisco Chronicle* newspapers were on strike, one group of striking news and editorial workers wrote and published an online newspaper on the Web. Management quickly countered with an electronic newspaper of its own (King, 1994).

In 1994, there were about 20 online newspaper services worldwide—mostly bulletin board systems[1] (BBS) with a handful of publisher alliances with commercial online services (Outing, 1995a). However, by the end of 1994, the Web had emerged as the favored online news medium, and online newspapers started to show signs of life, with about 100 newspapers operating or under development online. The year 1994 also not only witnessed online editions of major newspapers such as the *Los Angeles Times [http://www.la times.com/]*, but also saw the *Atlanta Constitution-Journal [http://www.ajc.com/]* operating as Access Atlanta *[http://www.accessatlanta.com/]* in partnership with Prodigy's Legacy online system. The Web also attracted other converts like the *Fort Worth Star-Telegram's* StarText; launched in 1982 as a dial-up, text-based BBS, it is one of the oldest surviving online news services (Outing, 1995b). In fall 1995, it made the transition to the Web *[http://www.star-telegram.com/]*, attracted by the Web's ease of use and potential to cover a vast audience. By August 1995, there were 313 online newspaper services across the globe (not counting another 100-plus college newspapers on the Internet). The online newspaper business, while still minuscule compared to the $44 billion core newspaper business in the United States, had grown more than 200 percent within eight months in 1995 (Outing, 1995a). By the end of 1995, newspapers on the Web were becoming numerous, and most BBS-based news services completed the transition to web-based platforms by 1996 (Outing, 1995a). Some newspapers like the *Los Angeles Times,* the *Milwaukee Journal-Sentinel [http://www.onwisconsin.com/]*, the *Washington Post,* and the *Minneapolis Star Tribune [http://www.startribune.com/]* abandoned deals with commercial online service providers to set up their own web sites (Outing, 1996b).

---

[1] Bulletin Board Services (BBSs) are electronic message centers on the Internet. Most bulletin boards, some of them web based, serve specific interest groups. They allow you to dial in with a modem, review messages left by others, and leave your own message if you want. Bulletin boards are a particularly good place to find free or inexpensive software products. In the United States alone, there are tens of thousands of BBSs.

In 1996, most of the nation's premier newspapers also staked out their domains on the Web. When *The New York Times on the Web [http://www.nytimes.com/]* began operating during the last week of January 1996, it had achieved 100,000 hits by 10:30 a.m. on its inaugural day (Outing, 1996a). The Web had established an online trend. Nearly 77 percent of U.S. newspaper and magazine editors surveyed in 1996 said they planned to have an online edition, compared with only 54 percent in 1995, according to a survey of newspapers and magazines (Middleberg and Ross, 1996). The survey determined that 15 percent of daily newspapers were already online, and an estimated 72 percent would have their web presence by 2001. Middleberg and Ross concluded that online technologies and the tremendous growth of online publishing from 1994 to 1997 had changed the nature of news operations more than the events of the previous 40 years (Ross and Middleberg, 1998). At least half of the journalists surveyed were using the Web to distribute news, and 55 percent said their publication, or portions of it, was already online. That was more than double the 25 percent reported in 1995. According to the study, only 9 percent of respondents in 1997 said their publication had no plans to go online at all (Ross and Middleberg, 1998).

Multimedia Streaming and Radio on the Web

1995, the emergence of rich multimedia capabilities, particularly streaming audio and video, continued to enhance the effectiveness of the Web as a communication medium. These technologies enabled the program content of the traditional television and radio media to be delivered over the Internet. Seattle-based Real Networks *[http://www.real.com]* makes software that enables computer users to hear audio and see video over the Internet. New streaming formats also enhance the Web with rich multimedia experiences ranging from the ability to tune in to real-time webcasts around the world, to the chance to sample music before buying, to the capability of multicast technology to connect multiple viewers and allow them to see the same video stream.

While viewing video is already possible and its use on the Internet is widespread at present, the image is small in size, halting, and unsynchronized when seen through most modems that operate at relatively slow speeds.

However, the day is not far off when the quality of audio and video on the Web will be as good as television quality on computer terminals.

In a historic first, the Internet helped National Public Radio's (NPR) stations to maintain uninterrupted service during a satellite outage. In May 1998, within an hour after the Galaxy 4 satellite unexpectedly turned away from Earth, NPR began using its web site [http://www.npr.org] to offer 600 member stations a backup feed of the radio network's regular programming. This included NPR's flagship program, "All Things Considered" (Wice, Mccullagh, and Grossman, 1998). In November 1998, with Internet webcasts of such major events as the Clinton grand jury testimony and with the possibility of streamed audio and video emerging as a mass-market phenomenon, Arbitron, the company known for rating radio station listenership, announced a set of partnerships for tracking usage of streamed audio sites. The new partners include Real Networks and Magnitude Network, two companies that, in one way or another, help radio stations put programming on the Net. While the web advertising market as a whole is expected to reach $2 billion this year, less than $25 million of it is likely to come from ads at streaming sites. In starting to flesh out the details of its upcoming service, Arbitron conceded that there has not yet been a real outcry for measurement services in Internet multimedia, a part of the market where file requests are typically measured in the dozens or hundreds, not millions. By mid-1999, Arbitron expects to introduce a password-protected web site that will provide streamed content sites with data on how their audience sizes compare with those of their competitors. That information will be derived from the log files of partner companies, such as Real Networks, that stream large amounts of audio.

In the past, the fleeting nature of television and limited broadcast time restricted the medium's impact on audiences and its effectiveness. However, interactive web sites offer television programmers a host of useful features. Web sites can provide greater mileage to the otherwise ephemeral programming content on television. More than eight years in the making, ABC's 12-hour special, "The Century," will offer an in-depth look at the past 100 years. The show features stories from people who witnessed major historical events of the 20th century. Online, TheCentury.com is telling those stories in greater detail (Kilsheimer, 1998). Television network web pages now feature original content and promos specially geared to attract a loyal following. NBC pioneered the development of web specials last year with the unveiling of Homicide, Second Shift [http://www.nbc.com/homicide/]. The site is based on the show "Homicide: Life on the Street." On the Web, Homicide, Second Shift was a fictional account of a graveyard shift working out of the same Baltimore precinct house featured in the prime-time show. The web version features fictional characters solving crimes as users click through the site. NBC also offers an interactive version of "Late Night with Conan O'Brien" (Kilsheimer, 1998).

Television viewers can now interact with news anchors, reporters, celebrity program hosts, and actors though e-mail or discussion forums. New searchable program guide web sites provide a ready reference not only for program time but for other details like trivia and profiles of actors. Some web sites have emerged as significant news sources providing updated news around the clock. Some television web sites have successfully facilitated efforts to address shared interests or used innovative ways to unite viewers into virtual communities with web-based discussion forums. Web sites provide value-added resources like access to archives of historical material, program transcripts, and even visuals. CNN's Cold War web site [http://www.cnn.com/coldwar/] was designed to augment the 24-part documentary series, which premiered September 27, 1998. The Cold War web site provides access to resources that depict how the Cold War affected nearly every aspect of our lives, from culture, technology, and economics to the pervasive uncertainty that came with the invention that changed the world forever: the atomic bomb. ABC's The Century [http://abcnews.go.com/century/] web site asked viewers to share memories for an online time capsule. Some web sites invite viewer participation and response from a worldwide audience, and viewers post their own firsthand accounts. Web specials have enabled television firms to do anything from selling products or promoting television shows to encouraging children to volunteer in their communities. Kids-oriented Nickelodeon [http://www.Nickelodeon.com/], for example, features a series of web specials including Nickelodeon—The Big Help [http://www.Nickelodeon. com/inits/ bh_dev/index.html] that encourages kids to volunteer in their communities and offers tips to get started. This site also allows kids to post messages about their volunteer projects.

All of the above examples illustrate how television web sites have finally tuned in to the unique capabilities of the Internet. According to Kilsheimer, "For years, television treated the Internet like an afterthought. Although the networks have posted web sites for a long time, much of the content was little more than an electronic rehash of their prime-time lineups. That's beginning to change. Television web sites are becoming more sophisticated, and the networks are unveiling 'web specials,' featuring content tailored to Internet audiences." Web specials have the same purpose as the sites the networks put up a few years ago: to promote prime-time shows. But now, the networks are beginning to exploit the Web's unique nature with bulletin boards, celebrity chats, streaming audio, interactive slide shows, and screensaver downloads. You cannot get any of those features on television (Kilsheimer, 1998). Such growth reflects the resolve of media organizations to utilize opportunities created by the rise in online usage by the American people. The next section covers trends in the growth of online news readership.

Growth in Online News Readership Affects TV Network News

The Internet is emerging as a supplement to, not a substitute for, other traditional news sources, according to the Pew Research Center's 1998 news use survey (Pew, 1998). With Internet use skyrocketing in virtually every major demographic group, more than one-third of Americans (36 percent) with a large appetite for news and information were turning to the Internet as another news source from work or home. Nearly 11 percent of those who go online for news said they used other news sources less often. More than half of Internet users (54 percent) said they accessed online sources to get more information about a story they first saw or heard from a more traditional news source (Pew, 1998). People reading news on the Internet also are disproportionately younger, better educated and affluent, and they place a higher value on getting up-to-date news. The most popular subjects online were science, health, finance and technology. The number of Americans going online to read news in 1998 increased at an astonishing rate, with one in five people using the Internet at least once a week to satisfy their appetite for information. The growth reflects the widespread adoption of the Internet by Americans. The Center's earlier study found only 6 percent went online for news in 1996.

The number of Americans going online for news and information more than doubled between 1994 and 1995, according to a 1995 survey on online usage by the Times Mirror Center for the People and the Press (Outing, 1995c). Nearly 60 percent of web users are avid readers of online news sites, according to a 1997 survey by the market research firm NPD Group; the survey also found that newspapers are the most popular type of publication for web news readers. Nearly 40 percent of those polled said they frequently read a newspaper online (Brooks, 1997). At least 67 percent of the online readers surveyed frequently read news on the Internet. Nine out of 10 consumers who read both print and online newspapers rated the two as comparable in terms of the accuracy and reliability (Brooks, 1997). In June 1998 a United Press International poll found that computer users put more confidence in information that they find online than that gleaned from more conventional sources such as newspapers and television. Forty-three percent of those polled said they trusted the accuracy of online information versus 35 percent for other media. And 59 percent of their computer time is spent doing work, versus 41 percent of time spent on recreational activities.

Research studies also indicate a decline in television network viewing associated with increased Internet use. While the Pew study (1998) found Internet use and cable television viewing were flourishing, it indicated declining viewership for nightly broadcast network news. Only 38 percent of Americans, mostly older women, describe themselves as regular network news viewers, down from 60 percent in 1993. But television newsmagazines like 60 Minutes, 20/20, and Dateline NBC were gaining popularity, especially among younger viewers. Readership of daily newspapers remained stable. The study found that Americans continue to rely heavily on their daily paper as a primary source of news, with 68 percent reading regularly, not much different than the center's 1996 study showed. But only 28 percent of people under 30 reported reading a newspaper within 24 hours of the survey, compared with 69 percent of seniors, "a far more dramatic generation gap than exists for television news consumption," the study said.

The growth of the Internet may affect TV viewership. For instance, web users said they spend as much time on the Internet as they do watching television, if not more, according to the 1998 WebCensus which broke down the time web users dedicated to various media during the course of a day. Respondents said 31 percent of their time was spent on the Internet, compared to 29 percent for television, 24 percent for radio, and 16 percent for print media such as newspapers and magazines. Nearly 58 percent of those surveyed use the Internet in addition to traditional media; but when asked which media Internet users gave up to go online, 22 percent said television, compared to 12 percent for newspapers and magazines and 3 percent for radio (Hu, 1998). In sum, all of these studies confirm a rise in the number of Americans using the Internet for news and information. The next section covers the social, political, and economic dimensions of the impact of the Web on the private sector.

Impact of the Web on the Private Sector

This chapter began with brief instances of how the Web has changed the way we live, think and communicate in the private sector. This section covers the social, political, and economic dimensions of the impact of the Web on the private sector at the individual, group, national, and global levels of analyses.

Individual Level

The advent of the Web has given individuals in the private sector the power to assume significant identities as entrepreneurs, activists, protesters, and informed citizens. The Web provides ease of access to information through portal web sites and online media. The Internet has also empowered entrepreneurs with new opportunities to achieve business success. Pierre Omidyar helped his girlfriend set up a web site in 1995 to sell her Pez dispensers. Soon, he had a bit of a following and allowed others to post at a small charge. The word traveled fast on the Internet, and eBay.com became Pierre's full-time job. Four years later, in 1999, eBay [http://www.ebay.com/] facilitates 400,000 daily online auctions for 2.1 million registered users and has built a worth of $7 billion. The Web in the private sector offers price advantages to consumers, with many vendors selling merchandise well below average retail prices. But considering how much web merchants claim they can save in costs by operating in cyberspace, true savings are rare once shipping costs are figured in (Green, 1998).

From online media to portal and corporate web sites, web developers in the public sector are attempting techniques to customize content that can be tailored to an individual user. This is being done to bring about a sense of community and belonging for people who fit similar psychological and demographic profiles online. For instance, Micromass Communications programmed the American Heart Association web site [http://www.american heart.org/] to generate pages for visitors based on individual profiles developed during registration. The site can show users who are at risk of heart disease how likely it is that they will be able to change their lifestyle and reduce cholesterol. Different messages are presented to individuals, based on their answers to an online questionnaire (Koprowski, 1998).

▶ Group Level

At the group level, the impact of the Web has benefited diverse groups of people because the Internet has something to offer to everybody, from new forums for protest to news and information. Working at the group level, private sector companies with strong online communities can gain customer loyalty and huge profits. Several initiatives like eBay's virtual flea market, with lively chat and ratings systems, keep subscribers buzzing about shared interests ranging from memorabilia to stamps. "Recommender services" at sites track information about customers' tastes and suggest products that might be of interest (Green, 1998). A 1997 article in *The Economist* attributed the winning formula of Amazon [http://www.amazon.com/] to community building and participation ("A River," 1997). The notion of community has been at the heart of the Internet since its early days, when groups of scientists used it to share data, collaborate on research, and exchange messages, according to Armstrong and Hagel (1996). Companies that have used their Internet sites to build online communities have been successful because a growing number of web users seek out sites that put them in contact with others who share similar interests.

A 1997 Business Week/Harris Poll found that 57 percent of current Internet users repeatedly return to their favorite community web site. Almost one-third of the 89 percent of Internet users utilizing e-mail are linked to an online community (Hof, Browder, and Elstrom, 1997). Internet communities can also turn into successful businesses, particularly when they provide ways for site visitors to interact with one another. Armstrong and Hagel believe businesses can benefit from creating four types of online communities for users: communities of transaction, communities of interest, communities of relationship, and communities of fantasy. These communities provide opportunities for people with common interests to communicate and exchange ideas, or even support. Businesses can stand to gain if they create a mix of all these types of communities. Usage fees, content fees, advertising, and direct sales are some of the ways companies can expect to profit.

National Level

At the national level, the Web in the private sector has helped companies do business, unhampered by barriers of geography or time, offering consumers the benefits of simplicity and convenience. Through its web site, Recreational Equipment racks up 35 percent of its online orders between 10 p.m. and 7 a.m., when its stores are closed and its mail-order operators aren't available (Green, 1998). Another example of convenience is Dell's cyber shopping cart [http://www.dell.com/], which lets customers customize a PC online and then store the selection for up to two weeks. Variety, being the spice of life, attracts consumers. Companies like CDnow [http://www.cdnow.com/] and eToys [http://www.etoys.com/] enjoy unlimited shelf space online and thus can cram their web sites full of offerings. Amazon offers a selection of more than 3 million books, plus music and other products. Realtor.com lists 1.1 million homes, which it claims is more than 90 percent of all homes for sale in the United States. All these examples prove how companies can have national and even international reach because of the Web.

Global Level

At the global level, the growth of the Web in the private sector has yet to reach its true potential. But the emergence of the Web as a mass medium will have global ramifications. Spawned as a Pentagon-funded communications network for scientists and academics, the Internet has evolved into a mass medium and a global platform for everything from electronic commerce to dating. Spearheaded by the rapid adoption of the Web over three years from 1996 to 1998, the Internet accomplished several milestone moments to become a mass medium. Internet coverage of the death and funeral of Diana, Princess of Wales, brought mourners together in cyberspace. In the summer of 1997, NASA published the first pictures from Mars, and millions logged on to primary and mirror sites set up to handle the huge volume of web traffic. The gyrations of the stock market and the impeachment proceedings against President Bill Clinton have also generated huge spikes in Internet traffic (Harmon, 1998). The online media have enormous growth potential.

Summary and Conclusion

Based on analyses from a social, political, and economic perspective, the preceding sections examined how the growth of the Web in the private sector has changed the way we live, think, and communicate. The Web has made a significant impact in transforming the private sector in various ways including successful corporate efforts, astonishing growth of web portals, the emergence of Internet technologies in unifying activists worldwide, the new phenomenon of rogue web sites for online protest, and the proliferation of the online media. This chapter explored the impact of the Web in the private sector. The next chapter will cover culture and the Internet.

References

Armstrong, A., and Hagel, J. III. 1996, May-June. The Real Value of On-line Communities. *Harvard Business Review,* 74:134–41.

Briones, M.G. 1998, October 28. Internet Portals' Mad Dash for Cash. *Marketing News,* 32:1.

Brooks, W. 1997, April 4. 60% of Web Users Read Online Publications (Best Read News Nuggets—E&P Interactive). mediainfo.com. [Online] Retrieved August 15, 1998, from the World Wide Web: *http://www.mediainfo.com/ephome/news/newshtm/nuggets/ nug0409.htm*

Cameron, G.T.; Curtin, P.A.; Hollander, B.A.; Nowak, G.J.; and Shamp, S.A. 1996. Electronic Newspapers: Toward a Research Agenda. *Journal of Mediated Communication*, 11(1): 3–53.

Cortese, A. 1997, February 24. A Way Out of the Web Maze. *Business Week*, 94-104.

DeBare, I. 1998, April 21. Web Workers Command Higher-than-Average Wages. *The San Francisco Chronicle*, p. C1.

DeGeorge, G., and Byrd, V.N. 1994, April 11. Knight-Ridder: Once Burned, and the Memory Lingers. *Business Week*, pp. 74–75.

Gore, A. 1998, October 12. *Vice President Gore Announces Five Challenges to Build a Global Information Infrastructure*. The White House Office of the Vice President. [Online] Retrieved March 1, 1999, fromthe World Wide Web: *http://www.accessamerica.gov/docs/informa tiontechnology_gorespeech.html*.

Green, H. 1998, June 22. Cyberspace Winners: How They Did It. *Business Week*, pp. 154–60.

Harmon, A. 1998, 20 September. Access to Clinton Data Abets E Pluribus Unum, '90s Style. *The New York Times on the Web*. [Online] Retrieved February 5, 1999, from the World Wide Web: *http://www.nytimes.com/library/politics/092098clinton-internet.html*.

Hof, R.D.; Browder, S.; and Elstrom, P. 1997, May 5. Internet Communities. *Business Week*, pp. 64–73.

Hu, J. 1998, March 30. Study: Net Use Eclipsing TV. CNET News.com. [Online] Retrieved February 5, 1999, from the World Wide Web: *http://www.news.com/News/Item/ 0%2C4%2C20597%2c00.html?dd.ne.tx.wr*.

Imperato, G. 1999, April. Web Sites We Can't Live Without. Fast Company, 23:266.

Kilsheimer, J. 1998, August 30. TV Finally Tunes in to Power of the Internet *Orlando Sentinel*, p. D6B.

King, P. 1994, November 21. On Strike but Online, Too. *Newsweek*, 124:106.

Koprowski, G. 1998, August 25. A New Crop of Web Developers Wants to Get Inside Your Head. *The Wall Street Journal Interactive Edition*. [Online] Retrieved March 5, 1999, from the World Wide Web: *http://interactive.wsj.com/*.

Lyons, D. 1999, March 22. Desperate.com. *Forbes*, 163:50–51.

Maddox, K. 1997, October 6. Information Still Killer App on the Internet. *Advertising Age*, 68: 42–43.

Maloney, M.C. 1997. Intellectual Property in Cyberspace. *Business Lawyer*, 53(1): 225–49.

Media INFO Links Database Statistics. 1999, February 11. E&P Interactive Online Media Directory. [Online] Retrieved March 5, 1999, from the World Wide Web: *http://www. mediainfo.com/ephome/npaper/nphtm/statistics.htm*

Middleberg, D., and Ross, S. 1996. *The Media in Cyberspace*. New York: Columbia University.

Outing, S. 1995a, August 21. Join the Party! 300-Plus Newspapers Are Online. E&P Interactive. [Online] Retrieved July 29, 1998, from the World Wide Web: *http://mediainfo.elpress.com/ephome/news/newshtm/stop/stop2.htm.*

———. 1995b, August 28. Oldest Newspaper BBS Makes Transition to the Web. E&P Interactive. [Online] Retrieved July 29, 1998, from the World Wide Web: *http://www.mediainfo.com/ephome/news/newshtm/stop/stop7.htm.*

———. 1995c, October 27. Another Survey Paints Rosy Picture of Web Use. E&P Interactive. [Online] Retrieved July 30, 1999, from the World Wide Web: *http://www.mediainfo.com/ephome/news/newshtm/stop/stop1027.htm.*

———. 1996a, January 22. All the News That's Fit for the Web: *N.Y. Times* Online. E&P Interactive. [Online] Retrieved from the World Wide Web: *http://mediainfo.elpress.com/ephome/news/newshtm/stop/stop122.htm.*

———. 1996b, May 13. Newspapers Online: The Latest Statistics. E&P Interactive. [Online] Retrieved from the World Wide Web: *http://mediainfo.elpress.com/ephome/news/newshtm/stop/stop513.htm.*

Pew Research Center. 1998, June 8. Internet News Takes Off: Pew Research Center Biennial News Consumption Survey. [Online] Retrieved January 5, 1999, from the World Wide Web: *http://www.people-press.org/med98rpt.htm.*

Piirto, R. 1993, January. Electronic News. *American Demographics,* 15:6.

Richtel, M. 1999, January 28. New Domain Names Set a Record in 1998. *The New York Times,* p. G3.

A River Runs through It. 1997, 10 May. *The Economist,* 343:9–10.

Ross, S.S., and Middleberg, D. 1998, February 18. Middleberg/Ross Media in Cyberspace Study 1997, Fourth Annual National Survey. [Online] Retrieved August 15, 1998, from the World Wide Web: *http://www.mediasource.com/cyberstudy/INTRO.HTM.*

Scoblionkov, D. 1998a, July 14. FTC Exposes Spam Scams. *Wired News.* [Online] Retrieved March 5, 1999, from the World Wide Web: *http://www.wired.com/news/news/politics/story/13710.html.*

———. 1998b, 13 July. When Spam Goes Bad. *Wired News.* [Online] Retrieved March 5, 1999, from the World Wide Web: *http://www.wired.com/news/news/politics/story/13667.html.*

Stone, M.L. 1999, May 1. Pathfinder Loses Its Way. *Editor and Publisher,* 132:57.

Wice, N., Mccullagh, D., and Grossman, L. 1998, May 21. Webcast to Broadcast. *TIME Digital.* [Online] Retrieved March 5, 1999, from the World Wide Web: *http://cgi.pathfinder.com/time/digital/daily/0,2822,13486,00.html.*

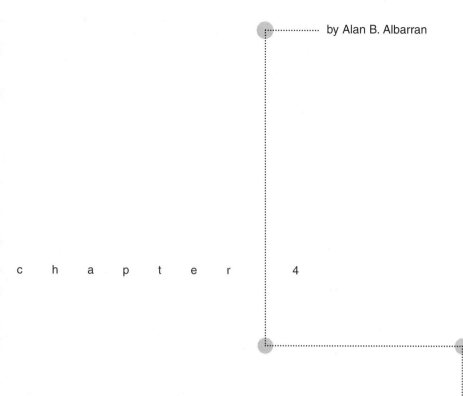

by Alan B. Albarran

c　h　a　p　t　e　r　4

Electronic Commerce

The buying and selling of goods and services via the Internet has escalated into a thriving economic force known as electronic commerce (e-commerce). Initially known as Internet commerce, e-commerce is a phenomenon that is revolutionizing business practices and reshaping traditional means of conducting business. Businesses and consumers use electronic commerce to overcome traditional time and space boundaries in ways not offered by other channels.

What exactly is electronic commerce? E-commerce can be defined in different ways. Kalakota and Whinston (1997) point out that electronic commerce can be defined four different ways, depending on the perspective. The communication perspective focuses on the delivery aspects of e-commerce, using telephone lines, high-speed computer networks, cable modems, and other forms of distribution. The business process perspective centers on transaction processing and automation. A service perspective looks at e-commerce from the standpoint of efficiency and improving the quality of service. Finally, an online perspective focuses on the ability to engage in commerce-related activities via the Internet and other online services.

Growth of Electronic Commerce

Many factors have influenced the growth of electronic commerce. The primary force driving e-commerce is the astounding growth of households acquiring personal computers to access the Internet. The U.S. Department of Commerce found that computer ownership grew an incredible 52 percent between 1994 and 1997, with more than 36 percent of all U.S. households now owning at least one computer (see *[http://www.ntia.doc.gov/ntiahome/net2/]*). Among U.S. households owning a computer, an estimated 28.7 million have online access. In the United States, online access is expected to reach 57 million households by 2002 (see Figure 4.1; Online U.S. Households, 1998).

Globally, the number of Internet hosts and users will also experience an explosive pattern of growth. By the close of 1999, half of the world's Internet users will reside outside the United States, growing to 60 percent by 2002 (In-

Figure 4.1.   Online household projections.

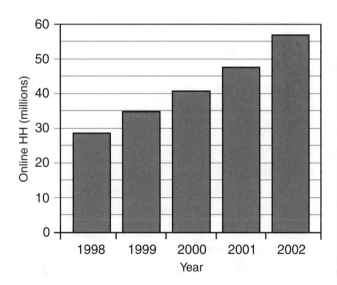

terconnect, 1999a). By the year 2000, the number of host computers is predicted to reach 254 million, while the number of worldwide Internet users may reach as high as 438 million (Cairncross, 1998).

Demand for Internet access has escalated for many different reasons. Declining prices for computing equipment, coupled with a strong economy and low unemployment, has enabled more households to jump online. For less than $1,000, a household can now acquire a complete basic PC multimedia system including a CPU and monitor, modem, and a printer. An even lower priced alternative can be found with a device called WebTV. Priced at around $250, the WebTV terminal can turn a standard TV set into a computer monitor with the ability to access the Internet.

Increasingly, Internet users are shopping for various types of products and services via the Web. A 1997 study by CommerceNet and Nielsen found that 73 percent of Internet users had utilized the Web for shopping during the previous month (Anderson, 1997). A larger study of 50,000 U.S. households conducted by Jupiter Communications found three types of Internet shoppers, which the study labeled buyers, browsers, and non-shoppers (Jupiter/NFO Consumer Survey, 1998).

This chapter looks at the subject of electronic commerce by exploring several different topics. First, existing models of electronic commerce are introduced. Next, following the pattern of the chapters in this section of the text, electronic commerce is discussed along four different levels of analysis: individual, group, national, and global.

Electronic Commerce Models

Electronic commerce has existed since the 1970s, when the financial community began using transactions involving electronic funds transfers (EFT), along with traditional electronic data interchange (EDI), to facilitate routine exchanges with other business partners (Kalakota and Whinston, 1997). This business-to-business commerce represents the oldest and largest model of electronic commerce activity. With the advent of the Web and corporate intranets, millions of dollars of business-to-business transactions are conducted every working day, involving every imaginable form of business activity.

A second model for electronic commerce is represented by consumer-to-business transactions. In this model, consumers shop for products and services via the Web both from established brands such as J.C. Penney, Eddie Bauer, and American Airlines and from new entities existing only in cyberspace such as Amazon.com, CDNow, and Reel.com. In 1998, the top consumer retail areas via the Internet included computer products and services, books and music, consumer goods, and travel. Consumer shopping escalated with the 1998 Christmas season, when an estimated $8.2 billion in purchases were made online (Online Holiday Shopping, 1999).

A third model for electronic commerce involving consumer-to-consumer transactions has emerged. In this model, consumers negotiate with other consumers for goods and services, usually through a third party acting in a brokerage role. Online auctions have become particularly popular, with web sites like eBay that serve as a virtual flea market to facilitate buying and selling. This model is difficult to track in terms of economic activity, because there are numerous web sites and no way to develop aggregate data among shoppers.

Of the three types of e-commerce models, business-to-business will continue to account for the bulk of the economic activity via the Internet. According to Simba Information, of the projected $28.2 billion spent in 1998, approximately $19 billion (67.3 percent) involved business-to-business transactions (Nichols, 1998). For the next decade, most analysts expect business-to-business commerce will continue to dominate e-commerce activity, although the consumer-to-business market appears to be growing at a much faster pace than originally predicted. The combination of instant choice, comparison shopping, and global reach shifts the balance of power to the consumer (Hof, 1999).

Electronic Commerce Predictions

Wall Street, the investment community, information technology research firms, and individual analysts anticipate robust economic growth for electronic commerce. The reasons are simple. Many businesses have made their way to the Web, but high start-up costs and marketing expenses have caused massive losses, even for major Internet brands like Amazon, eBay, and Broadcast.com. As a company, Amazon has yet to earn profits, yet its market capitalization (cost of a share of stock multiplied by total shares outstanding) exceeds that of many established companies like Sears, Delta Airlines, and J.C. Penny (Amazon.com, 1998).

E-commerce transactions are enabled by huge servers that provide many functions to a company web site. Server growth and diffusion illustrate the rapid growth of e-commerce. IBM projects that every month over 53,000 new servers are being connected to the Internet, approximately 1.2 servers per minute (IBM, 1999). Likewise, there are millions of households, both domestically and globally, that have yet to enter the online world. In 1996, worldwide households with Internet access totaled an estimated 23.4 million; by the year 2000 the number of worldwide households with Internet access may exceed 400 million (Anderson, 1997).

Revenue predictions vary considerably for both the business-to-business and business-to-consumer models. Research firms offer estimates ranging from a combined low of $349 billion to as much as $1.2 trillion by 2002. Earlier predictions have for the most part been far more conservative. The reality is that e-commerce on the Internet is growing at a phenomenal rate, much faster than originally anticipated. Several firms offer projections on electronic commerce revenues; these are listed in Table 4.1. Except where noted, the table includes revenues from both business-to-business e-commerce and consumer-to-business e-commerce.

Table 4.1.   E-commerce predictions for 2002 by various firms.

Company/Firm	Projected E-commerce Revenues—2002
Activmedia	$1.2 trillion
Forrester Research	$349 billion
U.S. Commerce Department	$300 billion
ZONA	$204 billion
Simba	$102 billion
Jupiter Communications	$37 billion (consumer only)
Average	*$365 billion*

Source: Data compiled by the author from numerous online sources.

Electronic Commerce Myths

The economic growth potential of e-commerce raises expectations that every type of business can make money via the Internet. This euphoria is understood given the success of firms like Amazon.com, E*Trade, and eBay. These companies have generated millions of dollars in revenues with brands that exist only in cyberspace. Likewise, the incredible growth of Internet-related stocks leads to expectations that any company can be an overnight success on Wall Street.

Reality suggests otherwise. A study by Giga Information Group suggests that only 5 percent of online efforts were expected to be profitable in 1999 (Clampet, 1999). The study concluded that many companies are expected to reach some level of profitability by 2000–2001, especially as established brands increase their net presence.

The belief that every business makes money on the Internet is just one of several myths associated with electronic commerce. An *InformationWeek* article identified eight myths regarding e-commerce (Wilder, 1997). Several myths are associated with performance (e-commerce is easy, cheap, lucrative), while others revolve around business practices (everybody is doing e-commerce; e-commerce levels the playing field; e-commerce leads to the demise of distributors and resellers), and product marketing (e-commerce means the end of mass marketing; e-commerce leads to product commoditization).

The myths regarding electronic commerce raise a key point. Electronic commerce reshapes business practices, but it doesn't change the fundamental rules regarding business. Electronic commerce requires considerable capital and investment in information technology, leadership, and marketing, but the principles guiding the right way to do business remain.

Online sales represent only part of what has been termed the *E-Business life cycle*, which refers to the ongoing relationships between customers and sellers (Blundon and Bonde, 1998). The life cycle approach suggests companies must differentiate, customize service, add value, and cross-sell additional products and services at each step of the cycle between the business and the customer. As businesses become more savvy in their understanding and application of e-commerce, many of these myths will give way to harsh reality.

Analyzing Electronic Commerce—Levels of Analysis ▬

To better understand the impact of electronic commerce, this section ana-
lyzes e-commerce along four levels of analysis. The levels of analysis include
individual, group, national, and global perspectives and are presented in the
following paragraphs.

▶ Individual Level

Three models of electronic commerce were introduced earlier in the chapter.
Recall that two of the models involve consumers, or individual users. In beginning our analysis, several questions deserve investigation regarding electronic
commerce at the individual level: Who is using electronic commerce? What type
of commerce activities are users engaged in? What advantages and disadvantages do consumers encounter when engaged in electronic commerce?

Who is using electronic commerce? The increasing numbers of households
equipped with personal computers and online access mean greater potential for electronic commerce at the individual level. For example, the total
of online households in the United States was expected to reach 34.9 million by the end of 1999, growing to 57 million by 2002 (Online U.S. Households, 1998). As more homes become Internet enabled, more individuals
will experiment with electronic commerce. Likewise, it is easy to forget
about the millions of workers connected to the Web while at work. In
many work locations, individuals can also purchase goods and services
while performing their occupations.

The electronic commerce user profile is beginning to take shape, thanks in
part to a number of different studies. Jupiter Communications completed a
study of 2000 Internet users that identified three distinct categories of Internet shoppers. *Buyers* consist of current shoppers who express a high degree of
satisfaction with their online experience. *Browsers* are individuals who shop for
goods and services online but don't actually make a purchase. *Non-shoppers*
are the households that do not browse or buy online (Jupiter/NFO Consumer
Survey, 1998). This study illustrates the simple yet complex challenge of electronic commerce at the consumer level, transforming non-shoppers into
browsers and ultimately converting more browsers to shoppers.

The 1998 Christmas shopping season produced several interesting findings that help profile individual electronic commerce consumers. Zona Research surveyed over 1,000 Internet users and found that shoppers over age 50 increased spending over 500 percent from 1997 (Who Shopped Online, 1999). While men spent more than women on online shopping in 1998, online buying by women rose over 300 percent compared to a 145 percent increase for men (Who Shopped Online, 1999). Shoppers aged 35–44 performed about one-third of their total shopping online, while the under-25 age group produced only a 36 percent increase in spending from 1997 to 1998 (Cox, 1999). Ethnic use of e-commerce is also increasing at a rapid rate, and groups such as African Americans are catching up with Anglo users (Crockett, 1999).

Synthesizing these findings, one can surmise that the individual electronic commerce user offers a very general profile. In reality, anyone old enough to have a credit card (typically 18 in most states) and basic computer skills is likely to someway be engaged in electronic commerce. There appears to be no significant gender, age, or ethnic gap such as are routinely found with adoption of other new technologies and practices.

What type of commerce activities are users engaged in? Retail sites represent one of the main areas for electronic commerce transactions, but consumers have not limited their e-commerce activity to retail shopping. In addition to consumer goods, several areas have proven to be extremely popular with Internet users, including computer products and services, finance and investment services, travel, and the growth of web portals as an entry point for Internet access.

Dell became the first company to successfully embrace the Web, and today a number of other competitors (Gateway, Compaq, IBM, etc.) sell custom-made computers directly to consumers. Online stock and investment trading is another area where commerce activity has flourished. A number of discount brokerage firms, including E*Trade, Schwab, and Ameritrade offer low-cost commission charges to investors and a wealth of research data. Not surprisingly, online pornography, which in early 1999 was represented by over 700,000 different web sites, is another category that has reached over a billion dollars in revenues (Schwartz, 1997).

The Web has revolutionized the travel industry, allowing consumers to bypass travel agents to make their own reservations. Delta Airlines became the first major airline to place a surcharge on tickets acquired from locations other than the company web site. Priceline.com became the first web service to allow customers to negotiate their own price for an airline ticket or a hotel room, tapping into the unsold inventory of airline seats and hotel beds that go unoccupied every day. In 1999, American Airlines announced the company would no longer print a directory of all American flights, instead moving all information to its successful web site *[http://americanair.com]*.

Many of the brands listed here represent categories of goods that are information intensive by their nature. In other words, consumers don't need to touch or hold these products as they might more personal goods and services. Text and graphic information provides all the detail needed to make buying decisions.

Perhaps the most interesting e-commerce development has been the development of portals, the entry point for many online users. A number of mergers and joint ventures have linked major players with various web search engines to enable more e-commerce transactions. Among the groups joining hands are Netscape and America Online; Yahoo! and GeoCities; NBC and Snap; Walt Disney and Infoseek (Go.com); and Lycos and USA Networks (Anders, 1999b).

What advantages and disadvantages do consumers encounter when engaged in electronic commerce? Electronic commerce offers both advantages and disadvantages to individual users. In terms of advantages, most users prefer the ability to browse, compare, and shop at anytime of the day or night. Many users cite time advantages, in that they can engage in commerce activities when it fits their individual schedule rather than having to conform to a brick-and-mortal business day. Products can be ordered and shipped anywhere in the world, allowing leisure time to be used for other activities. These time-shifting characteristics are similar to advantages identified with using a VCR to record television programs rather than having to adjust to rigid television program schedules (Levy, 1981).

Personalization, or customizing information for returning users, has become a key component of many web sites. Amazon.com was one of the first sites to engage in personalization. Once you buy your first item from Amazon, the company then greets you on returning visits with a list of recommendations based on past shopping preferences. Unlike many retail establishments, web customers are often greeted by name and delivered personalized information, including advertising messages designed for their demographic group (Peppers and Rogers, 1997).

Several disadvantages plague greater electronic commerce activities. Many users do not feel comfortable giving credit card information online. There is fear of hackers gaining access to the numbers, as well as concerns over fraudulent use of a person's credit card information. Security of transactions, discussed later in the chapter, is one reason many people use the Web to browse, but actually make their purchases from traditional business establishments.

There are also issues revolving around privacy. Many individuals are concerned about sharing personal information with one company, who may then sell that information to other companies. There also is the fear that these large database repositories of information may someway be used to harm or embarrass individuals.

Last, but not least, are problems related to customer service. Many web sites have provided poor to mediocre customer service, infuriating consumers and driving them back toward traditional business entities. During peak shopping periods, server problems have caused lost transactions and down time— also trying the patience of consumers. Web companies recognize that improving and maintaining a high level of customer service is as important in the online world as it is in the offline world.

Clearly, a number of barriers exist which limit the growth and potential of electronic commerce at the individual level. Some users will never be comfortable purchasing products over the Web due to privacy and security concerns, while others will fully embrace the technology and the flexibility it provides. Exactly how much of an economic impact electronic commerce will one day realize at the consumer level remains to be seen. But the aggregate impact of the individual user on the Web is certainly affecting the next level of analysis—the group or organizational level.

▶ Group or Organizational Level

In analyzing the group level, the focus in this section will be on the business aspects of electronic commerce. Business aspects of the Internet represent many different topics, so discussion in this section will be limited to three areas. First, the role of Internet Service Providers (ISPs) will be discussed. Second, individual business utilization of the Web is analyzed. Third, the development of portals as entry points for Internet access and as valuable tools for electronic commerce is examined.

Internet Service Providers (ISPs). Internet Service Providers play a key role in electronic commerce activity. The individual user must somehow be able to access the Internet from his/her home or office. The Internet Service Provider (ISP) fills that role by providing the software and physical connection from the user to the Internet, for a monthly fee. Today, many ISPs offer personalized service to their customers, and some contain advertising.

The ISP market is dominated by America Online, which boasts upward of 16 million subscribers (Anders, 1999b). While AOL holds a commanding position in the national ISP marketplace, there are an estimated 5,000 ISPs in operation in the United States alone (Wilde, 1998). These ISPs vary in size; some claim only a few hundred subscribers, while others have several thousand subscribers. To date, access has consisted of dial-up service using a modem, but there are other means of access, including cable modems, ISDN (integrated services digital network), ADSL (asynchronous digital subscriber line), and satellite/wireless access. Dial-up access will continue to be the primary means of interconnectivity for the next several years.

There has been a great deal of consolidation among ISPs, most notably the merger between America Online and Netscape, and further merger activity is anticipated (Wilde, 1998). Analysts expect smaller providers will continue to provide service in local and regional areas, but the larger ISPs will offer more of an economic advantage to their owners through economies of scale and scope (Albarran, 1996).

Business Utilization of the Web. Business users have found many advantages to conducting electronic commerce via the Internet. As for consumers, the Web allows a business site to be open 24 hours a day, seven days a week. Further, by tying transaction processing to their legacy database systems, businesses are able to personalize services toward each of their customers and provide better service, especially to high-volume customers. Companies have found web-based transactions more cost-efficient, allowing for higher profit margins in comparison to traditional brick and mortar establishments. Web sites can be expensive to maintain and require constant updating and development. But the advantages of having a web presence outweigh the disadvantages of having no presence on the Web. Customers can acquire information on an as-needed basis throughout the shopping and buying process, a clear advantage over companies not on the Web.

The development of corporate Intranets has allowed business-to-business e-commerce to flourish. For many businesses, electronic commerce has fostered globalization of operations, better sales management support, and new business opportunities (Ahikari, 1998). Companies in a variety of industries are finding e-commerce business practices much different than traditional business practices, as in sharing information with competitors. For example, a group of steel manufacturers created a web site that deals in single transactions and online auctions. Together the manufacturers share the risks and profits, and streamline their needs in a single web site rather than several competing sites (Wilder, Dalton, and Sweat, 1998).

The Growth of Portals and E-Commerce Potential. Portal sites are those web pages that users experience when they first log on to the Internet. By default, Netscape browser users are transported to www.netscape.com while Internet Explorer users are swept to www.msn.com until that time when the user learns how to change the opening page in a preference menu. Initially, the search engines were also recognized as key portal sites, primarily because these sites were the first to effectively develop Internet advertising. Search engines like Alta Vista, Lycos, and Excite were "hit" by users who conducted a search to find whatever subject matter they were seeking on the Internet.

The Web portals are seen as the gathering point for many Internet users. A developing strategy is to now place as much content as possible on the portal site in hopes of keeping users logged on to each portal for longer periods of time. In regard to E-commerce, the portals become launching points, through both advertising and click-through buttons, for attracting consumers to various points of interest. A series of acquisitions that began in 1998 has produced seven leading players in the portal market:

- America Online and Netscape Communications
- Microsoft and its acquisition of HotMail
- Yahoo! and GeoCities Yahoo! and Broadcast.com
- USA Networks and Lycos
- At Home Corp. and Excite
- Walt Disney Company and Infoseek (Go.com)
- NBC (a unit of General Electric) and Snap (a division of CNET)

What is particularly interesting in the makeup of the portals is the integration of three television-rich companies. Disney, the owner of the ABC network (as well as the ESPN cable networks), NBC, and USA Networks are no doubt interested in tie-ins with their television operations, and they may use the sites to stream video content to Internet users. To what extent the portal strategy will be successful in developing electronic commerce deserves more observation. Further consolidation may be necessary. It will also be interesting to see if companies like Fox, CBS, and Time Warner attempt to align their operations with an existing portal.

As presented in this section, business applications of electronic commerce are varied and occur in many different forums. No one model of business use has emerged as the de facto standard, and there is a great deal of ongoing innovation and experimentation. Companies will continue to invest heavily in e-commerce technology and software in an effort to find optimal business models. Business expenditures on Internet-related technology are estimated to exceed $85 billion in 1999, growing to $203 billion by 2003 (Interconnect, 1999). The extent to which e-commerce at the group or business level is affected by happenings at the national level is presented next.

▶ National

This section focuses on electronic commerce at the nation-state level by examining three topics that impact e-commerce at all levels of analysis: security, privacy, and the threat of taxation on goods and services acquired over the Internet. Each area represents a barrier to e-commerce achieving its full economic potential. In 1998, a group of Internet, media, and telecommunications companies formed a coalition to address a number of key issues affecting e-commerce, including consumer privacy, security, and taxation (Petersen, 1999). The group, known as the Global Business Dialogue on e-commerce, will be refining their agenda in 1999 and focusing on a number of self-regulatory issues.

Security Issues. Security represents one of the major barriers to e-commerce growth and development. Web sites have become easy targets for a number of security breaches, ranging from the planting of various types of disabling computer viruses to loss of data, fraud, manipulation of software and operating system applications, and of course, loss of revenue. One survey conducted in 1998 found that 59 percent of all sites selling products or services on the Web experienced one or more security breaches, resulting in an identifiable loss of between $1,000 and $100,000 per occurrence (Dalton, 1998).

Digital certificates, also called public key certificates, are one of the main tools businesses utilize for effective e-commerce transactions, both in the world of corporate intranets and the public Internet. Used in combination with various public-key cryptography applications, digital certificates identify and authenticate appropriate users, servers, and other network entities (Levitt, 1998). By 1999, a new public key infrastructure (PKI) to manage digital certificates should be available to help increase secure transactions.

Fraud complaints regarding Internet transactions increased six times from 1998 to 1999, according to Internet Fraud Watch, an online reporting system established by the National Consumers League (Hendren, 1999). The top complaints revolve around online auctions, general merchandise sales, computer equipment/software, Internet services, business opportunities, and marketing schemes, most occurring at the consumer level. The complaints have caught the attention of the Federal Trade Commission, who has announced plans to launch a 24-hour Internet fraud detection group (Hendren, 1999).

Efforts to improve Internet security continue, both with the advent of new software tools and technologies and with actions taken by web sites and the online industry to provide more secure transactions. For example, eBay initiated new efforts at the beginning of 1999 to eliminate fraud and misrepresentation among users (Anders, 1999a). Security issues will continue to plague the growth of electronic commerce. Industry self-regulation and government intervention will help address some security concerns, although response may be slower than desired.

Privacy Issues. As consumers interact with web sites and ultimately engage in business transactions, companies have the ability to gather a great deal of data about individual consumers and their consumption habits. Online privacy has become a key issue in electronic commerce. Many online companies fail to provide specific privacy policies on their web sites and do not explain what data is gathered from consumers or how that data may be used in the future. A number of companies sell the data they gather to other companies, who can use the data in their own strategic planning and marketing initiatives (Petersen, 1999).

In addition to monitoring what users encounter as they move through a specific web site, online companies can also record what the users clicks on and even what topics they search for via search engines. The end result is a possible data set including considerable personal information about individual consumer tastes, preferences, and buying/shopping habits. Consumer advocacy groups are demanding Internet companies develop specific consumer protection policies, rather than a commitment to self-regulatory efforts (Petersen, 1999). This could create a backlash effect for some e-commerce users.

Ensuring online privacy remains a stumbling block which prevents many users from engaging in electronic commerce (Kalakota and Whinston, 1997). Self-regulatory efforts will help, but unless some sort of national standards are enacted, the only true protection consumers have is to choose not to disclose personal information on the Web—which is increasingly difficult to avoid—or engage the old caveat, "let the buyer beware."

Taxation. Web taxation has emerged as a key electronic commerce issue, especially at the state level. The problem is that few companies engaged in e-commerce collect state sales tax on items sold over the Internet. In fact, it is up to the buyer to remit any local taxes due to taxing authorities at the state or local level. The reality is that few, if any, buyers follow through on this requirement. The states, which on average draw nearly half of their budgets from sales taxes, feel they are missing out on millions of dollars of revenues (Simons, 1999).

In October 1998, Congress passed the Internet Tax Freedom Act that established a three-year ban on any new Internet sales taxes. In short, the ban inaugurated a tax-free shopping spree on the Web. Business wanted a longer ban, as did the While House, but the National Governors Association and the National League of Cities were successful in lobbying for a limited three-year moratorium (Simons, 1999).

Most online businesses don't want to play tax collector/distributor for all 50 states and thousands of local tax jurisdictions. The states, on the other hand, argue they need and deserve the revenues derived from e-commerce consumers and are entitled to the funds. Consumers simply ignore the law, knowing there is little danger of facing any type of prosecution. Congress and the White House want to encourage e-commerce as a means to fuel the national economy and are hesitant to impose further regulatory controls. Thus, taxation is yet another key issue that will be undertaken by the Global Business Dialogue in hopes of developing solutions that will appease all concerned parties (Petersen, 1999).

▶ Global

Because the Web and e-commerce are inherently global in nature, many of the topics discussed at the individual, group, and nation-state levels also apply here. This section will focus on two topics: the growth of worldwide Internet e-commerce and the differing concerns over the issue of privacy, especially with regard to the European Union.

Worldwide E-Commerce Growth. While the Web's growth and impact have been predominantly a U.S. phenomenon (see Chapter 1), the rest of the world is quickly catching up. Projections suggest that by 2001, more Internet users will reside outside than inside the United States (IDC Predictions, 1999). In 1998, worldwide electronic commerce revenue was estimated to be around 11 percent (approximately $3 million); by 2002 worldwide e-commerce is expected to grow nearly 23 percent (Wreden, 1998).

The development of the global Internet audience brings with it many challenges. While a web site potentially offers a global marketplace, it doesn't necessarily mean it is easy to conduct business at a global level. There are differences in regards to business practices, infrastructure, and culture, which complicate marketing and sales efforts. There are other logistics related to various types of regulations, currency conversion, and language differences (Wreden, 1998).

One way around some of these problems is to enter partnerships with companies based in other countries/regions. These strategic partnerships lower the economic risk and increase the probability for success outside the domestic home base. Web sites also need to be available in other languages than English, a lesson learned decades earlier from the automotive industry, which fared poorly in efforts to sell cars, in part because owners' manuals were only in English (Wreden, 1998).

Global Privacy Issues. Many U.S. Internet companies are concerned about a European Union policy that went into effect in October 1998. The EU Data Protection Directive forbids companies from sending any personal information out of Europe unless the destination company has "certain privacy protections" (Petersen, 1999, p. B3). Businesses in the United States feel the policy is too restrictive and inhibits e-commerce potential with European Union customers.

The directive has several requirements. First, web sites have to allow users to consent to any type of data collection. Second, it gives users the right to receive an explanation of how the information will be used. Third, it allows users to access their individual data in order to correct or delete information. Finally, the directive allows for recourse if the data is used without permission

(Evans, 1998). The U.S. Commerce Department is negotiating with the European Union to develop principles that provide compliance with the EU law, but it is anticipated that these efforts to reach a compromise will take time.

An Electronic Commerce Research Agenda

This analysis of electronic commerce issues at the individual, group, nation-state, and global levels illustrates the need for additional research and study in this very fascinating yet complicated field. In this section, some possible areas for future study to learn more about electronic commerce and its impacts are offered.

At the individual level of analysis, research needs to go beyond descriptive analysis to understanding consumer motivations for using e-commerce. Theoretical domains such as uses and gratifications research would help establish linkages between motivations for using e-commerce, gratifications obtained from using e-commerce, and expectations associated with e-commerce. Media system dependency theory is another area that could provide insight on e-commerce usage at the individual level. Here the research could explore and identify the relationships among e-commerce companies, ISPs, individuals, and society. Both of these research areas would yield valuable data for marketers and Internet businesses.

At the group level, we need information on market structure and industry practices for many types of groups engaged in electronic commerce. Studies could focus on portals, ISPs, and specific Internet business markets, such as computers, books, and financial services. How do industry structure and practices differ between the online and the nonwired world? To what extent are conduct, structure, and performance analyzed differently?

The nation-state level offers other opportunities for study, such as the impact of the Internet economy on gross national product, domestic production, and labor and capital. Most of the topic areas here would be built around macroeconomic perspectives. Policy analysis is also needed, especially when considering topics related to security, privacy, and taxation.

Finally, the global level offers opportunities for cross-cultural comparisons of e-commerce activities, ranging from individual activity to national and regional policy initiatives. Business partnerships between global partners provide opportunities for case study analysis.

In summary, there are numerous opportunities for further study and investigation regarding electronic commerce at the individual, group, nation-state, and global levels of analysis. More work is needed in terms of theoretical development, descriptive information, and business/policy analysis.

Conclusions

Electronic commerce is one of several forces driving the growth and refinement of the Internet. Electronic commerce has enormous economic potential in both business-to-business transactions and consumer-to-business categories, in both domestic and nondomestic markets. There is little doubt that electronic commerce will forever change the way many companies do business and alter the way many consumers acquire goods and services.

Despite optimistic economic projections, many issues regarding electronic commerce will take time to resolve. The major barriers that limit the growth of e-commerce revolve around topics related to security and privacy. Taxation is another issue that could present problems for continuing e-commerce expansion. Policy initiatives, such as the Data Protection Directive established by the European Union, present ramifications regarding the growth of e-commerce at the global level.

Finally, a serious research agenda is needed to better understand the role, function, and impact of electronic commerce at all levels of society. Scholars from all fields, including business, engineering, and communications, should consider multi-disciplinary research projects which look at e-commerce from different perspectives and theoretical orientations. By engaging in systematic study and analysis, we will gain a better understanding of electronic commerce and the role it will play in developing a global information marketplace.

References

http://www.americanair.com

http://www.ntia.doc.gov/ntiahome/net2/

Ahikari, R. 1998, July 27. E-commerce Impact. *InformationWeek*, pp. 77–81.

Albarran, A.B. 1996. *Media Economics: Understanding Markets, Industries, and Concepts*. Ames, IA: Iowa State University Press.

Amazon.com. 1998, December 14. The Wild World of E-Commerce. *Business Week*, pp. 106–19.

Anders, G. 1999a, January 15. How eBay Will Battle Sham Bids, Mislabeling. *The Wall Street Journal*, pp. B1, B4.

_____. 1999b, February 11. The Race for Sticky Web Sites. *The Wall Street Journal*, p. B1.

Anderson, C. 1997. In Search of the Perfect Market. [Online] Retrieved from the World Wide Web: *http://www.economist.com/editorial/justforyou/14-9-97/index_survey.html*

Blundon, B., and Bonde, A. 1998, November 16. Beyond the Transaction. *InformationWeek*, pp. 5SS–6SS.

Cairncross, F. 1998. *The Death of Distance*. Boston: Harvard Business School Press.

Clampet. E. 1999, January 4. E-Commerce to Be Profitable in the Distant Future. [Online] Retrieved from the World Wide Web: *http://www.internetnews.com/ec-news/1999/01/0402-ec.html*

Cox, B. 1999, January 6. Report: Online Holiday Spending Grew Nearly 200%. [Online] Retrieved from the World Wide Web: *http://www.internetnews.com/ec-news/1999/01/0602-report.html*

Crockett, R.O. 1999, March 22. A Web That Looks Like the World. *Business Week E-Biz*, pp. EB46–47.

Dalton, G. 1998, August 31. Acceptable Risks. *InformationWeek*, pp. 36–48.

Evans, N. 1998, December 7. U.S. Needs to Tighten Privacy to Match EU. *InternetWeek*, p. 21.

Hendren, J. 1999, February 24. Internet Fraud Complaints Increase Sixfold, Group Says. *The Dallas Morning News*, p. 10D.

Hof, R.D. 1999, March 22. The Buyer Always Wins. *Business Week E-Biz*, pp. EB26–28.

IBM. 1999, January 11. Advertisement. *The Wall Street Journal*, p. A13.

IDC Predicitions '99: The "Real" Internet Emerges. [Online] Retrieved from the World Wide Web: *http://www..idc.com/idc7/EI/content/123198EI.htm*

Interconnect@mindspring.com. 1999, January 25. E-mail service available from Arthur Anderson Company.

Interconnect@mindspring.com. 1999, March 1. E-mail service available from Arthur
Anderson Company.

Jupiter/NFO Consumer Survey. 1998. Volume 1, New Research Study. [Online] Retrieved from
the World Wide Web: *http://www.jup.com/store/studies/jup_nfo1/*

Kalakota, R., and Whinston, A.B. 1997. *Electronic Commerce. A Manager's Guide.* Reading, MA:
Addison Wesley.

Levitt, J. 1998, August 31. The Keys to Security. *InformationWeek* , pp. 51–60.

Levy, M.R. 1981. Home Video Recorders and Time Shifting. *Journalism Quarterly* 58:401–05.

Nichols, P. 1998, August 14. Report: E-Commerce To Reach $28 Billion This Year. [Online] Re-
trieved from the World Wide Web: *http://www.internetnews.com/ecnews/article/
0,1087,archive_4_29671,00.html*

Online Holiday Shopping Is Pegged at $8.2 Billion. 1999, January 14. *The Wall Street Journal,* p. B6.

Online U.S. Households [Table]. 1998, November 15. 1998 Annual Report. *tele.com,* p. 84.

Peppers, D., and Rogers, M. 1997. *Enterprise One to One: Tools for Competing in the Interactive
Age.* New York: Currency Doubleday.

Petersen, A. 1999, January 15. Electronic-Commerce Initiative Launched by Officials of 17
Firms. *The Wall Street Journal,* p. B3.

Schwartz, E.I. 1997. *Webonomics: Nine Essential Principles for Growing Your Business on the World
Wide Web.* New York: Broadway.

Simons, J. 1999, January 26. States Chafe as Web Shoppers Ignore Sales Taxes. *The Wall Street
Journal,* pp. B1, B4.

Who Shopped Online in '98? 1999, January 4. [Online] Retrieved from the World Wide Web:
http://cyberatlas.internet.com/market/retailing/whoshop.html

Wilde, C. 1998, November 15. Shake-up, Not Shakeout. *tele.com,* pp. 71–76.

Wilder, C. 1997, December 7. E-Commerce Myths and Realities. *InformationWeek,* pp. 52–63.

Wilder, C., Dalton, G., and Sweat, J. 1998, August 24. Changing the Rules. *InformationWeek,*
pp. 18–20.

Wreden, N. 1998, November 16. Internet Opens Markets Abroad. *InformationWeek,*
pp. 2SS–4SS.

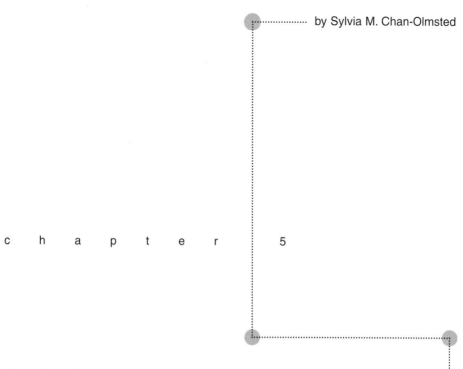

by Sylvia M. Chan-Olmsted

c   h   a   p   t   e   r   5

Marketing Mass Media on the World Wide Web:

The Building of Media Brands in an Integrated and Interactive World

The converging digital worlds of telecommunications and computers are amplifying the strategic importance of the Internet in the success and even survival of many businesses, including mass media firms. The same technological advances are blurring traditional market boundaries and fostering competition between firms that did not previously compete with one another. Broadcasters, cablecasters, telephone companies (telcos), and the World Wide Web offer each other's services, and the Web is experiencing growth in scope and in significance to the global economy. As these trends continue, traditional media practitioners need to improve their understanding of the Internet, not only as an emerging new media system, but also as a strategic tool for gaining competitive advantages.

In essence, the Internet poses both threats and opportunities to the traditional media as it, to some degree, substitutes, as well as complements, the existing communications functions provided by these media. The Internet offers traditional mass media online distribution of content that is enriched by the new medium's capacity for interactivity and personalization. As a marketing medium, the Web combines elements from various traditional media but becomes more than the sum of its parts. For example, the Web offers the relatively short-term exposure along with the concise information content and impact of broadcast media as well as the long-term exposure with high information content of print. Nevertheless, traditional media firms are asking themselves how their media will co-exist with the Internet: Does the Internet siphon readers/audiences and advertising revenues away from them? Can or should they extend their brands into the Internet? If so, how many resources should be devoted to this effort and what kind of result should they expect?

Regardless of the answers, many media firms are rushing to establish a presence on the Internet through either web sites or portal services because they see the Net as an inevitable force that has permanently changed the rules of competition in the marketplace. Most major newspapers like *USA Today* and *The Wall Street Journal* have set up popular online sites; NBC has invested heavily in MSNBC (online and cable) and has an equity stake in Snap, a new portal that is being promoted heavily on the NBC network. Disney, partnering with Infoseek, is developing its Go.com, trying to build a new brand name portal service, with marketing support from its ABC and ESPN properties (Girard and Paikert, 1998). Most media firms seem to agree that while they do not know the secret of winning in this converging marketplace, they simply cannot afford to stay still and risk losing what they have.

A New Communication and Economic Paradigm

Morris and Ogan (1996) suggest that the major constraints on doing mass communication research about the Internet has been the lack of theoretical models, and this new communication technology requires rethinking and redefinition of communication as the Internet conveniently combines various forms of communications such as interpersonal and mass communication. Indeed, discussions of media application and integration of the Internet should begin with a re-examination of the economic and communication premises of the Internet and how they are different from those of the traditional media.

It is said that in the broadcast and cable TV age, we moved the printing press from the newspaper factory to the home, while in the Internet age, we continue to move the editorial office into the consumers' homes (Ducey, 1997). In the World Wide Web, a consumer is no longer a passive receiver of content; he/she can actually access personalized digital copies of content from various web sites and create his/her own content, which is impossible for traditional media to accomplish. In addition, traditional media firms distribute content in real time. The Internet, on the other hand, allows a consumer to access content continuously in his/her own time. In the Internet age, the premise of scale economics of mass production or mass distribution is no longer relevant. The Internet enables a distribution mechanism that is efficient for all modes of communications, including one-to-many, many-to-one, many-to-many, and one-to-one. Such a paradigm shift in communication patterns and economics means that media practitioners need to realign their existing management and marketing strategies in order to benefit from this new medium.

Internet Media Consumers

Started as an elite medium used mainly by upper middle class, educated media consumers, the Internet has grown to be a mainstream medium as more than 72 million American adults were already online by the end of 1998. According to an Internet Tracking Service report, 51 percent of the users are now over the age of 35, almost half of the users have a high school education, and more and more women are going online. The Internet media consumer profile will soon closely resemble the profile of traditional media users as 70 percent of Internet users access the Net from home, a significant increase from the previous year (CyberAtlas, 1998b). Contrary to other new media, the Internet seems to be increasing in use among long-term users, indicating the significance of a learning curve to its utility and the potential for more growth. Newcomers are different from long-term users in terms of both makeup and behavior. The broadening of the base suggests that the Internet is expanding beyond early adopters, according to a longitudinal study of Internet use conducted by Nielsen Homevideo Index (Lindstrom, 1997).

As for online usage patterns, a field trial of home Internet usage conducted by Carnegie Mellon University discovered that different demographic groups used the Internet differently at home. Teenagers are much heavier users than their parents, and among teenagers, boys are heavier users than girls. Among adults, women are somewhat heavier users than men, especially in the use of e-mail. As reasons for going online, participants reported that they were more likely to use the Internet for enjoying themselves, for obtaining information relevant to a hobby or personal interest, and for communicating with friends and family (Kraut et al., 1997).

Web-based Businesses' Use of Media

The role of traditional media may also be reevaluated as important marketing communication tools for web-based businesses. The fact is that with millions of web sites available on the Net, the Internet is the most cluttered medium in the world. To succeed in marketing an online brand, a marketer most likely will need distribution of communication messages via mass media to create broad awareness of the product or service. Leading Internet brands such as Amazon.com and Yahoo! are advertising extensively on traditional mass media. The Internet's global reach and 24-hour accessibility also make it an invaluable tool for direct marketing. Direct marketers have observed that advertising for products on the Internet has to come from channels outside the Internet, such as TV spots and infomercials. Many marketers have realized the importance of advertising on traditional media to generate traffic to their web sites (Frederiksen, 1997).

Among all media, TV seems to deliver the best promotional results for online marketers. According to a study of web advertising, when asked where they noticed advertisements with a web address, television was mentioned the most by the respondents (60 percent), followed by magazines (20 percent), newspapers (17 percent), and radio (16 percent). One out of eight who remembered seeing an ad actually visited the web site, and this tendency increased slightly among those who use the Internet more. However, the research also suggested that noticing a web address is not enough to attract someone to the site. After a consumer notices a web address, he/she will visit the site only when he/she seeks detailed information or has an interest in a particular product. The research also concluded that people, both Internet users and nonusers, perceive differences between advertisers with web sites and those without. Over 60 percent of the respondents felt that advertisers with web sites are more customer-oriented than those without them (Maddox and Mehta, 1997).

Internet's Marketing Value

So exactly what marketing values can the Internet bring to traditional media marketers? Many marketers are including web addresses in their ads. Both practitioners and academics have suggested the value of having a web site and advertising on the Internet (Maddox and Mehta, 1997; Pallab, 1996; Pattinson and Brown, 1996; Raman and Leckenby, 1998). A 1997 content analysis of the home pages of the Fortune 500 companies revealed that companies which have higher market performances, as measured by revenues, are more likely to use web sites to reach their customers. Also according to the research, the goals of the home pages were mainly to have a web presence, to promote the companies' image, to enhance public relations, to attract users to browse products and services, and to collect user responses and other related data (Liu et al., 1997). Pitt, Berthon, and Watson (1996) suggested that web sites can generate awareness, explain/demonstrate the product, provide information, help in the evaluation and selection process, provide feedback, and help project a favorable corporate image.

Regardless of the exact impact of the Internet on TV viewership, TV audiences are embracing the Net while maintaining or reducing their viewing time. At this time, the Internet demographics are still a marketer's dream: the Web attracts the hard-to-reach, well-educated, high-income population most coveted by marketers. The Web also attracts hard-to-reach young consumers.

Strategically, personalization and targeting on the Net through effective collection and use of demographic and online behavioral data from a company's customers are likely to build competitive advantages. Finally, the Internet has empowered consumers, giving them a more active role in the marketing process. Each consumer creates his/her own original content, which is much more involving and thus more valuable to both the consumer and the marketer.

The marketing value of the Internet may again be amplified by the use of traditional advertising media, which attract attention, convey a brief message, and trigger initial interest to go online for in-depth, detailed information. At times and for certain markets, the Internet can be valuable in attracting initial consumer interest, but its real power is the ability to provide almost infinite layers of detail about a product or service interactively. The Internet is a valuable extension of traditional media. With the increased appearances of web addresses in traditional media, the consumer can continue a brand relationship initiated in an ad in an established medium and extend it to a closer relationship on the Net.

Despite its interactive and personalization aspects, the Internet as an advertising medium has been criticized as lacking intrusiveness, creativity in banner ads, and reliable measurement for web visitors (McDonald, 1997). Historically, the majority of online ad spending has been on banner ads, although banner ad click-through rates and revenues are down recently. In searching for more intrusiveness, involvement, and branding potential, advertisers are looking into sponsorship and "intermercials" (Cleland, 1996). The five- to 10-second animated intermercials, which resemble a short TV commercial and appeared originally in popular sites like pointcast.com, are expected to become more popular as they offer more creative message flexibility. On the other hand, sponsorship offers co-branding opportunities with compatible, favorable content providers. By sponsoring a site that consumers value, the marketer may build positive associations for the brand and capitalize on the long-term relationships that the content provider already has established with users.

How to best harness the branding value of the Internet has become the Holy Grail of marketing as many have found that creative web sites do not necessarily increase brand awareness or brand loyalty (Newborne and Hof, 1998). Some have argued that the traditional, offline branding tactics such as demographic targeting do not necessarily translate well online and that companies should focus on psychographics more than demographics (Montalbano, 1999). The most recent attempt from the marketers is to combine the emotional sell of traditional brand marketing, such as the appeal that links Disney with family or Volvo with safety, with a rational, concrete service offered exclusively online. In essence, a marketer "pays" a consumer to endure the brand message with some kind of useful service for the consumer as, for example, Saturn does by providing an interactive design shop for choosing options and a lease-price calculator on its web site (Newborne and Hof, 1998). The Web is both a competitor and a natural complement to traditional media. Therefore, a traditional media firm needs to carefully examine the value of the Net in relation to the firm's current assets and design an online extension plan that combines the best of the two to increase readership/audience, loyalty, and eventually, profitability.

Impact of the Internet on Traditional Mass Media

So, has there been a decline in the consumption of traditional media as a result of the increased popularity of the Internet? A Forrester Research, Inc. study found over 78 percent of its respondents admitting that the first activity they drop to go online is watching television (Use the Internet, 1997). In addition, PC usage peaks right in the middle of network TV's prime time viewing. Nevertheless, there have been contradictory reports about the impact of online usage on media usage, particularly television viewing. Based on its People Meter sample panel, Nielsen Media Research first found that households with Internet or online access watched 15 percent less TV over the course of a week than non-online households. In later research measuring the relationship over time between Internet and TV usage, Nielsen found that in its People Meter sample households, Internet access at home had little impact on overall household TV tuning levels (CyberAtlas, 1999).

Some have asserted that people have limited time to allocate between online and TV use and that an increase in online time will reduce TV time.

Others have argued that typical PC/online users are already light TV users and that a large amount of PC/online use is devoted to activities which have nothing to do with TV viewing. In fact, the use of online resources may actually save time and increase available TV time. The Internet may foster an increase in multitasking, enabling consumers to perform a number of activities at the same time while consuming media. Coffey and Stipp (1997) suggested that media organizations, especially TV broadcasters and cablecasters, should focus on studying the interactions between TV and the Internet, since 47 percent of computer owners had a PC and a TV in the same room, with both running simultaneously in 1998, compared with 40 percent in the previous year (CyberAtlas, 1999b).

The growth of online services may actually be good news for the multi-channel media industries: one report concluded that households equipped with PCs and online subscriptions are more likely to spend money on cable TV and related services. Data gathered in the Yankee Group's Technologically Advanced Family (TAF) survey of over 2,000 U.S. homes found that subscription rates for basic cable as well as enhanced services like premium channels, Pay-Per-View, and Direct Broadcast Satellite (DBS) ran significantly higher among PC and online homes than for the overall public (CyberAtlas, 1999a).

As for web impact on other media, research has shown that online users are more likely to be heavier newspaper readers or radio listeners and light television viewers, suggesting that the Web is more likely to reduce newspaper readership. At the same time, online users are more likely to be prospective home buyers, new car buyers, and job seekers, all targets of traditional newspaper classified advertising (Consoli, 1997). It seems that a sound battle plan to combat the potential threat posed by the online medium is a much more urgent issue for newspapers than for other media.

On a positive note, instead of replacing the traditional media, the emerging Internet medium may actually complement them. The "old" media are likely to continue to flourish because of their unique attributes and contents, which appeal to different audience wants and needs. And the arrival of the Internet actually enhances the existing media's ability to better serve these wants and needs. For example, while the Internet is a better choice for providing communication and information functions, television is better at offering entertainment (Stipp, 1995). The availability of online programming schedules and content information heightens the entertainment value of the program. "There is a synergy between broadcasting and the Internet which may well be a critical success factor for future growth," exclaimed Dr. Richard Ducey, the senior vice president of Research and Information Group at the National Association of Broadcasters (Ducey, 1996).

Current Use of the Internet by Traditional Media

Regardless of how they view the impact of the Internet, traditional media firms cannot afford to dismiss the continuous growth of this new medium. Newspapers are one of the earliest traditional media to embrace the Internet. Fueled by development abroad and in smaller U.S. markets, there were about 5,000 newspapers online worldwide by the fall of 1998, of which over half were based in the United States. While many continue to see online publishing as an opportunity for expansion and fending off competition, some U.S. newspapers have closed unprofitable web sites, claiming insufficient advertiser support. Some have raised questions about the long-term viability of web use by newspapers in a market in which less than one-third of all online newspapers expect to be profitable at this time (Meyer, 1998).

On the other hand, broadcast media are becoming more active in using the Internet for marketing, programming, and communication purposes. Radio stations today are using web pages for promotion and marketing; e-mailing clients and agencies; selling ads and sponsorships, Internet classifieds, and personals; webcasting; and participating in various sales projects. A content analysis of TV station web sites in 1996 revealed that the majority of the stations had as high as 95 percent of their online content in text form, much of it archived news material and community outreach and calendar pages. The report also found few national advertiser tie-ins on stations' web sites (Freeman, 1996). However, the pattern of Internet use by TV broadcasters changed rapidly in two years; another summary of the web activity of TV stations prepared by the NAB in 1998 found that over two-thirds of all TV stations have web sites. Noncommercial stations were more likely than commercial stations to have a web site. Of the commercial affiliates, CBS stations (97.2 percent of all CBS affiliates) are the most likely to have a station web site, followed by NBC (89.4 percent), ABC (82.5 percent), WB (56.5 percent), UPN (55.7 percent), and Fox (55.1 percent) (Savoie, 1998). TV broadcasters are using the Internet to provide station and personality information; promote and market news and other programming; communicate with audience, clients, and agencies via e-mail; sell online ads and sponsorship; and engage in webcasting and video-streaming (Baker, 1998).

As for specific web strategies, a content analysis of 300 TV stations discovered that broadcast TV stations prefer to acquire their domain names to reflect their local station IDs rather than their network affiliation in their URLs. Less than 4 percent of these stations actually engage in webcasting of their programs. However, almost 25 percent of them are offering online merchandise shopping functions. These web sites are used mostly to provide station and personnel facts, program schedules, and news and weather information. Approximately 47 percent of the station web sites contained banner ads (Chan-Olmsted, 1999).

The major broadcast networks are approaching the Web with various degrees of investment. CBS was the first of the four broadcast networks to open a web site. In 1995, CBS presented three alternative web packages to affiliates interested in setting up Internet sites. The packages cost a station from $5,000 to about $15,000 (for a more developed site). The network viewed the creation of Internet sites for the affiliated stations as an extension of its network-affiliate relationship and as a means to enhance its affiliates' relationships with local audiences, improve ratings, and boost revenue through the sale of online advertisements. Nevertheless, CBS has made limited investments in such online ventures as CBS Sportsline, and CBS Marketwatch, a financial site (Berniker, 1995).

NBC is apparently more aggressive than others in investing in the online world, partnering with Microsoft to create MSNBC, a cable and online joint venture, in addition to NBC.Com, beginning in 1996 (Ross, 1996). NBC has also created fresh online content for two of its series, "The Pretender" and "Homicide," that allows users to get involved in solving crimes with a set of detectives not featured on the show (Tedesco, 1997a). NBC offers advertisers, like Pontiac and Oldsmobile, sponsorship opportunities on the web sites for these two shows, in which advertiser products are woven into the story lines. NBC executives have repeatedly claimed that they are racing to catch up with dominant online companies like America Online and Yahoo!, and they are determined to leverage their brand power from television to the Web. To create an instant presence in the online world, NBC purchased a fledgling portal site, Snap, built by CNET. NBC has also acquired stakes in a host of Internet businesses, ranging from a popular-music site to a new-media production company to a technology firm that delivers Internet video. NBC seems to see the Internet as a part of achieving a strategic objective that is fundamental to its growth (Gunther, 1998).

Disney, the parent company to ABC, is also expanding its empire into the Internet, buying 43 percent of the portal and search engine Infoseek in 1998 and launching a new consumer portal brand, Go.Com (Gunther, 1998). Both NBC and ABC seem to be developing a convergence strategy that begins with portals, which serve as a gateway to and a return from an emerging universe of integrated digital text, sound, and video offerings. However, some argue that building a portal gateway is not what broadcast networks should be doing; instead, they need to refocus on the development of quality entertainment, especially products for high definition television (Rothenberg, 1998). Regardless of the strategic approaches, profitability for online businesses seems to be a long-term process. ABCNews.com, which began operations in April 1997, lost $21.5 million in 1998. ABC's ESPN.com also lost $7.2 million over the same time. ABC attributed the loss to the lack of advertising sales (Evans, 1998).

As for the nonprofit PBS, its online efforts have concentrated on extending the value of its current programming. In addition to the high-traffic web sites of its signature children's programs, PBS has created web sites that build on its documentaries to strengthen the relationship between online and on-air content and extend its programs' shelf lives. For example, one of the PBS web sites contains community artwork, photos, and poetry collected in relationship to the urban violence topic covered in one of its documentaries. Another site tracks the lives of four working-class girls who were featured in another documentary, "Girls Like Us" (Tedesco, 1997b).

Broadcasters' counterpart, cable television, is aggressively experimenting with the interactivity of the Internet and focusing on building online sports franchises. For example, Flextech, a cable and satellite programmer, is introducing a video-streaming version on the Web of a live afternoon show on Trouble, a teenage-oriented cable channel. Flextech also plans to use its web sites to test program formats such as game shows for its cable channels before investing in a TV pilot (Grande, 1998). Learning from the success of espnsportzone.com (in terms of traffic), BSkyB in the United Kingdom is focusing its online efforts on sports-related content such as its football (soccer) site (Grande, 1998). Even Lifetime's web site (*[www.lifetimetv.com]*) is focusing on sports and fitness, in addition to female-oriented content such as health and medical features (Tedesco, 1996b).

So, what is the path to prosperity for traditional media firms as they try to take advantage of this emerging new medium? Experts have pointed out that several elements drive consumers to return to particular web sites: continuous updates, topical issues, easy navigation and reading, and ability to customize information. According to another online survey of media services conducted by Editor & Publisher Co., Inc., most media web sites are concerned with staffing, pricing, alliances, marketing, content, sales, and, most importantly, return on investment questions. The survey project concluded that three components—balanced content, proper user measurement, and savvy marketing—are critical to the profitability of a media web site. The research also found that a web site is likely to be more profitable if it develops original editorial content; provides advertisers with demographic measurements of users, click-through data, and page view data; offers online surveys from users for content development; uses online traffic usage reports; has voluntary registration; and provides secure electronic transactions of products or services. In general, print media are more active in providing user data to advertisers and selling merchandise online. Interestingly enough, an increase in online promotion budgets or investment budgets did not lead to an increase in profit (Dahlin, 1999).

Promoting Media Web Sites

Though an increase in online promotion budgets has not been proven to increase a media web site's profitability, promotions of media web sites, especially on TV, have generated a substantial increase in web site traffic. The use of TV in promoting web sites creates an interactive promotional loop. For example, ABC News links the Internet to TV sets with its frequent references to its web site as a source of more in-depth reports. This interactive promotional loop is most evident when major sports events bring a tremendous increase in traffic to many media sites. MSNBC's web site broke quickly to the second spot among news/info/entertainment sites in July 1996, the height of the Summer Olympics, reaching 6.1 percent of the Internet users, according to PC Meter's household Internet usage survey (Tedesco, 1996a). Fifty percent of the respondents in a Jupiter Interactive survey indicated that they had visited a sports-related web site as a direct result of the mention of a URL during a sports broadcast. Furthermore, 33 percent of online users surveyed said they had visited a sports-related web site while simultaneously watching sports on television. Sports sites such as ESPN's SportsZone and CNN/SI have labored to leverage their online presence by creating cross-platform campaigns with broadcast partners. Cross-promotional campaigns between TV and the web can drive traffic and exposure when the broadcast event refers back to the site and vice versa.

Traditional media firms have also utilized established Internet brands for promotional purposes. CBS has partnered with AOL to promote its fall lineup to AOL subscribers in 1998. Yahoo! was used to market Fox Sports when online users used search words pertaining to sports. Traditional mass media need to take their web sites seriously to create an online environment that is a comprehensive extension of their off-Net world, using their web sites to accomplish their business strategies and fortify their current brand strength online.

Strategic Functions of the Internet for Media Organizations

As media options continue to proliferate, traditional media are fighting to amortize their content investments across platforms. The arrival of the Internet extends traditional media's capabilities and business models. Specifically, the availability of the Internet allows traditional media to perform the following marketing functions necessary to prosper in today's marketplace:

▶ Brand Image Building

As indicated earlier, a traditional media firm such as CBS may extend its brand into cyberspace or use its web site to build favorable brand images. Note that strong TV brands do not necessarily translate successfully onto the Internet, as BBC Online has demonstrated (Grande, 1998).

▶ Complementary Content/Content Support

Complementary content or content support appears to be most useful in traditional media's quest to extend their brands online and build a closer relationship with their current readers/audiences. While *USA Today* offers extensive news reports online, cable TV networks such as ESPN use video streaming to display some of its game coverage on its SportsZone web site (Girard and Paikert, 1998). Such a content strategy strengthens the brand in both media.

▶ Original Content Development

Some aggressive media firms have ventured to develop original content for Internet use in an attempt to offer current added value and eventually to fortify their existing brands into online territory. Cable networks such as Discovery and MTV actually manage their web sites as totally different business ventures, offering original content and custom programming. The push for original programming on the Internet has put new pressure on traditional video producers. Some TV networks like PBS now require program producers to develop separate Internet applications (Hall, 1996). The NAB has recommended that online sports content rights be negotiated in a separate contract from their on-air rights (Ducey, 1996).

▶ Local Content Development

Research has shown that many online users value local information. To fend off competition for local advertising dollars from the new media and to expand their services, many traditional media are aggressively developing local online information. The revenue sources for such a local content element may include media buys, classifieds, directories, and commerce and transactions. Such broadcasting-related initiatives as CBSNow, CityWeb (Warner Bros.), and NBC Interactive Neighborhood are competing with local ports of call on the Net such as Cityscape, Sidewalk, Digital City, and Cityweb.

News, Weather, and Sports Information

Because of their well-established content franchise in the news area, traditional media are most aggressive in providing news, weather, and sports-related information online. While a news-based web site enables the print media to remain competitive in this interactive online world, it moves broadcast and cable media into the "in-depth" franchise that was previously the exclusive domain of print media, thus making them more powerful competitors in both worlds. At the same time, the Web offers print sources the ability to capture the immediacy of sound and moving images and to update content immediately.

Promotion

The Internet provides an excellent opportunity for media promotion as it not only offers in-depth information on the media product but also reaches hard-to-reach segments of the population like teens. The cross-promotion between old and new media may promote more focused and integrated brand images in an increasingly cluttered media environment.

Communications

As in many other businesses, the e-mail and forum capability on the Internet substantially improves client, consumer, agency, and media communications.

Advertising

Traditional media may extend their classified and sponsorship ad opportunities online as both are content-based and are historically the franchise of print and broadcast media. Commercial media will be able to harvest the best of both worlds by offering advertising packages that take advantage of the Internet's interactivity and personalization and traditional media's mass reach and impact.

▶ E-Commerce

Mass media firms may use the Internet for online transactions for novelty merchandise or other consumer items, generating both additional revenues and sales promotion opportunities. Note that a favorable, trusted brand image is a necessary ingredient for the success of e-commerce for a media firm.

▶ Product Information Distribution

The Internet offers mass media an efficient information distribution system. The Internet not only enables the distribution of more product information but also enhances the value of traditional media products by offering traditional media another outlet for their content products.

▶ Customer Service

Because of the interactive nature of the Internet, it is an excellent customer service tool for media firms, which may use this personalizable distribution system to provide value-added customer services. KCTS, a Seattle PBS affiliate that produces the popular "Bill Nye the Science Guy," developed a Nye Labs site (*[http://nyelabs.kcts.org/]*), which offers audio clips for download and experiments for online participation, making its web site a customer service vehicle (Hall, 1996).

▶ Public Relations Enhancement

The Internet's capacity to distribute product and company information and improve customer services enables important activities that build and maintain public relations for media firms.

▶ Market Research Tools and Consumer Database Building

The Internet offers an opportunity of market testing for media firms. New media service or content may be tested online before larger scale implementation. Furthermore, a media firm may use its web site to gather reader/audience demographic, lifestyle, and behavioral information for product design and other marketing purposes.

Internet Economic Issues for Media Organizations ▬

The strategic functions available through the Internet delineate the importance of this emerging medium for individual media organizations in an increasingly proliferative, competitive media marketplace. In fact, the Internet has established a relatively level playing field that may discount the benefit of media group ownership and allow the development of innovative content providers such as web-based radio stations. On the other hand, the strategic functions of the World Wide Web also suggest an urgent need for strong brand identities for media organizations. In the online world, media consumers are the initiators of brand contacts, and a weak, indifferent brand will be less likely to induce consumer actions in a world full of content choices. At the global level, the need for branding presents a special challenge to multinational media conglomerates. While strategies that integrate multiple media content to build strong brand identifies are essential, these media organizations need to, at the same time, customize and localize online information for individual users, taking advantage of the interactive nature of the Internet. In a nutshell, the World Wide Web offers media organizations the never-before-experienced opportunity of marketing a global brand with interactive, individualized content/utility capacity, an obvious competitive advantage in an increasingly crowded global market.

Concluding Analysis ▬

This chapter has examined the relationships between existing mass media and the Internet and, in particular, the strategic utilization of the Internet by commercial media firms and industries. The issues raised are largely economic, but the increasing commercialization of the Internet raises important social and political concerns as well. In keeping with the format of this volume, this final section examines the social, political, and economic consequences of the integration of traditional and online media at the individual, group, national, and global levels of analysis.

▶ Individual Level

The most successful brands in the world of integrated and interactive media will be those perceived by individuals as offering something of value. The interactive nature of the Internet changes the relationship between individuals and media, requiring media to shift their efforts from persuasion to relationship building. As communication channels continue to proliferate and fragment, successful media firms will have to focus on consumers, rather than on systems of distribution or types of media content. The unique ability of the Internet to allow online users to customize web sites to better serve their interests will further force media firms to consider consumers as individuals rather than as audiences.

▶ Group Level

The strategic functions available through the Internet delineate the importance of this emerging medium for individual media organizations in an increasingly proliferative, competitive media marketplace. In fact, the Internet has established a relatively level playing field that may discount the benefit of media group ownership and allows the development of innovative content providers such as web-based radio stations. On the other hand, the strategic functions of the World Wide Web also suggest an urgent need for strong brand identities for media organizations. As noted above, in the online world, media consumers are the initiators of brand contacts and a weak, indifferent brand will less likely induce consumer actions in a world full of content choices.

The Internet should not be regarded as a marketing handicap for traditional media firms but rather as an excellent way to differentiate media organizations and improve services to both advertisers and media consumers. Traditional media need to anticipate the extent and rate of growth of this new medium. Rather than producing specific content for a specific distribution system, tomorrow's media will be in the business of producing media assets that can be accessed and served in customized packages specified by the consumer via multiple platforms, including the Internet.

▶ National Level

Around the world, national media industries are being restructured by the interaction of technology, competitive marketplace forces, and policy.

While the Internet is an important element of change, the full extent of its impact on national media will not be known for some time. Nonetheless, successful strategic use of the Internet by media industries is likely to be an indispensable element in the long-term survival and prosperity of existing and new media firms in the increasingly competitive and crowded media marketplace.

▶ Global Level

At the global level, the need for branding presents a special challenge to multinational media conglomerates. While strategies that integrate multimedia content to build strong brand identities are essential, these media organizations need to, at the same time, customize and localize online information for individual users, taking advantage of the interactive nature of the Internet. While the World Wide Web offers media organizations the opportunity to market a global brand, such opportunities usually are accompanied by problems.

The global marketing of media brands is likely to face both political and cultural challenges. The dominant global media organizations are Western, and the majority are based in the United States. Even though the global distribution and openness of the Internet levels the playing field shared by international media competitors, the decades-old concern with American cultural imperialism is likely to be heard again, given the tremendous head start enjoyed by U.S. media firms in the online global marketplace. While the clash of American and Western cultures with those of other nations is a familiar political and social issue, cultural differences have economic consequences as well. As media firms find it easier and increasingly attractive to operate at a global level, they will increasingly experience the need to adapt content and practices to other cultures, especially as the Internet becomes more multilingual. This adds yet another level of complexity associated with the Internet's role in changing the relationship between media and consumers.

References

Baker, J. 1998, October 21. Internet and Broadcasters. [No pagination] [Online] Retrieved October 21, 1998, from the World Wide Web: *http://www.nab.org/ Research/RIBriefs/ presentatons/ BCFM98/sld032.htm*

Berniker, M. 1995, June 5. CBS Expands Plans for Affiliate Web Sites. *Broadcasting & Cable*, 28. Retrieved January 10, 1999, from online database ABI/INFORM [UMI Company].

Chan-Olmsted, S.M. 1999. Branding Television Stations on the Internet. Manuscript in preparation.

Cleland, K. 1996, July 15. AT&T, Modem Ring Up a Big Olympics Web Buy. *Advertising Age*, 67:16.

Coffey, S., and Stipp, H. 1997. The Interactions Between Computer and Television Usage. *Journal of Advertising Research*, 37(2): 61–67.

Consoli, J. 1997, February 22. Online Users Turn Off TV. *Editor & Publisher*, 36–37. Retrieved January 10, 1999, from online database ABI/INFORM [UMI Company].

CyberAtlas. 1998, November 20. Net Has Little Effect on TV Viewing. [Online] Retrieved January 12, 1999, from the World Wide Web: *http://www.cyberatlas.com/big_picture/demographics/article/0,1323,5901_150201,00.html*

———. 1999a, January 14. PC vs. TV: Yankee Group Report Finds Target Customers Spending More, But Watching Less [No pagination]. Retrieved January 14, 1999, from online database ABI/INFORM [UMI Company].

———. 1999b, January 8. Market Demographics: Television and PCs Receive Equal Time. [No pagination] [Online] Retrieved January 14, 1999, from the World Wide Web: *http://cyberatlas.com /big_picture/demographics/article/0,1323,5901_15034/00.html*

Dahlin, T.C. 1999, January. *Editor & Publisher* 10th Annual Online Media Services Free Survey Results, *Editor & Publisher*.

Ducey, R.V. 1996. Multimedia Broadcasting and the Internet. INET '96 6th Annual Internet Society Conference Montreal, Canada June 25–28, 1996. [No pagination] [Online] Retrieved January 7, 1999, from the World Wide Web: *http://www.nab.org/Research/RIbriefs/Presentations/isoc_b3.htm*

Ducey, R.V. 1997. What's Next in Consumer Media! Keynote speech, Broadcast Engineering Conference NAB '97, LasVegas, Nevada, April 6, 1997. [No pagination] [Online] Retrieved January 8, 1999, from the World Wide Web: *http://www.nab.org/Research/RIbriefs/bec.htm*

Evans, J. 1998, October 22. The Industry Standard: Losing $21.5 Million: As Easy as ABC-News.com. [No pagination] [Online] Retrieved January 8, 1999, from the World Wide Web: *http://www.thestandard.net/articles/display/0,1151,2168,00.html*

Frederiksen, L. 1997, January 20. Internet or Infomercial: Which Will Turn Your Audience On? *Marketing News*, 15. Retrieved January 10, 1999, from online database ABI/INFORM [UMI Company].

Freeman, M. 1996, August 19. Neuralgia in Repland. *Mediaweek*, 22–23. Retrieved January 10, 1999, from online database ABI/INFORM [UMI Company].

Girard, T., and Paikert, C. 1998, October 12. Cable and the Internet: Friends or Foes? [No pagination] [Online] Retrieved October 16, 1998, from World Wide Web: *http:// cvmag.com/feature.htm*

Grande, C. 1998, August 20. Channels Turn to Internet for Program Launches. *New Media Markets,* 6–7. Retrieved October 5, 1998, from online database ABI/INFORM [UMI Company].

Gunther, M. 1998, August 17. NBC Is Old Media, But Its Web Plans Are Real Smart. *Fortune,* 138(4): 191–194.

Hall, L. 1996, March 11. Cable, Broadcast Online Sites Come into Their Own. *Electronic Media,* 15(11): 42.

Kraut, R.; Lundmark, V.; Kiesler, S.; Mukhopadhyay, T.; and Scherlis, W. 1997. Why People Use the Internet. [No pagination] [Online] Retrieved October 20, 1998, from the World Wide Web: *http://homenet.andrew.cmu.edu/progress/purpose.html*

Lindstrom, P.B. 1997. The Internet: Nielsen's Longitudinal Research on Behavioral Changes in Use of This Counterintuitive Medium. *Journal of Media Economics,* 100(2): 35–40.

Liu, C.; Arnett, K.P.; Capella, L.M.; and Beatty, R.C. 1997. Web Sites of the Fortune 500 Companies: Facing Customers through Home Pages. *Information & Management* 31:335–345.

Maddox, L.M., and Mehta, D. 1997, March/April. The Role and Effect of Web Addresses in Advertising. *Journal of Advertising Research,* 37(2): 47–59.

McDonald, S.C. 1997, March. The Once and Future Web: Scenarios for Advertisers. *Journal of Advertising Research,* 37(2): 21–28.

Meyer, E.K. 1998. Unexpectedly Wider Web for the World's Newspapers. [No pagination] [Online] Retrieved January 14, 1999. from *http://www.newslink.org/emcol10.html*

Montalbano, L. 1999, March 11. Building Brands in Cyberspace. [No pagination] [Online] Retrieved from the World Wide Web: *http://www.frankel-anderson.com/phoneplus.html*

Morris, M., and Ogan, C. 1996. The Internet as Mass Medium. *Journal of Communication,* 46(1): 39–50.

Newborne, E., and Hof, R.D. 1998, November 9. Branding on the Net. *Business Week,* pp. 76–86. Retrieved January 10, 1999, from the online database ABI/INFORM [UMI Company].

Pallab, P. 1996. Marketing on the Internet. *Journal of Consumer Marketing,* 13(4): 27.

Pattinson, H., and Brown, L. 1996. Chameleons in Marketspace Industry Transformation in the New Electronic Marketing Environment. *Journal of Marketing Practice: Applied Marketing Science,* 2(1): 7.

Pitt, L.; Berthon, P.; and Watson, R.T. 1996. From Surfer to Buyer on the WWW: What Marketing Managers Might Want to Know. *Journal of General Management.* 22(1): 1–13.

Raman, N.V., and Leckenby, J.D. 1998. Factors Affecting Consumers' "Webad" Visits. *European Journal of Marketing,* 32(7): 737.

Ross, C. 1996, November 4. TV Networks Struggle with Internet Role : Promo Purposes Central, But Other Avenues, Alliances Are in the Works. *Advertising Age,* 16. Retrieved January 10, 1999, from online database ABI/INFORM [UMI Company].

Rothenberg, R. 1998, December. Go Ahead, Kill Your Television, NBC Is Ready. *Wired.*

Savoie, B. 1998. Summary of the Web Activity of Television Stations. [No pagination] [Online] Retrieved January 10, 1999, from the World Wide Web: *http://www.nab.org/Research/webbriefs/WebActiv.html*

Stipp, H. 1995. I Want My Old TV! *Forecast* 3(2): 18–28.

Tedesco, R. 1996a, September 30. NBC Makes Olympian Showing in 'Net ratings.' *Broadcasting & Cable,* p. 83.

_____. 1996b, March 25. Lifetime Revs Up Website With Auto Race. *Broadcasting & Cable,* p. 70.

_____. 1997a, July 28. NBC Pushes On-air/Online Content Crossovers. *Broadcasting & Cable,* 127: 72.

_____. 1997b, June 30. 'POV' Online Content Connects to Air. *Broadcasting & Cable,* p. 79.

Use the Internet to Reach Upscale, Techno-savvy Households. 1997, August. *About Women & Marketing,* 10(8): 7.

by John V. Pavlik and
Steven S. Ross

c   h   a   p   t   e   r   6

Journalism Online:
Exploring the Impact of New Media on News and Society

Introduction

No longer are journalists and the news constrained by the technical limitations of analog media boundaries of print, television, or radio. Instead, all modalities of human communication are available for telling the story in the most compelling, interactive, on-demand, and customized fashion possible. Of course, newsroom traditions and training, as well as newsroom economics, may ultimately determine whether journalists fully utilize these online capabilities to create better, more complete and contextualized news reports. Nevertheless, the technology makes improved journalism possible. Consider the following example comparing how an Internet-original news operation covered a major news story with how a newspaper covered that same story online.

Frank Sinatra's FBI file became public property on December 10, 1998. News organizations across the United States and internationally reported on the release of the file and the various allegations it contained. These allegations ranged from reports of Sinatra's alleged mob connections, to his arrest for "seduction," to his 4F status for psychological instability that made him ineligible for the draft during World War II.

The New York Times provided a standard journalistic accounting of the 1,300-page file, exploring each of these allegations in an approximately 2,500-word account. *The Times'* report, available in both the print and online editions of the paper, represents a good example of how most general interest newspapers or news magazines would approach a story such as this. A primary source makes certain information available, and news organizations report on the release of the report and provide an overview of its contents, pointing out certain notable items.

Contrast *The Times'* report with that of a web site launched in the fall of 1998 from New York's Silicon Alley (an area of Manhattan south of 41st street). Apbonline *[http://www.apbonline.com]* is a new news web site covering crime throughout the United States and internationally. It is an Internet-original, or purely online, news product; it has no print or broadcast parent.

Apbonline covered the Sinatra report in quintessential Internet fashion, using a wide range of online media capabilities. Not just confined to text reporting, the site utilized interactivity, images, and all 1,300 pages of the FBI Sinatra file scanned in electronically and made available to anyone visiting the web site, thus placing the news story into the full context of the original source material. Although *The New York Times* did make the several hundred pages of the Starr report available on its web site and in the paper, it did not make the Sinatra file available. Apbonline didn't stop with just making the 1,300 pages available. It also annotated the file and included several sidebar reports about each of the most important sections of the report.

Apbonline illustrates the unique capabilities of online news. Some advantages apbonline has are that it is edited by Columbia Journalism School graduate Mark Sauter, it features among its contributing editors journalist George

Lardner, Jr., Pulitzer Prize winner at *The Washington Post*, and it has an experienced team of technical designers and programmers.

Consider another example from apbonline. One sometimes-heard criticism of American news media is that they tend to focus on events to the exclusion of processes and trends. Events make better, or at least easier, stories than broad social trends. Of course, the best journalism uses an event-based story to illustrate a broader trend. But, be that as it may, a December 1998 report in apbonline illustrates how new media, especially online news, can make trend reporting more palatable, at least to the editors who sometimes shy away from publishing it. Apbonline also published a story about an FBI crime report released that month. The FBI reports, flawed as they may be in overreporting certain types of crimes and underreporting other types, are the best single source of crime data for the United States. Most news organizations typically publish or broadcast a story about the issuance of such a report, followed by a "local" angle story. At the local level the reporter might examine the data about the local geographic community and perhaps interview some local residents or officials to elicit their reactions to the FBI data that shows their community as either more or less safe than average or than other communities in the report. Apbonline took this model one important step further: it published the entire report online. That means, anyone visiting the site can not only get the best available journalistic intelligence about the data in the report, but also look up data about any community, county or state in the United States, their own or any other, and evaluate the significance of the data for themselves.

MSNBC on the Web *[http://www.msnbc.com]* took this same idea of reporting on federal databases even further than apbonline. On its cable channel, MSNBC transmitted a report about the five most dangerous roads in America. On its web site, not only did MSNBC provide the text of this report, but producers also linked to a federal traffic database that permitted visitors to the site to enter a zip code (theirs or any other). This allowed the user to obtain traffic fatality data for their community and see which roads are the most dangerous in their town.

This form of making better connections between news analysis and primary source materials is one of the most important emerging trends in online journalism. It is important because it helps to place stories in better context and can hold journalists accountable for their reporting by enabling the audience to compare a journalist's report with the actual primary source material he or she is reporting about. This may help slow or even reverse the steady decline in credibility suffered by U.S. news organizations the past quarter century.

A 1998 study by the American Society of Newspaper Editors, in which 3,000 adult Americans were surveyed, confirms the credibility crisis in U.S. news media, finding that "78 percent of U.S. adults believe there's bias in the news media" (Journalism Credibility Project, 1998). Most (59 percent) see this bias as stemming in large part from the belief that news media (including newspapers) "are concerned mainly with making profits, rather than serving the public interest." A 1998 study by Jupiter Communications places these findings in the context of online journalism, revealing that the 80 percent of adult Americans who use online media (2,200 were surveyed) rate online news sources as just as credible (i.e., they trust them to the same degree) as traditional news providers, with the remaining 20 percent relatively evenly split (12.7 percent say they trust offline sources more, 7.3 percent say they trust online sources more) (Mooradian, 1998).

But there are other important developments in online journalism, as well. Some of these are positive trends and others raise serious and troubling questions. The remainder of this chapter examines these trends and questions in the context of four areas of impact of new media, and online communications in particular, on journalism and society. The four areas of impact are

1. How new media developments are affecting the content of news,
2. Implications of online communications for the way journalists do their work,
3. Implications for newsroom structure and the structure of the news industry overall, and
4. Implications of online developments for the relationships between news organizations, journalists, and their many publics, including the audience, competitors, sponsors/advertisers/partners, news sources, government regulators, and the like.

Redesigning News Content ▬

As outlined above, online communications, including but not limited to the Internet and the World Wide Web (America Online *[http://www.aol.com]*, for example, is another important online development that is not limited to the Internet and the Web), are transforming news content. As of March 1999, some 4,925 newspapers around the world (the total number of news sites is much higher because it includes a variety of sites created by broadcast and cable magazine parent news organizations as well as many Internet originals, such as apbonline, salon, and thestreet.com) had created online news sites (see *[http://www.ajr.org]* for the most current information). Virtually all of these sites feature content that in some way utilizes the unique capabilities of online media. Most, for example, use pointers or hyperlinks that allow readers easy access to related online news and information. This hypermedia capability gives online news the unique ability to place news stories into greater context than in traditional media by making connections and associations with related developments, facts, and stories.

Online media also permit news reports to provide layers of content that can include text, audio, and video, as well as graphics and animations, permitting readers to access news content in considerably greater depth than traditional news stories can provide. The character of online news varies somewhat by whether the online news provider is an Internet original such as apbonline, the product of a broadcast or cable news parent, or the product of a print operation, either newspaper or magazine. By and large, Internet originals are the most creative in their use of new media storytelling tools, such as interactivity, customization, and multimedia because they are not concerned about protecting any existing franchise. In contrast, online news offerings published by print, broadcast, or cable parents are often concerned about cannibalizing their existing audience, so they often proceed rather cautiously in breaking news (they don't want to "scoop" themselves) and in other news decisions and story designs. Salon.com, an online original magazine, or "zine," illustrates this tendency. Salon.com broke the Henry Hyde extramarital affair story during the Clinton investigation, when no established news operation would. Subsequently, many other news organizations ran the story. Operations such as

MSNBC.com or CNN.com are among the most progressive in their use of multimedia and interactivity among sites with a parent content company. CNN.com benefits from a central newsroom organization that allows all six CNN networks (including online and on TV) to share central news-gathering functions.

Moreover, emerging new media tools permit online news providers to deliver content using new media formats, such as 360-degree images and object-oriented video that gives readers greater control over the news, giving increased access to news on demand.

Online news also permits a greater level of customization and localization than is ever possible in traditional media. For example, Pavlik and Feiner (1998) have developed the notion of dynamically updated news delivered to a mobile augmented reality system (see Feiner, MacIntyre, Höllerer, and Webster, 1997) which allows for the delivery of customized news information to a mobile news consumer. The content is localized to the exact location of that person, as well as to that person's orientation to the environment around her or him.

To illustrate and test this notion, a group of students in the News Lab at Columbia University developed, under Pavlik's direction, an "immersive" documentary using the Mobile Journalist's Workstation (MJW) developed in Feiner's Computer Graphics and Animation Lab at Columbia. The documentary explored the 1968 student revolt at Columbia in which students took over control of much of the campus in protest of the University's plans to build a gymnasium in Morningside Park, an area not owned by the University. The documentary permitted an individual wearing the MJW to walk the campus today and relive the revolt of three decades ago. As designed in Feiner's lab, the MJW involves a wearable computer, a see-through, head-worn display (with orientation tracker) and audio playback system, a spread spectrum radio communication link for Internet access (two megabits per second wavelan system), a hand-held personal digital appliance (PDA), and a global positioning system (GPS) receiver. The system uses "augmented reality" to allow the wearer to see the campus as it exists today, and it layers additional information upon that view. Linked to the GPS and head orientation tracker, the MJW-delivered immersive documentary allows the wearer to see the campus and overlays graphics, text, images, video, and audio from the student revolt approximately where they actually occurred in 1968, all placed in journalistic context by the student news team.

This three-dimensional news experience could also be delivered in a virtual reality environment, as well, by overlaying the MJW content onto an opaque, 360-degree view of the campus. The MJW technology could be used to deliver interactive 3D news reports for any news event or process in either an augmented reality (i.e., to allow a user to visit the location of an event and relive it) or a virtual reality format (to allow people the same type of experience without having to go on location).

Online news can offer readers other means to participate in the news, as well. Most news sites host a variety of reader forums that invite readers to comment on news reports and issues. At many news sites, these forums have become extremely active. *The New York Times on the Web*, for example, hosts more than 100 forums daily, with some 3,000 or more postings daily. Elizabeth A. Osder, former content editor for The New York Times Electronic Media Company (now vice president for iXL-Media and Entertainment) observes that these are typically not just rantings, but well-informed, articulate soundings from a diverse array of readers concerned about the news and public affairs (Osder, 1998). Overall, these developments create the possibility of reengaging an increasingly alienated citizenry.

Will the content capabilities of online media be realized in online journalism? The technological developments of new media make possible a better format for news content, one richer in context, interactivity, and use of multimedia, and all on demand 24 hours a day from anywhere in the world. But these possibilities will likely not be realized, at least on a widespread basis, for a variety of reasons. Three of the most compelling reasons are uncertain economics (i.e., will it make a profit?), fear of change, and three centuries of tradition (*Publick Occurrences Both Forreign and Domestic* is the earliest-known newspaper printed in British North America in 1690).

Transforming How Journalists Do Their Work

Perhaps no technological development since the invention of the telephone has influenced the practice of journalism more than the convergence of the computer and telecommunications, as manifested in the Internet, the World Wide Web, and other forms of online communication. With the vast repositories of databases and other information available online, the asynchronous communications capabilities of electronic mail, and the ability to deliver news online to audiences anywhere, journalists have rapidly embraced online media for their news-gathering and delivery potential. Consider data reported by Dan Middleberg, Chairman and CEO, Middleberg + Associates, and Steve Ross, Columbia journalism associate professor of professional practice, in their annual national survey of the "media in cyberspace" (Middleberg and Ross, 1998). The authors' five-survey trend data are based on more than 2,500 responses and reveal that journalists are making increasing and significant use of the Internet and other online resources in their work. The most important findings of the landmark study are reported below.

- Almost all journalists now use online tools for researching and reporting. Fully 93 percent of respondents say they or their staffs in some way use online services at least occasionally. Almost half the respondents say they or their staffs are online every day (more than half for newspapers). Only 2 percent say they or their staffs absolutely never use online technology.

- When reporting a breaking story after hours, journalists try for the source first, almost every time, but indicate they turn to company web sites second for information. During nonbusiness hours, or when live sources are not available, web sites are playing a significant role in delivering information to media.

- The trend for online scoops continues. Almost one-third of publications' web sites allow the Web to scoop their print product, at least sometimes.

- Many journalists are going online to get story ideas. Amazingly, LIST-SERVS, e-mail, the Web, and Usenet Newsgroups together were named by only 9 percent of respondents as their primary source of story ideas—together about the same as newswires. But live sources remain far and away journalists' biggest sources of story ideas.

- The growth of online publishing is simply tremendous. More than half the responding journalists indicate they use the Web to distribute news. Fifty-five percent say their publication, or portions of it, are already online! That's double the 25 percent reported at the end of 1995. And only 9 percent of respondents at the end of 1997 said their publication had no plans to go online at all.

- Original content being published online has seen significant growth. In 1996 only 7 percent of newspapers with web sites said 50 percent or more of the site's content was original and not appearing in their print version. By late 1997 almost 20 percent of newspapers with web sites said original content was at least 50 percent. For magazines, 48 percent said their web sites are at least 50 percent original, up from 17 percent last year.
- Over 40 percent of editors or their staffs write copy that ends up on their own publication's web site.
- Journalists cite financial information as being the most useful element of a web site, followed by photos and press releases. Journalists expect complex sites to have a search engine.
- Most respondents indicate that they are using the Web for gathering images and other materials that had to be physically carried to the newsroom just a few years ago.
- More than half of all respondents can now access the Internet from work, compared to a bit more than a third of the entire sample in 1995. And only 9 percent of the respondents said they had no individual Internet access.
- Preference for online submissions rather than paper submissions jumped to 29 percent from 1995's 20 percent.
- Yahoo!, which used AltaVista as a web catalog and search system when the survey was done, and AltaVista, itself, have become dominant as entry points for journalists on the Web. Combined, they get about half the search activity by journalists.

Changing Newsroom and News Industry Structure

Although these changes in how journalists work are remarkable and important, other aspects of the new media transformation of journalistic work are only beginning to take shape. Perhaps the most important of these are the capabilities of journalists in the field to have full access to online information and collaborative work groups in the field. Mobile, wireless access to online information and high-speed communications are poised to transform both the work of the field reporter and the structure of the newsroom. Consider the implications of the Mobile Journalist's Workstation (MJW), the 360-degree "omnicamera," and other emerging new media as described in the following journalism scenario developed by Steve Ross (1997).

Head: The Atlanta Olympics of 2004

"Phew! I'm really exhausted, Dick. Covering these nighttime concert security gigs after doing crowd control all day down at the stadiums is really getting to me."

"The computer really is doing most of the work. We just ride shotgun, so to speak. Those three Omnicams up on those poles take in the whole park. That little black box under the desk processes all the images and suggests suspicious items for us to investigate."

"Yeah, Jim. Every time a guy or gal puts down a purse for a minute or two, the computer goes nuts and the Omnicam zooms in, thinking it might be a bomb! I'm going out into the park. Just feed me anything REALLY weird; I'm carrying Mobile-3."

Dick Jowell walks out of the security office and meets a German TV-web team. Standing by the door, Jowell compares his small, specialized security video specs—eyeglasses with built-in video screens—to the Germans' fancier hand-held Mobile Journalists Terminal, when Jim yells. Dick hears him through the door and on his video pad speaker. The video screen alternates between a view of the small black bag propped up against the back of the concert stage and a map of the area with the bag's location marked. It is only 100 feet away. The computer had automatically detected the object in the

Omnicam's 360-degree field of view as "not moving, artificial, and not part of the stage" and had zoomed in on it. The third "real" alert in two hours.

Jowell walks briskly, deliberately toward the bag, telling concert patrons quietly and firmly to move out of the area. Unless someone claims the bag quickly, the bomb squad, already alerted, would be there in three minutes. The German camera crew was picking up the security video and audio feed as well now, while following Jowell as he moved people away.

Kabloom!

The German TV team, more used to reporting on jazz concerts than on bombings, swings into action. The chief producer dictates a quick news bulletin into the MJW base station, a large laptop. The audio, video, and a text translation of her voice are all immediately sent to other news organizations in the Olympic Games news pool and to the wire services.

The team's three reporters scatter with wireless mikes and eyeglass-like video screens to three injured bystanders. The team's single Omnicam focuses in on all three. The terminal, tied to the Germans' satellite-linked car a block away, is already receiving a message from the TV-web office in Munich. One of the injured is German, also a reporter, and willing to talk. He knows his family back home will be able to see him within minutes and see that he was not seriously hurt. The MJW processes all of it into three separate, simultaneous video cuts from the one camera. Other reporting teams are already sprinting to the scene. The big story tonight is not the concert!

In the security shed, Jim replays the video of the bag, to see who put it there. A playful young couple. There! They are carrying a leather bag. They stop by the wall at the back of the stage. They put the bag down behind them. They kiss. They laugh. They walk off slowly. "They are smart," Jim thinks. "Never once did they turn their faces away from the wall during the bag placement. But not smart enough."

Jim now directs the video system to track the couple as they had moved in the park before the blast and to access the feed from Jowell's up-close video camera, the one mounted in his eyeglass frames, as he had walked toward the bag. Within 20 seconds, he has two excellent, full-face images. Another 10 seconds and his computer is searching Georgia driver's license records for picture matches. There's the gal! No match on the man yet. The system automatically starts searches in other states and in passport and immigration files. Four minutes! There are six possible matches on the guy!

Jim issues photos of the two bombers to the news teams and police all over the city, by video link. The police, but not the journalists, also get a list of possible suspect names. A federal judge gets the details and issues a warrant for authorities to search credit card databases. Perhaps they are from out of town and have been using their cards. Perhaps they are more careful. The FBI is already trying to match them with known terrorists and international terrorist organizations. The German TV-web crew is already searching its files in Europe.

Within hours, there are hundreds of gigabytes of text and video on the bombing. The reporters covering it, in turn, are searching hundreds of terabytes of material—everything from personnel records, to stories of similar bombings, to histories of violence in Atlanta or violence at Olympic events. At the MJW and in newsrooms all over the world, software summarizes key points about incoming data and outgoing stories to make the flow easier to manage.

Back at the security shed, an FBI official linked over Jim's computer asks if it is all right to upload the complete digital record of the night's happenings to the FBI's central computer banks. The video feed, digitally watermarked, will be kept as evidence. Jim makes a permanent copy for his superiors on a DVD-II disk, just in case something goes wrong.

"That guy Jowell is a hero," the FBI officer says. "From the video, we estimate that the bomb has 40 grams of C4 explosive. Our scenarios say 20 or 30 people could have died. Instead, you had three injured, only one seriously, and no panic." *The Atlanta Constitution*'s reporters already have Jowell's biography on their terminals. His mother will be interviewed within the hour for the newspaper, the web site, and a video feed they'll broadcast and sell to other news organizations as well.

The bombers will be caught within four hours, as they drive through Rome, Georgia, on the way to their farm in Montana. "They look just like the picture those guys in the park sent," says one police officer in Rome.

The technologies described in this scenario are real, and their application to journalism is beginning. The notion of a "virtual newsroom," or a newsroom without walls, may become real in the next decade, as reporters in the field gain access to powerful, lightweight, computing and communications devices supporting mobile Internet access.

The virtual newsroom has important implications at a number of levels of analysis, including the individual, group, national and global levels. At the individual level, it is the journalist who is most affected, especially working as a freelancer. The freelance reporter in the field can use tools such as the Mobile Journalist's Workstation to support the news gathering and production process, link to online databases, interview remote experts, and compile and distribute multimedia news reports. Traditionally, the best journalism is based on good "shoe-leather" reporting, and providing tools to support the reporter in the field can only enhance the quality of that journalism. At the group level, the newsroom is transformed from an organization largely disconnected from its reporters in the field. The virtual newsroom can facilitate the move away from a model in which news stories are managed by a disconnected central newsroom to a model in which stories, especially breaking stories, are managed from the field.

At a national level, the virtual newsroom suggests the possible emergence of new news "networks" that can effectively coordinate over a large physical distance, yet distribute customized news to a national audience. This is clearly occurring on a national level with the development of "portals" as news destinations by many Internet users who now go to sites such as Yahoo! to get their news from Reuters, Associated Press, or even the PR Newswire (this also underscores the increasing commoditization of news). Finally, this same notion extends to an international level in which news organizations will be able to extend their network on a global scale. This is well illustrated by the development of the international audience of *The New York Times on the Web* [http://www.nytimes.com], which now has an online international audience of more than 300,000 subscribers.

Reinventing Relationships between News Organizations and Their Publics

Although new forms of news content, new ways of reporting and new newsroom structures are all vital to the future of journalism, perhaps the most important changes are those occurring in the relationships between news organizations, journalists and their many publics. As Michael Schrage (1998) of MIT has written,

There may be a small irony in an "Information Revolution" being little more than media hype, but the consequences here might be more tragic than ironic. *In reality, viewing these technologies through the lens of "information" is dangerously myopic.* The value of the Internet and the ever-expanding World Wide Web does not live mostly in bits and bytes and bandwidth. To say that the Internet is about "information" is a bit like saying that "cooking" is about oven temperatures; it's technically accurate but fundamentally untrue. ... *The so-called "information revolution" itself is actually, and more accurately, a "relationship revolution."* Anyone trying to get a handle on the dazzling technologies of today and the impact they'll have tomorrow, would be well advised to re-orient their worldview around relationships. *Along every conceivable dimension—from the intimate to the institutional—digital media force both individuals and organizations to redefine what kind of relationships create value.*

In journalism, the most important relationships are being transformed by the new media. Consider the relationship that has existed throughout most of the past century among news organizations, their audiences, or public, and the sources of news. For the most part, news organizations gathered information from news sources, who frequently sought to be either in or out of the media spotlight. They then packaged that information in a manner palatable to the public, who consumed the news in linear format (i.e., as stories told sequentially with a beginning, middle and end), as delivered via a variety of traditional analog media. The dramatic rise of the Internet and the World Wide Web in the 1990s as media of mass communication has inexorably altered this triangular relationship of interdependency. By empowering the public and redefining the reporter-source relationship in an age of direct public access to primary news sources, the Internet and WWW have challenged journalistic organizations to reinvent their role in this relationship. Not only that, but they must also re-invent their business model, since the media's relationship with their primary sponsor, advertisers, is fundamentally altered as well.

Other relationships are also transformed. News audiences are no longer necessarily determined by the geographic, political, or cultural (e.g., language) boundaries predominant in the world of analog media. Consider how English-speaking journalists and news consumers alike can make use of online tools such as the free, real-time, translation capabilities of AltaVista (using Systran) to read web sites published in French, Italian, Spanish, and several other languages (see *http://www.altavista.com*).

Governments around the world have taken a special interest in regulating online communications, thus confronting journalists with a whole new set of legal challenges. How do notions of freedom of speech extend to a global publishing medium such as the Internet? Do newspaper journalists reporting online enjoy the same First Amendment protection as when they report the same news in print? Do broadcast journalists enjoy greater First Amendment protection than they traditionally receive over the airwaves? What is the proper balance among online law enforcement, digital security, privacy, and the public's right to know?

Problems of equity of access to online news sources will not disappear soon, and cyber journalists concerned about their role in a democracy must be aware of the uneven distribution of computers and online services both throughout the United States and around the world.

These are just some of the opportunities and problems facing journalism and the public in a digital age. Whether democracy ultimately will be better served by an Internet-connected society is impossible to say. The only certainty is that journalism and society are undergoing a fundamental transformation. Journalists who fail to meet the challenges of the digital age will likely find themselves as obsolete as a Royal typewriter in an online newsroom.

References

http://www.ajr.org
http://www.altavista.com
http://www.apbonline.com
http://www.msnbc.com
Feiner, S.; MacIntyre, B.; Höllerer, T.; and Webster, T. 1997. A Touring Machine: Prototyping 3D Mobile Augmented Reality Systems for Exploring the Urban Environment. In *Proceedings ISWC '97 (International Symposium on Wearable Computers)*, October 13-14, 1997, Cambridge, MA. Also in: *Personal Technologies*, 1(4): 208–17. [Online] Retrieved from the World Wide Web: *http://www.cs.columbia.edu/graphics/projects/mars/mars.html*
Journalism Credibility Project. 1998, December 15. American Society of Newspaper Editors. [Online] Retrieved from the World Wide Web: *http://www.asne.org*
Middleberg, D., and Ross, S.S. 1998. Media in Cyberspace Study. [Online] Retrieved from the World Wide Web: *http://www.mediasource.com/intro.htm*

Mooradian, M. 1998, December. Digital News: Revenue Strategies, Consumer Usage, Case Studies. *Jupiter Communications,* New York, p7.

Osder, E.A. 1998, October 2. Online Democracy Forum. Panel hosted by the Columbia University New Media Technology Center, New York, NY.

Pavlik, J., and Feiner, S. 1998. Implications of the Mobile Journalist's Workstation for Print Media. Presentation at the The Future of Print Media: A Virtual Symposium on the Digital Transformation of Printing and Publishing, School of Journalism and Mass Communication, Kent State University, Kent, OH. [Online] Retrieved from the World Wide Web: *http://www.jmc.kent.edu/futureprint*; *http://www.cs.columbia.edu/graphics/projects/mjw*

Ross, S.S. 1997. Atlanta Olympics News Scenario. Developed by the Engineering Research Center Proposal at Columbia University, 1997.

Schrage, M. 1998. The Relationship Revolution. The 1998 Merrill Lynch Forum. [Online] Retrieved from the World Wide Web: *http://www.ml.com/woml/forum/index.htm*

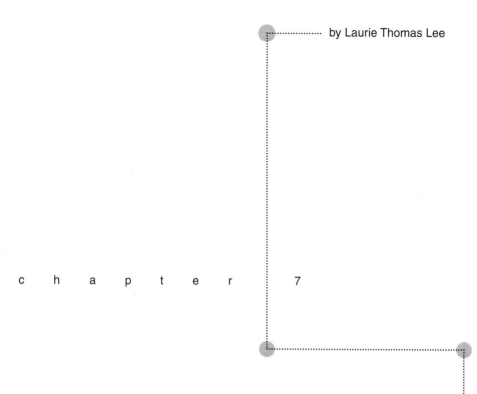

by Laurie Thomas Lee

c   h   a   p   t   e   r   7

Privacy, Security, and Intellectual Property ▼

The Internet creates new issues and poses new questions when it comes to online security and privacy rights. Individuals have come to enjoy the opportunities of online socializing, community activism, education, and shopping, yet they fear they are losing their privacy to businesses and government agencies able to take advantage of the Internet's enhanced tracking and record-keeping capabilities. The economic efficiencies of mass commercial e-mails are weighed against the privacy concerns of recipients. The prospects for e-commerce and the needs of law enforcement are also simultaneously weighed against interests in encryption and security. While some nations have already created online privacy policies, the United States grapples with a political hotbed of privacy and security issues, debating whether to create new laws or rely on industry self-regulation.

Intellectual property rights also face similar conflicts. The Internet affords authors and creators expanded opportunities to share, publicize, and exploit their works while making it much easier for others to steal, manipulate, and distribute the proprietary material. Legal protection serves to encourage the development of more intellectual property and a free flow of information, which is socially, politically, and economically desirable in a democratic market economy. Existing legal principles and precedents may certainly govern many of the rights and responsibilities, but digitized information and online distribution present new challenges and uncertainties.

The Internet essentially presents a kind of trade-off between incredible gains in economic, political, and social opportunities and corresponding losses in privacy and intellectual property rights. While the Internet offers exciting new ways to communicate and collect, market, and deliver information, some of the information is considered proprietary. Who has the right to access, collect, and exploit this online, digital material? This chapter explores privacy and security and then examines intellectual property, focusing on the legal contexts, issues, and responses at the individual, organizational, national, and international levels.

Privacy and Security

Internet security and privacy rights are leading topics of concern among consumers and have prompted some of the most intense policy debates in the United States and abroad. In the 1970s, about one-third of Americans said they were worried about threats to personal privacy (Dorney, 1997). Today, over 80 percent are concerned (Allard, 1998), saying that privacy protection is "important" or "very important." At least one study indicates privacy is the number one issue among online consumers (Tweney, 1998).

In general, studies show people are troubled by such matters as public access to personal and corporate data from online databases and government access to private information (Lawton, 1998). Specific complaints include the collection and transfer of private information identifying buying habits, the development of programs that can access or monitor personal files, and the invasion of junk e-mail or "spam." The concerns are not unfounded. One study by the Federal Trade Commission discovered that many web sites collect personal information from users and release the information without the users' knowledge or permission. Other studies reveal that more companies are accessing employee e-mail files, and the incidence of unsolicited e-mail is increasing at alarming rates. The development of full-scale e-commerce and other Internet growth opportunities may be hindered when many people choose to steer clear of the Internet, citing personal privacy concerns as their single biggest reason for staying off-line (Allard, 1998). Nearly one in four Americans say they would use the Internet more if their privacy were protected (You Are Being Tailed, 1998), and nearly two-thirds believe Internet privacy legislation is needed (Net Surfers Anonymous? 1998).

▶ The Right to Privacy

Privacy is a very broad concept that has many meanings and definitions (Lee and LaRose, 1994). Westin (1967) was among the first to study the nature of privacy, defining privacy as "the claim of individuals, groups, or institutions to determine for themselves when, how, and to what extent information about them is communicated to others." Others have defined privacy as an interest in managing transactions or interactions (Margulis, 1977). Still others have considered privacy to include a desire to control inputs from others (Altman, 1975) and maintain freedom from surveillance and unwanted intrusions (Burgoon, 1982).

A *right to privacy* is relatively new and not well articulated in the law. There is no right to privacy expressly guaranteed in the United States Constitution, although privacy interests are found in some provisions such as the Fourth Amendment, which forbids searches and seizures by the government without a warrant. Not until 1965 did the Supreme Court recognize a fundamental right to privacy, inferred from the Bill of Rights (*Griswold v. Connecticut*, 1965). Today, courts will generally consider a fundamental privacy right based on such factors as whether there is a "reasonable expectation of privacy." Privacy rights grounded in the Constitution, however, protect individuals from intrusions by the government, not by private parties.

A number of state and federal statutory laws serve to govern the interception, collection, use, and distribution of certain types of information by either government or private parties. The Electronic Communications Privacy Act of 1986 (ECPA) and many similar state wiretapping laws protect against unauthorized interception and disclosure of electronic communications while in transit or storage. The Privacy Act of 1974 provides limited privacy protection against government collection and disclosure of certain personal records held in government-maintained databases. Other laws that may serve as models or indirectly affect privacy and the Internet include

- The Fair Credit Reporting Act (1970) (governing the disclosure of information by consumer credit reporting agencies),
- The Right to Financial Privacy Act (1978) (restricting government access to financial institution customer records),
- The Telephone Consumer Protection Act (1991) (prohibiting unsolicited commercial faxes),
- The Telecommunications Act of 1996 (limiting the use of customer proprietary network information by common carriers),
- The Cable Communications Policy Act of 1984 (restricting the collection and disclosure of subscriber information), and
- The Video Privacy Act of 1988 (restricting the disclosure of information about videotape rentals).

Finally, privacy rights may be found in common law, protecting against the conduct of private parties. This type of law can be traced back to a famous law review article published over a century ago that recognized "the right to enjoy life—the right to be let alone" (Warren and Brandeis, 1890). Since then, the courts have recognized four widely accepted privacy torts: (1) misappropriation of a name or likeness for commercial purposes, (2) publicity that places a person in a false light, (3) public disclosure of embarrassing, private facts, and (4) intrusion upon seclusion or solitude (Prosser, 1960; *Restatement of the Law, Second, Torts*, 1977). Here, the courts will generally consider such factors as whether the privacy invasion was "highly offensive to the reasonable person." Each of these torts has implications for Internet privacy.

▶ Privacy Dimensions and Issues

In the context of the Internet, several dimensions of privacy interests emerge:

- Freedom from intrusion of unwanted information into one's personal space,

- Freedom from surveillance and improper access by others,
- Autonomy over personal information collected and disclosed by others, and
- Anonymity.

Intrusion. The first dimension focuses on concerns such as "spam" or unsolicited commercial e-mail (UCE). Spam is becoming a major concern among Internet service providers (ISPs) and users. Up to one-fourth of all messages handled by ISPs is thought to be junk mail. Companies complain that it clogs the network, increases Internet costs, and reduces employee productivity, while many users complain that spam is a nuisance and an intrusion into their system, demanding that it be stopped. In the meantime, spammers enjoy this new opportunity to reach thousands of potential customers at little or no cost, essentially shifting advertising costs to ISPs and recipients. The extent to which spam is a form of trespass or recipients are captive audiences is not yet clear. Several court cases have considered spam as trespassing onto proprietary networks. One model for legislation may be the Telephone Consumer Protection Act of 1991 (TCPA), which prohibits sending unsolicited advertisements to fax machines because of the unfair cost-shifting to consumers.

Surveillance/Improper Access. The second dimension of Internet privacy interests concerns improper monitoring and tracking as well as interceptions and computer hacking. Employee e-mail monitoring, the use of "cookies," and encryption fall under this category. Employee e-mail monitoring concerns arose in the early 1990s when employees at Epson American, Inc., and Nissan were fired after discovering and complaining about supervisors reading their e-mail (Lee, 1994). At that time, a survey of large and small companies found that over 40 percent had searched employee e-mail files (Piller, 1993). The Electronic Communications Privacy Act (1986) prohibits the interception of electronic communications and therefore applies to private e-mail over the Internet, although it may not protect e-mail within intracompany networks. Internet service providers may disclose information with the originator's consent. They may also intercept, disclose, or use any communication while engaged in an activity that is part of the normal course of business, such as performance control checks. As a result, systems operators and employers may monitor employees' e-mail, provided that employees are given prior written notice that their e-mail may be monitored in the normal course of business (Lee, 1994). Several lawsuits have emerged, and more companies now post policy statements indicating that e-mail on company-owned systems is not protected.

Another privacy controversy centers on a unique characteristic of the Internet called "cookies." Cookies are essentially small strings of text characters that are sent to a person's hard disk via his or her browser while visiting a web site. The cookies store certain pieces of information about the person which are passed back to the web server when the person returns to the site. Cookies and other similar tracking systems are meant to help consumers by remembering preferences and eliminating repetitive tasks such as signing on. But cookies also place information on one's personal hard disk and function largely without one's knowledge. They also pose a privacy concern as they track usage history and preferences, eventually building detailed user profiles (Randall, 1997).

Data security is another prime concern among Internet users, who fear their messages and files will be broken into or intercepted. Strong encryption standards are demanded by users and required by online companies offering such services as banking and Internet stock trading, which need guaranteed data integrity in order to survive. A 56-bit data encryption standard (DES) has sufficed since the 1970s, but a 128-bit standard is now coveted, particularly since the Electronic Frontier Foundation and Distributed Net demonstrated they could crack a 56-bit DES encrypted message in less than 23 hours (Encryption, 1999). Ensuring both security and a robust Internet marketplace is not a simple matter, however. For example, a system of public and private keys may be necessary. Under this scheme, a person has a public key that he or she gives out to anyone who wishes to send that person an encrypted message. The person then uses his or her private key to open the message encrypted with his or her public key (Ouellette, 1999). This way, by avoiding a myriad of private-only keys, communication is enhanced while confidentiality may remain relatively secure.

Perhaps a bigger problem facing encryption, though, is the conflict between individual and corporate security needs and the needs of law enforcement and national security. With greater security come more opportunities for drug dealers, terrorists, and other criminals to shield their communications from the law. United States policies to restrict encryption have garnered the support of law enforcement and the wrath of privacy advocates and industry. Only recently has the United States begun to back down, relaxing its 1996 policy that required U.S. vendors exporting strong encryption software to make duplicate keys available to law enforcement. The administration now says vendors can ship products with keys as long as 56 bits without a license or key-recovery plan to as many as 45 countries for use by insurance, health, and medical companies and online merchants (Machlis, 1998; Bureau of Export Administration, 1999). The policy change still prohibits stronger encryption, such as 128-bit, which has yet to be broken. In the meantime, other countries have put pressure on the United States to further ease its export restrictions.

Autonomy. The third privacy dimension relates to the desire to control the collection, compilation, and transfer or sale of one's personal information to others. This includes the desire to keep one's name and other tracking information off of marketing lists, for example. Data integrity also comes into play where personal data maintained by others is expected to be secure, with limited access available to others. These types of privacy issues are not new, but with the Internet the potential for infringement and the magnitude of the concern have increased.

In terms of data collection, such private entities as banks, insurance companies, department stores, credit card companies, and credit reporting agencies maintain extensive databases of information on individuals that can be compiled, cross-referenced, and potentially used in a discriminatory manner. Government agencies also collect information through social security records, tax payment, medicare payments, and military records. Individuals are often not aware that the information is collected or to what extent or how it is used. Likewise, they may not know whether or how they can access and correct their records.

Subsequent distribution of personal data is also a concern, particularly when it is done for financial gain and for purposes other than the purpose for which it was collected. Once consumers are aware of the practice, however, their complaints may attract attention. A noted case involved America Online selling its subscriber contact information, financial information, and information about Internet activities (Wang, Lee, and Wang, 1998). Another case that gained national notoriety involved the Lexis-Nexis database service which began selling personal information about citizens, even though the information was pulled together from publicly available sources (Richards, 1997). In yet another case, a class action suit was brought against American Express, which gathered and sold data on cardholders' spending habits. But because the court reasoned that the information was given by cardholders voluntarily, the claims were dismissed.

There is no single statutory law or policy that regulates the collection, use, and distribution of personal information. The Electronic Communications Privacy Act (1986) prohibits the intentional disclosure of the contents of a personal electronic communication intercepted or reviewed while in storage by system operators, employers, and the like. The Privacy Act of 1974 restricts government collection and disclosure of personal records, requiring that the data be relevant and accurate and that individuals have the right to review, copy, and correct the information as well as control disclosure. The Act does not govern collection and disclosure by private parties, however. Specific policies already exist pertaining to financial, insurance, employment, education, health, and medical records, but individuals must rely on industry self-regulation when it comes to the collection and distribution of other types of personal information. The Federal Trade Commission is, however, considering drafting policies governing the privacy of consumer data.

Other related information autonomy concerns may be addressed by existing privacy common law, resulting in civil suits. For example, if information is gathered over the Internet in such a way that it is "highly offensive to the reasonable person," the tort pertaining to "intrusion upon seclusion" would apply. Tort law would also address the publication of embarrassing but true personal information that a scorned lover might spread over the Internet. If the image of a person is merged with offensive text, sounds, or other images, the tort of "false light" applies. Misappropriation of someone's name or likeness for commercial purposes is also recognized as a privacy tort. Here, a web advertisement that intentionally features a model who resembles a movie star could constitute misappropriation. Another example might include the Internet practice called "spoofing," which is the impersonation of a return-address in order to encourage recipients to view the contents.

Anonymity. The fourth dimension relates to a basic privacy interest in surfing the Web and communicating online anonymously. Anonymity is particularly useful for whistle-blowers, political and religious dissidents, shy individuals, and others who simply want to avoid a backlash of e-mails (i.e., sales calls) or having their personal data collected or movements tracked. Researchers from Vanderbilt University found that 94 percent of web users have refused to provide information to a web site, and 40 percent have given fake information. Indeed, people have come to expect a degree of confidentiality in private correspondence and telephone calls, and this expectation may carry over to the Internet (Lee, 1996).

Yet anonymity can also serve as a cloak for online harassers, pornographers, terrorists, and other criminals. The Supreme Court has recognized a First Amendment right to speak anonymously, but says a ban that is limited to fraudulent, false, or libelous speech may pass constitutional scrutiny (*McIntyre v. Ohio Elections Commission,* 1995). At least one state has unsuccessfully banned anonymous and pseudonymous online communication (Ban on Anonymous Speech, 1997), yet several states recently enacted statutory laws forbidding false headers and misleading subject lines in unsolicited commercial e-mail. Whether ISPs have an obligation to preserve subscribers' anonymity is also in question. When a Navy investigator contacted America Online to find out the name of a sailor who had identified himself as gay, he was given the name of a U.S. Navy senior chief petty officer who was subsequently discharged. Privacy advocates questioned whether or not there was a violation of the Electronic Communications Privacy Act (1986), which bars the release of customer information without a subpoena, court order, or customer consent. As a result, ISPs are taking greater strides in preserving online identities.

▶ Responses to Privacy/Security Issues

Even though privacy and security concerns appear as largely an individual matter, the impacts and effects are certainly felt in the business, national, and international arenas where a variety of responses are being considered.

Individuals. At the very basic level, it is the individual who obviously bears the brunt of privacy invasions, potentially losing a significant measure of information autonomy and anonymity. But to what extent might individuals be able to retain their privacy while reaping service benefits? There are many questions to consider. For example, to what extent do individuals have a proprietary right in their personal data collected by others? How might users technically maintain anonymity and data security? Who will bear the costs of protecting privacy online? Is spam an intrusion into proprietary systems or upon captive audiences who unfairly bear the costs? What are the available legal and technical recourses?

While some legislative bills, agency policies, and civil suits are testing the legal waters, many individuals are resorting to various self-help means. For example, individuals are learning to delete or disable cookies using certain technological tools and software options. They are also turning to (sometimes free) anti-spam software filters and encryption software such as PGP (Pretty Good Privacy). Other technological solutions include anonymous remailers and "anonymizers" (which give consumers control over their personal data by stripping away personally identifiable information) and pseudonymizers (which create an artificial identity). Some promising technological opportunities include the Platform for Privacy Preferences (P3P) and Trustlabels, which permit consumers to automatically determine the privacy policies of a particular web site and then choose whether or not to interact with or accept cookies. With P3P, users can select their privacy preferences, and P3P will warn them if they try to access a web site with a privacy policy that falls outside these preferences. Trustlabels go a step further by prompting users to accept or reject individual cookies whose trust labels fall outside the user's privacy preferences. All of these solutions give users greater control, effectively preventing the surreptitious collection and use of personal information. More individuals are also becoming better educated about data collection practices and avoiding e-mailing or giving out personal information. Assuming a more active role and complaining or boycotting offending businesses is also having some effect.

Organizations. At the organizational level, firms and industries play a major yet delicate role in the privacy equation, hoping not to alienate potential customers while seeking to maximize consumer data. How far can businesses go technically, legally, and ethically? To what extent must industry provide notice that data are collected? Must businesses afford people an opportunity to access, change, or determine the distribution of their personally identifying information? How far can businesses go in monitoring or tracking customers and employees online? Do companies have a First Amendment right to distribute unsolicited commercial e-mail?

The industry response in the wake of a groundswell of privacy complaints and potential legislation has been a resounding promise to regulate itself. Various industry coalitions and associations devoted to online privacy have formed, pledging to gain and restore consumer trust. The Online Privacy Alliance, for example, is a coalition of 50 Internet companies committed to fostering privacy online and engaged in certifying companies that abide by Alliance privacy policies. TRUSTe is a program that provides a third-party "trustmark seal" which allows web publishers to inform users of their site's gathering and dissemination practices, assuring users and providing a dispute resolution mechanism (see *[http://www.truste.org]*). The Association of Accredited Advertising Agencies (AAAA) has also issued privacy goals for electronic commerce aimed at ensuring full disclosure of marketers' practices and the appropriate use of personal information (TRUSTe, 1999).

In general, more Internet sites are posting privacy policy statements explaining how the data are collected, used, and disclosed. Greater strides are also being made to limit the use of the data and ensure accuracy. Some specific strategies include giving adequate notice such as "cookie prompts," which alert users that a web site wishes to place a cookie on their browser. Marketers are also offering opt-in and opt-out features to consumers reluctant to reveal information. Others are even offering incentives such as free online services in exchange for consumer data—essentially recognizing and paying for the value of the data. Still others are pulling back and practicing restraint by not selling consumer lists, avoiding spam, and limiting monitoring practices.

National. At the national level, legislators and other policy-makers juggle an onslaught of consumer complaints, industry pleas for self-regulation, and international pressures for conformance. The arguments raise a host of political, economic, and social questions. For example, what role should government play in preserving privacy interests while promoting a marketplace economy? Is privacy a commodity to be bought and sold in an open marketplace? Should there be more legislation protecting privacy, or will industry self-regulation work? How can a balance be achieved among commercial, privacy, law enforcement, and national security interests? How might U.S. policies come into compliance with stricter international privacy policies?

Despite a number of federal and state bills (Electronic Privacy Information Center, 1999), U.S. Internet privacy policy-making has primarily taken a wait-and-see approach in favor of industry self-regulation. United States policy-making has tended to support marketplace solutions, relying on legislation as a last resort. So it is not surprising that the White House formally called for industry self-regulation of Internet privacy. Now the effectiveness of this approach is being debated, with such agencies as the Federal Trade Commission announcing guidelines and scrutinizing the industry's response. Privacy advocates argue that the industry response has been inadequate and that without enforcement, privacy objectives will not be achieved.

Pressure from the European Union and others is also sparking some reaction. The European Union's Directive on Data Protection, which went into effect in late 1998, grants European citizens control over personal data and demands that foreign governments—including the United States—provide equal data protection under a similar regulatory structure. Countries that fail to adhere to the standards may be banned from doing business with the E.U. This puts both U.S. industry and the government in a precarious regulatory position. Some regulatory promises have been made, but proponents suggest they may not be enough. In the meantime, some U.S. companies are entering into contracts with European companies that provide the necessary protection in order to continue conducting business, effectively treating European customers differently. The U.S. Department of Commerce and the European Commission have also considered a "safe harbor" for self-certified U.S. companies voluntarily adhering to the principles.

The United States is also responding to international and domestic industry pressures to revise its encryption policies. The Administration's policy of restricting encryption exports is considered outdated and counterproductive, putting U.S. industry at a competitive disadvantage relative to its foreign counterparts. United States lawmakers face three basic choices when regulating encryption technology. First, they can do nothing, giving both consumers and criminals free access to these products. Second, they can bar encryption that the government cannot break, forcing private parties to use weak forms of encryption, rendering them vulnerable to security breaches and effectively stunting the growth of electronic commerce. Finally, a compromise approach may be followed, whereby strong encryption is allowed, but with some type of government access to keys (Allard, 1998). In late 1998, 33 nations agreed to the Wassenaar Arrangement (see [http://www.wassenaar.org]), which bans the export of encryption software with keys of 64 bits or longer. Nonetheless, some countries such as France have liberalized their encryption policies to allow 128-bit encryption. So far, the United States response has been to loosen its restrictions to permit the exportation of 56-bit encryption.

International. Considerable progress has been made in securing privacy rights in some parts of the international community. With the European Union's Directive on Data Protection and other countries' privacy initiatives, many foreign citizens may enjoy greater control over their personal data than U.S. citizens. The policies are generally in sync with the social, political, and economic philosophies of the concerned countries, where privacy is viewed as a fundamental right (Wellbery, 1997). Yet, how will enforcement occur when the Internet has no national boundaries? Can U.S. privacy policies coexist? How will international conflicts be resolved?

Over a decade ago, the European Union began an inquiry into the impact of technology on society, ultimately creating, in 1995, its Directive on Data Protection, which went into effect three years later. The E.U. Directive grew out of a need to harmonize the national privacy laws of the 15 member nations. It requires companies wishing to use personal data to first obtain permission, explain the specific purpose, and allow people to access and correct their personal data. The directive gives E.U. commissioners the right to prosecute companies and block web sites if they do not adhere to the data privacy standards (Baker, 1998). Furthermore, the data legislation prohibits the transfer of personal data to a third party country unless that country ensures comparable protection for the data. Other governments, for example, that of Hong Kong, are following Europe's lead, adopting similar laws.

Intellectual Property

Digital information and the Internet present special challenges when it comes to preserving intellectual property interests. Online information can be much more easily copied, edited, morphed, and otherwise manipulated than information in other media can, and a digital copy may be virtually flawless. It can also be instantly distributed to a worldwide audience at little or no cost. In the meantime, the source of the infringement may be untraceable, making enforcement and prosecution extremely difficult.

Based on the many infringement lawsuits filed in the past few years alone, billions of dollars are being lost to problems such as software pirating, domain name hijacking, and the unlicensed distribution of copyrighted music. In fact, the Software Publishers Association says online copyright infringement is a $13.2 billion annual problem (Packard, 1998). Intellectual property rights may be implicated when someone forwards e-mail, downloads web pages, uploads copyrighted photos, swaps files, scans photos, copies a web page, incorporates a movie clip, and posts links. The magnitude of the problem comes into focus when one considers, for example, that most of the text, images, sounds, and software communicated online consist of copyrighted material. Authors and creators presume traditional intellectual property laws apply in cyberspace, while the growing number of online users and infringers either do not understand intellectual property interests or believe their actions are somehow permissible, forgivable, or undetectable in the relatively new territory of the Internet.

▶ Intellectual Property Rights

Intellectual property essentially encompasses the intangible mental work products of authors and creators and includes writings, trade symbols, processes, and secrets. Unlike most tangible goods, information rights exist separately from any particular copy of the information, permitting the owner to maintain rights to the work while distributing copies. Property rights may also be spread across several individuals or organizations. For example, with a web site, one person may own the rights to a photograph posted, another person may have the publicity rights to his or her image in that photo, while yet another owns the patent rights to the GIF compression technique used. Someone else may have the rights to the recording of the music bed, while someone else may own the rights to its composition. Still, another individual may have pulled the elements together, while that person's employer ultimately controls the rights to the site design and its domain name.

Unlike privacy law, intellectual property law in the United States dates back to the Constitution and the nation's founding fathers, who established a concept of protection for authors and inventors by granting them exclusive rights in their writings and discoveries for limited periods of time. The U.S. Supreme Court has recognized that protection draws upon the economic incentives to ensure continuing innovation and the promulgation of creative works. Today, information rights essentially permit owners to control access to their work and its use, copying, and distribution.

Common law actions such as misappropriation and unfair competition address some intellectual property interests, and there are also some applicable state statutory laws. Most intellectual property interests, however, are governed by federal statutory laws such as the Copyright Act of 1976 (as amended), the Digital Millennium Copyright Act (1998), and the Lanham Act (1946, as amended). Other countries have similar laws, and there are a number of international treaties, such as the Berne Convention, that address the preservation of rights across borders.

▶ Intellectual Property Dimensions and Issues

Although there are intellectual property interests addressed as trade secrets, misappropriation, and unfair competition, intellectual property rights will fall primarily within the following areas of law: (1) Copyright, (2) Trademark, and (3) Patent.

Copyright. Copyright is governed by the Copyright Act of 1976, which protects "original works of authorship" (section 102a). Among the types of work granted copyright protection are literary and musical works, pictorial and graphic works, motion pictures and other audio-visual works, and sound recordings. Copyright protection was extended to software in 1980 and online digital recordings in 1995. Essentially, e-mail and other online text are protected, as well as certain compilations of data (databases), WAV files, GIF files, and other audiovisual elements. Not protected under copyright law is factual information like domain names, digital signatures, URL addresses, and encryption keys, as well as ideas, short phrases, and titles. The facts within a database cannot be copyrighted, for example, but the selection, coordination, and arrangement of the material may be copyrighted (*Feist Publications, Inc. v. Rural Telephone Service Co.*, 1991).

The law requires the work to be "fixed in any tangible medium of expression," which has posed some concern for online information. Essentially, information stored on a computer disk or CD-ROM qualifies, and even information stored briefly in RAM may meet the definition (*MAI Systems Corp. v. Peak Computer Inc.*, 1993; *Triad Systems Corporation v. Southeastern Express Co.*, 1994). Information transmitted live over the Internet, however, is not afforded protection unless it is simultaneously fixed.

Copyright owners have the exclusive right to control their work, including the ability to make copies and derivative works, as well as to distribute, display, and perform the work publicly. Here, the Internet poses unique challenges to users who may easily and even unwittingly infringe on these rights. For example, simply viewing a work online requires one to copy it in RAM, technically constituting a copyright infringement. While a 1980 copyright law amendment permits the owner of a *copy* of a software program to copy the program into RAM, the law does not address online transmissions where no physical copy exists. Thus, without consent or implied license, browsing a web site or downloading an e-mail attachment could be against the law.

Users may also be more tempted to lift and modify pictures, HTML code, and available material to incorporate into their own web sites, only to be infringing on the original authors' rights to make derivative works and adaptations. The Internet also makes it easy to forward e-mail, technically violating the author's right to distribute his/her work. At least one court has indicated that allowing subscribers access to copyrighted pictures over a computer bulletin board constitutes an unlawful display (*Playboy Enterprises, Inc. v. Frena*, 1993). In addition, playing someone else's video over the Internet might infringe a performance right. In fact, the Digital Performance Right in the Sound Recordings Act of 1995 specifically protects sound recordings performed publicly via digital audio transmission.

Copyright owners' rights are not absolute, however. The Copyright Act recognizes a number of exceptions, permitting some use of materials without permission. Aside from facts, ideas, and short phrases that cannot be copyrighted, individuals can use any material deemed to be in the public domain. This occurs when a work is created by the federal government, when copyright protection is waived or vacated, or the term of the copyright has expired (lifetime plus 50 years for individuals and 75 years for corporations and works for hire, with longer extensions now permitted). Also, works may be copied if there is "implied license." For example, putting up a web site essentially presumes users will, and may therefore permit users to, copy the contents to their RAM in order to view them (*Religious Technology Center v. Lerma*, 1995, albeit involving trade secrets). Although debatable, providing links to a copyrighted site should not result in liability if the linked site's home page is the destination (Sovie, 1998). Copying short, insignificant portions of a work may also be permitted, although this depends on the quantity and quality taken from the particular work.

Copyright law also considers "fair use" to be an exception. This applies to such uses as teaching, scholarship, research, news reporting, criticism, and commentary. Here the law considers the purposes and character of the use; the nature of the copyrighted work; the amount and substantiality copied; and the effect of the use on the market or value of the work. For example, if the copying is for educational purposes, very little is taken, and there is no market impact on the original, then the action may be permitted as fair use. The courts construe fair use narrowly, however. For example, no fair use existed when photographs from a magazine were digitized and offered online for a fee (*Playboy Enterprises, Inc. v. Frena*, 1993) and when entire documents were posted with little added criticism (*Religious Technology Center v. Netcom*, 1995).

One particular copyright concern has been the liability of ISPs that carry infringing material. The Digital Millennium Copyright Act (1998) relieves ISPs from liability for infringements where the ISP essentially serves as a conduit and does not financially benefit from or is unaware of the infringement, or upon actual knowledge acts expeditiously to stop the infringing activity. The law also frees service providers from liability for caching (temporarily storing material on the system's server) and linking to material that is infringing (Packard, 1998).

In most countries, including the United States, information is automatically protected by copyright from the moment it is created. Thus, a simple e-mail message is essentially protected by copyright. Affixing a notice and registration with the U.S. Copyright Office is not necessary, although it can help dissuade copying, and registration permits an infringement suit for more than actual damages. Copyright infringements are filed as civil suits, although criminal penalties can apply if infringements are willful and for commercial or financial gain. Yet, the No Electronic Threat Act (1997) makes it a crime to copy or distribute copyrighted software, music recordings, and other creative works with a retail value of more than $1,000, regardless of any direct financial profit. The law essentially protects software, music recordings, and other creative products easily pirated over the Internet. The Digital Millennium Copyright Act (1998) makes it a crime to possess and use tools that remove copyright protection mechanisms from software and digital media.

Trademark. Trademark protection applies to words and symbols used to distinguish particular goods and services. This includes words and phrases such as "United Airlines," pictures or icons such as the McDonald's arches and Mickey Mouse ears, numbers and letters such as MCI and 3M, as well as abbreviations, nicknames, and even colors. Trademark protection in cyberspace applies to domain names and online services such as Yahoo!, as well as existing products and services advertised online.

Trademarks allow consumers to clearly identify a good or service with its source and reputation for quality and value. Infringement occurs when another party uses the same or similar mark in that market, creating a likelihood that consumers may be confused as to source or sponsorship. For example, an individual offering unauthorized copies of Sega games over the Internet would likely cause consumers to erroneously believe the games came from Sega (*Sega Enterprises, Inc. v. MAPHIA*, 1994). A likelihood of confusion is not the only criterion, though. The Federal Trademark Dilution Act of 1995 provides trademark owners relief even if there is no product or service competition or confusion, provided the other mark somehow dilutes the original mark. Dilution includes "tarnishment" of the mark, essentially done in an immoral or otherwise unappealing way. For example, Hasbro, the maker of the children's game CandyLand, successfully sued a company based on this theory when the company used the domain name candyland.com for sexually-oriented products (McDonald, Reich, and Bain, 1997).

The owner of a trademark has the right to use the mark relative to specified goods or services in a particular market. Trademark protection applies only within the market in which it is recognized, whether a town, state, region, or nation. Therefore, it is possible for many "Al's Autoparts" to exist across the country, with each enjoying trademark rights within their respective markets. Expanding the business into new communities can pose trademark problems where similar goods or services with the same mark are offered. Trademark rights go to whoever was first to use the mark; conflicts may otherwise be negotiated or a new mark created. This has serious implications for online use, where creating a web site advertising "Al's Autoparts" now gives this business global reach, easily infringing on others' trademark rights in their respective communities locally and abroad.

Trademark law has particularly been an issue in the areas of domain names and web site links. Domain names present a unique trademark problem in cyberspace. *Domain names* are alphanumeric addresses for Internet sites and often consist of trade names. This can lead to disputes where companies with similar names but offering different products or services in different parts of the country battle over the rights to a single, abbreviated domain name. In addition, some people quickly secure domain names of well-known companies in the hopes of selling the name at a later date. For example, Microsoft is suing two men for registering the Internet domain names microsoftwindows.com and microsoftoffice.com. Calling them "cybersquatters," Microsoft complained that the men had also registered domain names such as AirborneExpress.com, AlamoRentalCar.com, AssociatedPress.com, and Hollywood-Video.com. Network Solutions, Inc., which had the monopoly in domain name administration, developed a policy requiring applicants to certify that they would not infringe on the trade name of others. A new, nonprofit corporation called the Internet Corporation for Assigned Names and Numbers (ICANN) is taking over, however, and some procedural changes may result.

Another problem implicating trademarks is the linking of one web site to another (Maloney, 1997). In *Washington Post Co. v. TotalNews, Inc.* (1997), the latter provided a link to the *Washington Post* web site while displaying the site within the TotalNews frame which obscured the Post's advertising and URL. The Post sued under the Federal Trademark Dilution Act of 1995, but settled out of court. Whether or not providing links or pulling a remote site into a frame is a dilution is not clear (Maloney, 1997).

Trademarks (and servicemarks) are obtained by applying the marks to the goods (or services) so that they are prominently displayed, and by using the marks in commerce. No registration is necessary in the United States, although under the Lanham Act (1946), registration with the U.S. Patent and Trademark Office (PTO) gives the mark nationwide rights and allows owners to sue infringers in federal court. Trademarks may be federally registered if they are distinctive and are used in interstate or foreign commerce. The strongest and most secure trademarks are those that are highly distinctive (e.g., AltaVista and Lycos) and unrelated to the nature of the product (e.g., Amazon.com and Sega). It is possible, however, for more generic names (e.g., America Online) to acquire distinctiveness after five years of exclusive use. New products or services such as software and online services may need specific trademark protection, even if the original good or service is already trademarked. It is possible to register in advance of intended use and hence reserve a trademark. Trademark registration only provides protection within the respective country, however; registration must be obtained in each and every country where protection is desired.

Patent. Patents are issued to a person who invents or discovers a new and useful process, machine, manufacture, or composition of matter, or any new and useful improvement. Unlike copyright, which is limited to expression, patent provides protection for the invention itself (or its functionality). Abstract ideas or laws of nature are not eligible for a patent, nor are methods of doing business or printed matter (which may otherwise qualify for trade secret protection or copyright) (Ellis, 1998). In addition, mathematical algorithms used in computer programs are not themselves patentable; however, the Supreme Court has ruled that utilization of algorithms in an original and useful computer program may rise to the level of a patentable invention.

A patent is a grant by the federal government to an inventor giving him or her the right to exclude others from making, using, or selling the invention throughout the country for a limited period of time. A patent provides a strong basis for licensing the technology to others. A patent also protects against the creation of similar versions or obvious improvements. Hence, an updated or enhanced computer program that simply manipulates more calculations or handles more accounts would not be patentable (Ellis, 1998).

There are two kinds of patents applicable to the Internet: utility patents, covering functional innovations in products or processes, and design patents, covering ornamental aspects of an article of manufacture. In both cases, to achieve a patent, an invention must be patentable by definition, useful, and truly novel. Utility patents must also be nonobvious.

Utility patents may apply to computer software, which was previously considered unpatentable. Now, the PTO and the courts recognize software patents if the software is characterized as a machine for performing certain functions or a process that manipulates or physically changes some physical structure. For example, certain interactive functions and interfaces, communications protocols, data compression techniques, and encryption techniques may be protected by patent law. One recently awarded patent, for example, was for an online system called "attention brokerage," created by CyberGold Inc., that lets web users earn money by clicking on banner ads and corporate web sites. Utility patents provide strong protection, giving the user an exclusive right to the idea embodied in the software, not just the code itself, therefore preventing competitors from creating new code to perform the same function (McDonald, Reich, and Bain, 1997).

Design patents can be obtained for computer screen icons, according to PTO guidelines (McDonald, Reich, and Bain, 1997). With respect to graphical user interfaces, design patents can provide stronger protection than copyrights. Design patents will not cover functional aspects of a display or Graphical User Interface (GUI), however.

Patents are granted through the Patent and Trademark Office pursuant to the Patent Act of 1952. Unlike other intellectual property registrations, the process usually takes two or more years, sometimes costing several thousand dollars. Notice of a patent must be affixed or damages for infringement may be limited. Falsely marking an item as patented is against the law. Utility patents expire 20 years after being filed, while design patents last 14 years from the date of issuance. Patents issued in the United States are not recognized in other countries. To protect inventions in other countries, applications must be filed separately.

▶ Responses to Intellectual Property Issues

The rights of authors and creators are certainly impacted by Internet intellectual property issues, but so are the interests of potential users and creators. Individuals, industry, and national and international policy-makers are responding in a number of ways.

Individuals. At the individual level, interests range from demanding maximum intellectual property protection for personal creations to seeking flexible protections and exceptions in order to access and use the works of others. There are many questions, but they are only sometimes answerable by existing law. The basic questions are these: Who exactly owns what information? What rights do they have? What rights do nonowners (users) have? How do the traditional laws apply to the Internet?

From the standpoint of intellectual property owners, the questions expand to how the information can be protected and how its value should be exploited. For example: How might implied license or fair use negate a copyright? Which owner of a trademark has priority when online advertising causes an overlap in markets? How can a mark now be used online without infringing on others' trademarks in the United States or abroad? To what extent can an existing interface or compression technique be incorporated into new software without infringing on existing patents?

While some copyright holders are refraining from online distribution, more are actively registering their copyrights, or limiting access and use to paid subscribers. Others are jumping on the Internet bandwagon and offering their information for free in exchange for viewing advertising or as an inducement to buy more information or other goods or services. Some people with trademark interests are adopting highly distinctive marks (to avoid potential territorial disputes over trademark) as well as registering for trademarks in advance of intended use and using the mark on the Internet to obtain national rights. Where conflicts arise, some owners are unfortunately negotiating rights or changing marks altogether, oftentimes at considerable expense.

More individuals are interested in intellectual property rights as potential users, however. In this sense, they are concerned about what information can be used without infringing owners' rights. How can users find out if a work is protected? When do fair use and other exceptions apply? When is permission implied or required?

The initial excitement of the Internet prompted many authors and creators to provide their works online, for free. As a result, many users have come to expect valuable information at little or no cost, with little effort, and with little or no negative consequence. Many individual users mistakenly believe that copying, using, and distributing online material is either permissible, tolerable, or essentially undetectable. However, more publicity of infringement cases and prominently displayed notices are causing more potential infringers to pause. While the average user does not understand intellectual property law or its implications, more are paying attention, particularly since knowledge of the law is not a requisite for a successful copyright infringement lawsuit. More users are also turning to the Internet for answers, using various search engines and available databases to quickly find out if particular information is proprietary or in the public domain. Seeking permission through the Internet itself is making the process much easier, quicker, and less expensive.

Organizations. Industry and other organizations face the same competing interests as both owners and users of intellectual property. As with individuals, the same basic questions apply. Yet with more invested and deeper pockets, the stakes for businesses are much higher. Companies also face additional concerns. For example: What are the liabilities of ISPs when subscribers infringe intellectual property rights? Might overly broad patents prevent interoperability between programs? Are there technological means or self-regulatory approaches that can be developed to address problems?

When it comes to collecting damages, ISPs are easy targets for lawsuits because they are more easily located than individual infringers and are well capitalized. Internet service providers may escape direct liability, but they may be liable for contributory or vicarious infringement—well-recognized doctrines applying standard tort law concepts (Maloney, 1997). In response, the industry lobbied hard for the Digital Millennium Copyright Act (1998), which now provides some protection. Still, ISPs are being more careful in regard to monitoring their services, since liability still applies if it can be shown that the ISP had knowledge of the infringing action, could have controlled it, or financially benefited.

When it comes to patent rights, there is a fear that broad patents might prevent programs from being able to interface or work together. As a result, interoperability is hindered, and the development of new software is stifled. The market will not accept programs that do not adhere to certain standards, and designing around the patents may be impossible without infringement. Some patent owners resort to injunctions while others demand royalties, costing prospective developers millions of dollars. In the meantime, computerized patent databases are helping businesses track patent activity to avoid problems. In some cases, patentees are focusing their enforcement efforts on suppliers, rather than company end users. Nonetheless, organizations need to be wary of using software from a vendor that did not secure a suitable license.

In response to the many challenges of a digital, online world, some organizations are working toward joint licensing or contractual limitations on use of works on the Internet, and others are developing technology that would permit practical enforcement of these limitations (Maloney, 1997). For example, in *Frank Music Corp. v. CompuServe* (1993), plaintiffs sued CompuServe, alleging copyright infringement of 947 songs that subscribers were uploading and downloading without permission. The suit was settled with the grant of a license to upload or download musical works (Maloney, 1997). Other organizations have established Internet licensing schemes, which ensure copyright holders are fairly rewarded for the use of their works. For example, the Copyright Clearance Center now licenses articles and pictures on the Internet, and Broadcast Music, Inc., (BMI) provides a blanket license to an ISP called Onramp (Packard, 1998). Some even envision a pay-per-use system, whereby users would license from a publisher each and every time for access to and use of protected works. This has implications for the need for the sweeping concept of "fair use" if immediate licensing of every work is possible.

National. At the national level, lawmakers are listening to, debating, proposing, and enacting various legal remedies in response to intellectual property concerns raised by owners and users as well as by the international community. How can conflicts over trademark rights be resolved domestically and internationally as more individuals and businesses go online? How can the works of authors and creators be protected and encouraged while furthering a free flow of information? Should more regulation be created or should solutions be market driven?

The White House has assumed a fairly active role in examining the issues, creating several initiatives, and issuing reports such as its 1995 White Paper. The administration encouraged the adoption of the World Intellectual Property Organization (WIPO) treaties and endorsed limitations on devices designed to circumvent copyright protection. Congress has likewise been active, putting these and other recommendations, such as the Digital Millennium Copyright Act (1998) and the No Electronic Threat Act (1997), into law. In addition, a number of bills have been offered, addressing such matters as database protections and the misappropriation of collections of information. National organizations such as Network Solutions, Inc. have also attempted to resolve problems like the battle for domain names, where more subdomains or suffixes are being created to alleviate conflicts.

International. The international community is faced with the problem of reaching consensus and uniformity in protection and enforcement across borders. A variety of social, political, and economic factors contribute to the differing types of protections available in each country. For example, Europe has historically recognized the existence of moral rights, which has not gained support in the United States. On the other hand, policies in the United States are more likely to be driven by marketplace interests in the free flow of information. The sociological, political, and economic effects of cross-border information flow must be considered as national barriers are broken down by the Internet. Can international conflicts over rights be resolved? What protection is there for information copied and distributed in another country? In which countries must registration be obtained in order to receive protection? How might trademarks, copyrights, and patents be enforced internationally?

Different international policies have only created confusion among intellectual property owners and users. For example, users are discovering that works created by other governments are not necessarily in the public domain, as government works are in the United States. Moreover, works that fall into the public domain in the United States may still be copyrighted in another country, making online availability a difficulty. Trademark rights may be infringed in other countries once the trademark is available globally on the Internet. Even policies regarding web caching vary, as the Internet Society is urging the European Parliament to ease provisions of a directive that would make web caching illegal.

Despite the various approaches, several international treaties have been successfully created to establish minimum standards for protecting works across borders. The Berne Convention, for example, extends a country's copyright protection to foreigners whose works are infringed in that country. In addition, the Agreement on Trade-Related Aspects of Intellectual Property Rights (TRIPS), effective 1995, was a major development with regard to harmonizing intellectual property rights. Over 100 countries signed on to TRIPS, which recognizes software as literary works and protects certain compilations of data.

Two 1996 World Intellectual Property Organization (WIPO) treaties—the Copyright Treaty and the Performances and Phonograms Treaty—addressed literary and artistic works in cyberspace and were ultimately incorporated into U.S. law (Digital Millennium Copyright Act, 1998). They encouraged nations to provide effective remedies against technologies designed to defeat protections. A controversial measure considering RAM as potentially infringing copyright was dropped (Maloney, 1997), as was a proposed treaty to provide protection for nonoriginal databases. More WIPO conferences are being held to negotiate international policies, including the 1999 International Conference on Electronic Commerce and Intellectual Property, which addresses the impact of electronic commerce on intellectual property.

Conclusions

Information over the Internet has considerable value, whether it is a personal data profile, a web document, software, or a trade name. Companies are able to easily target and reach customers, information providers are able to distribute their content quickly and globally, and users are able to enjoy a wealth of information at the click of a mouse. Yet there exist varying degrees of proprietary interest in this online digital information. These proprietary interests are manifested in such rights as privacy, copyright, trademark, and patent, which recognize the rights to maintain autonomy and to control access, use, copying, disclosure, and distribution.

The Internet presents new challenges when it comes to balancing these proprietary interests against the competing interests of users in a democratic, market economy. Interests in a free flow of information must be balanced against intellectual property rights and the desire to stimulate new intellectual property development. Perhaps one of the most challenging public policy issues of the information age is balancing the benefits realized by data collection, distribution, and monitoring with the privacy rights of individuals. Adding to the difficulty is the changing nature of these interests relative to the rapidly evolving Internet. For example, marketplace forces, social pressures, and new laws may shift the privacy balance back, or individual privacy expectations may change and adapt. Likewise, the free nature of the Internet has been changing the dynamics of intellectual property rights, although shifts toward a pay-per-use system may further change the nature of the debate.

The stakes are high in the trade-off between Internet market opportunities and intellectual property and privacy rights. How to achieve a balance is a challenge facing individuals, organizations, and national and international policymakers, as the Internet and interests in privacy and intellectual property evolve. While the courts struggle to understand the nature of the Internet and how traditional guidelines fit, lawmakers are considering new laws and international agreements. It is vital that industry self-regulation, legislation, education, and technological solutions be coordinated to ensure a framework satisfactory to all.

Online Sources

As these issues evolve, some online sources for further information about privacy and intellectual property rights include

Electronic Privacy Information Center *[http://www.epic.org]*
Internet Privacy Coalition *[http://www.privacy.org/pi]*
Consumer Project on Technology *[http://www.essential.org/cpt/cpt.html]*
Center for Democracy and Technology *[http://www.cdt.org/]*
Electronic Frontier Foundation *[http://www.eff.org/]*
American Intellectual Property Law Association *[http://www.aipla.org]*
Copyright Clearing Center *[http://www.copyright.com]*
Intellectual Property Owners *[http://www.ipo.org]*
International Trademark Association *[http://www.inta.org]*
U.S. Patent and Trademark Office *[http://www.uspto.gov]*
U.S. Copyright Office *[http://lcweb.loc.gov/copyright/]*
World Intellectual Property Organization (WIPO)
  [http://www.wipo.org]

References

http://www.truste.org

http://www.wassenaar.org

Allard, N. W. 1998. Privacy On-line: Washington Report. *Hastings Communications and Entertainment Law Journal,* 20: 511–40.

Altman, I. 1975. *The Environment and Social Behavior.* New York: Wadsworth Publishing Company.

Baker, S. 1998, November 2. Europe's Privacy Cops. *Business Week,* pp. 49–50.

Ban on Anonymous Speech, Use of Trade Names Ruled Unconstitutional (Georgia). 1997, Summer. *News Media & The Law,* 21(3): 20–21.

Bureau of Export Administration; Office of Strategic Trade and Foreign Policy. 1999. *Commercial Encryption Export Controls.* [Online] Retrieved from the World Wide Web: *http://www.bxa.doc.gov/Encryption/Default.htm*

Burgoon, J.K. 1982. Privacy and Communication. In M. Burgood, ed., *Communication Yearbook,* Volume 6, 206–49. Beverly Hills, CA: Sage.

Dorney, M.S. 1997. Privacy and the Internet. *Hastings Communications and Entertainment Law Journal,* 19:635–660.

Electronic Privacy Information Center. 1999. *EPIC Bill Track.* [Online] Retrieved from *http://www.epic.org/privacy/bill_track.html*

Ellis, D. 1998. Cyberlaw and Computer Technology: A Primer on the Law of Intellectual Property Protection. *Florida Bar Journal,* 72(1): 34–38.

Encryption Standard Cracked in Record Time. 1999, January, 28. *Computer Weekly,* p. 40.

Lawton, G. 1998, June. The Internet's Challenge to Privacy. *Computer,* pp. 16–18.

Lee, L.T. 1994. Watch Your E-mail! Employee E-mail Monitoring and Privacy Law in the Age of the "Electronic Sweatshop." *The John Marshall Law Review,* 28(1): 139–77.

————. 1996. On-line Anonymity: A New Privacy Battle in Cyberspace. *The New Jersey Journal of Communication,* 4(2): 127–46.

Lee, L.T., and LaRose, R. 1994. Caller ID and the Meaning of Privacy. *Information Society,* 10(4): 247–65.

Maloney, M. 1997. Intellectual Property in Cyberspace. *Business Lawyer,* 53: 225–49.

Margulis, S.T. 1977. Conceptions of Privacy: Current Status and Next Steps. *Journal of Social Issues,* 3 (3): 5–21.

McDonald, D.; Reich, J.; and Bain, S. 1997. Intellectual Property and Privacy Issues on the Internet. *Journal of the Patent and Trademark Office Society,* 70(1): 31–60.

Ouellette, T. 1999, January 25. Encryption. *Computerworld,* 33(4): 75.

Packard, A. 1998. Infringement or Impingement: Carving Out an Actual Knowledge Defense for Sysops Facing Strict Liability. *Journalism & Mass Communication Monographs,* p. 168.

Piller, C. 1993, July. Bosses with X-ray Eyes. *MacWorld,* 10(7): 188.

Prosser, W.L. 1960. Privacy. *California Law Review,* 48:383–423.

Randall, N. 1997, September 9. Cookie Managers. *PC Magazine*, 16(15): 159–62.

Reinstatement of the Law, Second, Torts, Section 652B (Vol. 3), 1977, Philadelphia, PA: American Law Institute.

Richards, J. 1997. Legal Potholes on the Information Superhighway. *Journal of Public Policy & Marketing*, 16(2): 319–26.

Sovie, D. 1998, December 14. Downloading from the Net is Dangerous; Well-intentioned Companies that Download or Hyperlink to Copyrighted Material Online May Find Themselves Liable for Infringing. *The National Law Journal*, B5.

TRUSTe. 1999. [Online] Retrieved from the World Wide Web: *http://www.truste.org*

Tweney, D. 1998, June 22. The Consumer Battle over Online Information Privacy Has Just Begun. *InfoWorld*, 20 (25): 66.

Wang, H., Lee, M.K.O., and Wang, C. 1998, March. Consumer Privacy Concerns about Internet Marketing. *Communications of the ACM*, 41(3): 63–70.

Warren, S., and Brandeis, L. 1890. The Right to Privacy. *Harvard Law Review*, 4:193.

Wellbery, B. 1997, December. 'For Your Eyes Only' Means What in Cyber Age? The Gap between What 'Privacy' Means in the U.S. versus the European Union Must Be Addressed. *ABA Banking Journal*, 89(12): 30–34.

Westin, A. 1967. *Privacy and Freedom*. New York: Atheneum.

You Are Being Tailed. 1998, June 27. *The Economist*, 347: 62.

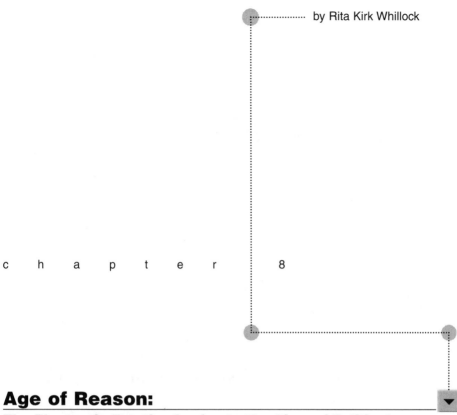

by Rita Kirk Whillock

c　h　a　p　t　e　r　　8

Age of Reason:
The Electronic Frontier Confronts the Aims of Political Persuasion

> I know of no safe depository of the ultimate powers of the society but the people themselves; and if we think them not enlightened enough to exercise their control with a wholesome discretion, the remedy is not to take it from them, but to inform their discretion by education.
>
> —Thomas Jefferson

During the 20th century, discussions about newly emerging technologies and their effects upon the political process have been ongoing. In 1917, less than a week after war was declared on Germany, President Woodrow Wilson established the Committee on Public Information (CPI) by executive order. Believing that effective national policy depended on an informed electorate, he hired the nation's top strategists in rhetoric, advertising, journalism, and public relations to set about the task of selling the "American" story of war to the public, and the idea of America to the world. The CPI was so effective that Congress banned Administrative fiat of such public relations tactics without the express consent of Congress. Their argument was simple. Since there is no one point of view in the United States, no one course of action can be empowered by the Administration for national consumption. Such empowerment would stymie debate and undermine the free choice of U.S. citizens. That action effectively terminated the government-sponsored disbursement of information until another world war emerged.

Embracing the new technology of the day, public information efforts sponsored by the government to advance America's case for prosecuting the war utilized the relatively new technologies of radio and film, while refining the use of those media through which the CPI worked. Post–World War II use of new technologies continued to develop but typically followed the use patterns necessitated by war. The media were largely dominated by government and big business, which catered to the tastes of a public willing to be led.

The development of the Internet emerged in much the same way as radio. It emerged first as a public vehicle through mostly academic venues. Like radio, its early days have been marked as an era for unprecedented free speech. And, as for radio, the economic potential has become so clear that people are rushing to discover how to control it for profit. This task is not simple. There are those who argued seven decades ago that the airwaves could not be controlled, so radio would be safe as a vehicle of oppositional thinking. They were wrong. Regulatory control and big business tamed the medium. Today, there are those who argue that control of the Internet cannot be sustained. I suspect that they, too, are mistaken. But there are serious questions to be asked as this medium takes shape. Concerns over the effects of this medium on our lives should not be taken lightly. By understanding the inherent risks of the medium, we become more educated citizens, which is perhaps capable of influencing the direction of the Internet.

This chapter examines the political uses of the Internet. Following the pattern suggested by the editors, I explore the impact of the Internet on the individual, groups, and national and global society. I argue that the greatest negative impact is on the individual. While giving individuals the illusion of self-destiny, the Internet segments the public into interest groups that have little need of each other. Further, I argue that the ideas of the individual continue to be devalued in the political process, depriving them of an effective deliberative voice and of their individual identity. Finally, I contend that this medium removes the individual from the time-and-place community that is the basis for political organizations. By doing so, this medium provides only the illusion of community while further isolating citizens from those who govern them.

The Internet is far more conducive to the advancement of group goals. Interest groups are able to mobilize and sustain contact with like-minded individuals. Similarly, political campaigns and their support organizations are able to explore the uses of the Web to develop constituent groups. The press is yet another important constituent group for the Internet; they are finding ways of investigating and reporting that have been reserved for those with money to fund the research and access to the printing and distribution channels.

The final section of this analysis considers the impact on national and global objectives, what I term national internal and external policies. A nation's first objective is to sustain itself. Little wonder, then, that in our capitalistic society there is a premium on granting a favorable commercial climate. Simultaneously, as a democratic institution, the government is also committed to enabling the free exchange of ideas. Maintaining these issue identities while attempting to advance the nation's policies is an enigma. External policy is also driven by the goal of sustaining international influence and protecting national borders. Challenges to national security are examined as evidence of international terrorism as a tactic for international control emerges.

Politics, the Internet, and the Individual

In each new media revolution, there is an implied threat against the reigning powers. As individuals gain access to means of public persuasion, power is thought to be diluted. Fears arise about the power of public opinion and the ability of government to construct meaningful responses. Most authoritarian regimes attempt to apply strict controls over media use for this very reason.

The Internet is not unique in this regard. The power to communicate and express ideas has been placed in the hands of individuals. However, the Internet's unique power is the inability of a central authority to control speech and its effects. The obviously liberating power of the media at times overshadows some of the less obvious, but equally serious, effects on individual lives. One of the more positive ramifications for the media on the individual is control over time.

▶ Time Shifting and the Impact of the Internet

In the medium's infancy, users began turning to the Internet to facilitate personal communication. Often, users wished to have immediate contact with colleagues in a mostly work-related environment. As the medium progressed, an interesting phenomenon occurred. It permitted people to communicate without reference to actual time. People could send or retrieve messages at their discretion. Similarly, with the addition of web pages, users did not have to wait for conventional office hours to access basic information on subjects ranging from corporate financial data to campaign speeches. Such "time shifting" is similar to the pattern that arose from programmable videocassette recorders (VCRs). Suddenly, the user was not bound by conventional schedules or predetermined work hours.

Time shifting holds one of the greatest potential assets of this medium for political operatives at a variety of levels. The primary advantage is that information is available to users when *they* want the information. For years, campaign strategists have planned their persuasive efforts around decision-timing issues. Strategists attempt to determine when voters will be ready to pay attention to information and campaign claims, placing persuasive information in their voters' hands as close to the time of decision as possible. Over the last two decades, campaigns have spent enormous amounts of the campaign budget on get out the vote (GOTV) drives in the last 72 hours before the election. That strategy emerged from polls indicating that a large percentage of people decide who to vote for close to the time of the election. Yet the truth is that strategists never know at what point in the election individuals are ready to make decisions. Nor do they know how events arising during the campaign will affect supporters. The use of e-mail and the Web is changing the decision scenario. Voters, the press, and opposition can access campaign information when they have decided the information is useful. This shift of timing marks a strategic placement of information that—at least in theory—aids in the decision-making process.

Control over time is a relatively positive trait for Internet users. But control over time does not suggest that users are more open to ideas.

▶ Selective Use

For the most part, rules of selective perception and selective attention are as operative in campaigns as they are in people's daily lives. People are drawn to messages that are important to them, that reflect their interests, and that do not challenge the basic tenets upon which their psychological stasis depends. The individual citizen-consumer of mass mediated messages is not necessarily jaded, critical, or judgmental of the messages encountered on a daily basis. But they are selective about the information to which they pay attention.

There are exceptions to these patterns of selective media use. Most everyone can find information or images on the Web that disturb their psychological equilibrium. Many feel that the uncontrolled, unregulated nature of the medium is a factor in unwanted information finding its way to the user. One of the defining characteristics of this medium of communication is that the individual seeks out sites of interest. Users flock to the medium, in part, because they get to choose information they want. For the most part, information is not "broadcast," as seeds are across a potentially fertile field. Yet consumers are increasingly disgruntled by the fact that they may inadvertently access disturbing sites as a result of the skillful manipulation of others. For example, many consumers are so accustomed to accessing corporate web sites that they routinely end web addresses with dot com (.com). If the consumer were to forget that government sites end with dot gov (.gov), they could wander into territory they had not intended. For example, one site has adopted the *[www.whitehouse.com]* address as a pornographic outlet. Individuals who inadvertently type .com instead of .org find themselves in potentially embarrassing—or titilating—territory.

Consumers are so accustomed to finding intended materials that they are upset when incongruous messages appear on their screens. For example, parent groups have sounded alarm that their children, hoping to find information about their government, could so easily stumble upon a pornographic site.

Few of these activists consider an alternative course. They could, for example, become better, more savvy web consumers who learn to find the materials they want while avoiding those which are offensive.

Rather than regulate their own behavior, such groups are asking for regulatory intervention. In acts of self-interest and domination, a variety of individuals (such as Professor Catherine Mackinnon or Nebraska Senator James Exon) and groups (such as Internet Watch Foundation or the Citizens Internet Empowerment Coalition) are attempting to regulate free speech on the Web. Such advocates have introduced legislation such as the Communications Decency Act, lobbied Congress, or filed lawsuits in efforts to prevent offending words and images from being inadvertently accessed on the Web. Their attempt is a clear effort to relegate divergent—perhaps even offensive—voices to channels that virtually ensure that opposition thinking/morals will not be voiced or, if voiced, not heard. To a medium whose charm has been the empowerment of individual voices, such attempts at regulation are debilitating.

Importantly, free speech issues regarding the Internet constitute a major political issue for the individual. Regulating the content of the Web is a political issue that churns a great deal of debate (e.g., Davis, 1999). However, many scholars confirm that such regulations are not feasible since there are no borders with the Web. Regulating interstate or international commerce has proven nearly impossible. Restricting free expression of ideas is even more daunting. In some foreign countries such as China, Russia, and India regulators have been so unsuccessful in regulating web access that they have resorted to restricting computer access instead (see Janda, 1999; Richter, 1999). Beyond the most obvious issues surrounding free speech and regulation, there are far more complex and potentially critical issues that affect the individual.

▶ Devaluation of the Individual

In the political arena, the use of the Web has suppressed the value of the individual to the political process. There are several ways this is evidenced.

First, the use of the Web has deprived the individual of intrinsic worth within the political process. Even before the use of Internet, the mass media had learned to target the specific needs of individual consumers. Strategists had become so sophisticated with their use of various media that the resulting communication appeared personal and sincere. For example, direct mail campaigns have provided people with the appearance, without the substance, of genuine communication. Individuals may receive numerous birthday cards from people who neither personally know them nor personally sign the cards. There is the appearance that the individuals are of personal concern to the communicator, although they are not. The Internet is starting to follow such target use patterns. Today, software programs are available that permit political operatives to scan thousands of chat groups for key words. Targeting individuals by searching their missives for various "hot words" on specific issues, users can be surreptitiously targeted to support a particular candidate or donate to a specific cause without ever knowing that the message was not from a like-minded individual, but from a sophisticated political operative. The use of finding individuals, then, is to assist them in becoming a member of a cohesive, user group. Concern for the individual voice is not a priority. A similar argument could be made for the way "cookies" are used to track web site visitors. Once a user has been identified, he/she can also be targeted for future communications. Some capitalistic ventures are currently attempting to develop cross-referencing tools that will permit users to be identified via the Internet and targeted through other, more conventional communication vehicles. Should these and similar tracking programs be developed, the individual will again become a target of communication and will have less of an opportunity to exercise true deliberative exchanges with others.

Second, political uses of the Web have deprived individuals of a deliberative voice. Political operatives usually define a *public* as a group upon whom success or failure depends. In this decision-making vacuum, the only thing that matters is who holds the voting majority. Once a majority is achieved, dissenting viewpoints are merely noise in the channel. Dissent does not precipitate thought. It does not compel thoughtful discussion. It does not warrant compromise. Individuals are important only to the extent that they may influence those who exercise authority. Noted theorist Hans Speier (1980) contends that "public opinion, so understood, is primarily a communication from the citizens to their government and only secondarily a communication among citizens" (p. 27). Such a view of public opinion is subject to manipulation, for it prevents the effective presentation of alternative views and becomes a ready tool to autocratic personalities. Speier (1980) continues, "there can only be suppressed, clandestine opinion, no matter how ingenious or careful the government may be in permitting an organized semblance of truly public opinion for the sake of democratic appearances" (p. 27). Some have referred to the outcome of such a limited public voice as the tyranny of the masses. De Tocqueville (1948) eloquently explains the impact for the individual:

> There is, and I cannot repeat it too often, there is here matter for profound reflection to those who look upon freedom of thought as a holy thing and who hate not only the despot, but despotism. For myself, when I feel the hand of power lie heavy upon my brow, I care but little to know who oppresses me; and I am not the more disposed to pass beneath the yoke because it is held out to me by the arms of millions of men. (pp. 11–12)

Third, political uses of the Web have deprived individuals of an effective public voice while perpetuating a voice that is of more value to the propagandist than to the group of individuals involved. The rise of niche publics in politics gives rise to what Todd Gitlin (1995) describes as *identity politics*. Political figures no longer speak to deliberative groups who value compromise and attempt to decide matters based on a vision of the common good. The good of the group takes precedence. The result is that politicians customize messages to targeted groups, even when the unifying message demonizes those who do not hold similar opinions. Such a unifying strategy results in an isolationist rhetoric that pits one special interest group against another. This isolationist rhetoric and its devaluation of the common good encourage self-promotion rather than public service.

Fourth, uses of the Internet have devalued individual identity. We no longer know with any certainty to whom we are speaking or if the identity as presented is a true representation of the person sending the message. The Internet has perpetuated an explosion of cyber personalities, personalities invented solely for online communication. Such fantasy personalities permit individuals to role-play in anonymity but lessen the intrinsic importance of the individual living in a real time-and-place community and seeking to find a purpose among those with whom he/she interacts daily in the real world. There are those who argue with this position. They claim that disjoining speaker from message permits us to view ideas for what they are without the innate prejudice we may have toward the speaker. In theory, these critics are correct. However, such criticism devalues the role of motive. Assessing the motives of the speaker is one of the critical tools for determining the impact of the message. Classical theorists from Plato to Aristotle would argue that determining speaker ethos (or character) is a critical ingredient in assessing the proper weight of an argument.

Finally, the most potentially damaging political function of tools like the Web is that it connects us to others who share similar points of view, but not necessarily to others who are linked by voting district. Whether we like to admit it or not, we live in communities, not virtual communities. There are real problems with infrastructure (like water and sewage), taxes (to support school systems and civic projects), and community values (that are as unique and impassioned as those of the original thirteen colonies). Individuals only linked through portals in computers are deprived of a community identity that has real borders and a distinctly physical space. Critically, politics is territorially based. People vote in districts where they live. For our system of government to function effectively, living and reasoning together in that space is critical. "Cohabitation of a territorial space" (Gumpert, 1987, p. 78) is a requirement of community building. Virtual communities only contribute to the individual's loss of connectedness with local politics. "Our connections with virtual others in nonplace communities stand in opposition to the community building communication needed to enact governing policies that regulate our day-to-day environment in the place where we live" (Whillock, 1999, p. 26).

Individuals may well lose political ground if use of the Web begins to take an increasingly more important role in politics. While individuals are devalued by this medium, the importance of the Internet for facilitating and empowering group communication is greatly enhanced.

Group Uses of the Internet

Use of the Internet for political purposes has been a feature of the medium almost since its inception. Initially, early academic and military uses of the medium that placed a premium on sharing information were mirrored as a broader public gained access. Web sites were designed that permitted access to a variety of sources of government information. Census data, legislative calendars, information about historical sites such as the White House, government documents ranging from The Declaration of Independence to proposed legislation, and the names and contact information for legislative officials became available for easy public access.

Recognizing that information is not neutral and may, in fact, encourage particular points of view, the information dispersal function of the medium soon became a political value. Information is, of course, value laden. Four specific groups made particular political use of information: interest groups, campaigns, campaign support groups, and the press.

▶ Interest Groups

Interest groups were quick to offer context while granting the public access to information they sought. There is little doubt that groups deliberately present information in a manner that places a particular spin on it.

To date, no one has substantiated the direct effects of the medium on the political process. Yet everyone senses that the use of the Web may prove valuable one day, so no one wants to be without it. Minimally, having a web page indicates that the candidate is up-to-date and sometimes even "cutting edge."

One of the great values of the Internet is the ability to advocate group values, develop the medium's innate potential to be reached by thousands of users, and do so at very little expense to the advocating group. Such access has not been replicated since the early days of radio (Engelman, 1997). As a result, issue advocates found the Web a ready place to advocate their points of view.

Perhaps even more important than low-cost access is the benefit such access provided user groups. In an almost unprecedented opportunity, groups could organize without charging membership fees. Membership could be solely determined by level of interest rather than ability to pay. The American

Communication Association *[http://www.americancomm.org]*, for example, be-came one early advocate of free speech on the Internet. The uniqueness of this group was that it was a virtual organization with no membership dues and no annual meetings. The group functioned, quite literally, in a virtual environment as activists for a particular point of view. The proliferation of interest group sites today is explosive. Most every cause and point of view can find representation on the Web whether it is pro-choice/pro-life groups, animal rights activists, en-vironmental activists, or a myriad of other committed advocates.

Groups also advance their causes to those users who might otherwise dis-tance themselves from groups with whom they have uncertain identification. Due to the supposed anonymity of the user, people are permitted the oppor-tunity to explore divergent groups and ideas. (Though, as we have discussed, users can be tracked, there are also programs available that protect the anonymity of the user.) So common is this form of idea-shopping-in-anonymity that these virtual-searchers/game-players have a name: avatars. Avatars often adopt various personalities or identities in order to role-play in game environments and chat rooms to experiment with roles, conversations, and ideas. On the positive side, such anonymity permits people to play games but also explore ideas and identities that they would never explore in person (Barrett and Wallace, 1994; Escobar, 1994). Some researchers suggest that im-munity from physical reprisal is one reason that anonymous users can freely explore ideas (Rheingold, 1993; Serpentelli, 1993). Others contend that anonymity protects the user from social isolation (Whillock, 1997). Whatever a user's actual reason, understanding the point of view of others who hold di-vergent opinions permits the individual to consider counter claims or to find arguments to support already held propositions.

For groups who hope to persuade others to their points of view, gaining an individual's attention is the first step. For example, right-to-life and pro-life groups each have developed visually compelling web sites to attract attention while attempting to persuade viewers to adopt their points of view. Recogniz-ing that users may be drawn to the sites when considering pregnancy termi-nation, the groups provide access to a wealth of information supporting their particular points of view. They also provide access to (approved) chat groups where the users can discuss issues facing them. As in actual groups, online groups can also bring to bear the power of public opinion. Links to notable others who share the group's point of view as well as testimonies of those who have faced similar decisions can help add group pressure to an individual's decision process.

▶ Political Campaigns

Other groups that found the use of the Internet useful were political campaigns. Groups of people using the Internet to assist their candidate or ballot initiative quickly took advantage of this low-cost means of conveying specific points of view and conducting research. Similarly, candidates for most major offices have home pages. Notably, this was not the case in 1996 when web page experimentation was mostly used by Presidential candidates and in a handful of the better financed state races.

To date, no one has substantiated the direct effects of the medium on the political process. Yet everyone senses that the use of the Web may prove valuable one day, so no one wants to be without it.

The producers of political web sites often design their products assuming that the greater percentage of people who access the site will be supporters or "leaners" (those that are "leaning" toward support of the person or view advocated). Appeals to voters are largely based on *judgmental heuristics* that encourage Democrats to vote as Democrats and unionists to vote the union line or that unite people of particular moral points of view to act on those stated beliefs. Although designers are aware that not everyone who attends the message will be a leaner, the presumption is that those who are against the campaign will not be persuadable any way. Therefore, the goal is to provide information that will have a persuasive effect on those who are still considering options. Once there, voters will be exposed to a lot of things. Surfers may find today's headlines, the candidate's proposals, testamonials from well-known supporters, ways to volunteer, ways to contribute, and places to find further information. In essence, most of the site is devoted to engaging and involving the user.

Campaigns can use the medium to their advantage in two distinct ways. First, they can provide information in the manner they believe is most conducive to voter learning. Second, they can present an unfiltered argument that some third party journalist has not edited into an eight-second sound bite. Those accustomed to using the Internet expect to find information readily available. In a single click of the computer keyboard, those with a passing interest, supporters, or opponents can access information related to the campaign at the user's particular level of interest.

Campaigns have begun using their web pages as surrogate cottage presses. Rather than having reams of printed position papers, campaigns are using the Web to catalog the candidate's issue stances. Most web sites include photos of the candidate with key constituents. Others include candidate quizzes that users can take to determine their political awareness. Several include full texts of speeches and position papers to explain the candidate's view on specific subjects. Given the complexity of issues, embedded web page designs permit the reader to go as in depth on an issue as the candidate is willing to take them. This allows for users to absorb information at various levels of complexity.

The downside to web pages, according to many consultants, is that they can be primary targets for opposition research. Opponents can find a candidate's daily schedule, for example, which would let them know the audiences being targeted by the candidate. This could be particularly useful to underdogs who can rarely entice their powerful opponents into a debate. Typically, a debate-chase strategy ensues, where the underdog chases the front-runner around while asking, begging, pleading for a debate. The idea is that a failure to accept the challenge implies the leader has something to hide.

Some web-page appeals are based on rational arguments. These appeals are frequently limited to fund raising, party building, and issue selection early in the political race. The justification for existence (raison d'être) is to appeal to those who have made a prior commitment that the political process is important, as is their involvement—at least by the minimal effort of exercising their right to vote.

Some judgmental heuristics are less rational. Richard Brookhiser (1996) argues that "the body is the basic unit of all human intercourse, including politics. Civilization modifies or suppresses the fact, in the interest of cultivating other qualities. Yet even rulers who are intelligent, prudent, or visionary must make a sensual impact if they are to lead. If their bodies cannot command attention, they must compel it by secondary physical means such as eloquence or by props—masks, regalia "Air Force One" (p. 113). Image factors have always served as an ingredient of political decision making. The image-laded use of the Internet is but an additional use of the image campaigns that have dotted the political landscape since our nation's inception.

Often, rationality is a second place appeal in political campaigns. So much so that one joke going around in political circles is "only 10 percent of the voting population thinks wrestling is a real sport but 90 percent of them vote." Anecdotal evidence of the absence of rationality abounds. For example, in the 1998 Oklahoma race for the U.S. Senate, one of the candidates who made it to the runoff was dead. Jacquelyn Ledgerwood died July 15, 1998, but got enough votes on August 25 to make it to the runoff. According to the Oklahoma Attorney General, if she won the runoff, her name would be placed on the November ballot against the Republican contender (Dead Woman, 1998). Those familiar with political campaigns suggest one reason Ledgerwood garnered so many votes was the high name-recognition resulting from statewide coverage of her death.

Strategists often cater to this anti-intellectual constituency in the way they approach elections. Clearly, there is a distinctly anti-intellectual bias in the way political persuasion is utilized, particularly the campaign commercial. Endemic to the success of an ad is that it promote a visual (availability heuristic) and a catch argument (one that is easily repeatable). They are often designed as "talking points" for people at cocktail parties who need no more than a few glib phrases to get through the evening.

Yet rationality, while not a commodity of the public phase of the campaign, serves a vital campaign function. Information is often the coin of the realm. Who has it and who can afford it often determines election outcomes. By way of example, consider the role of research in a campaign.

Research is expensive. Focus groups, polls, and opposition research range from $10,000 to $30,000 each for simple Congressional elections. For campaigns to efficiently use their financial resources, they must concentrate on targeting their message to people who actually vote. Though we prefer to argue that educating the citizenry is a valid function, few people have the money to do that even if it were a valid outcome measure. Instead, the primary objective of the campaign is winning the election. Research worth the expenditure is goal driven—it assists the strategist by reducing uncertainty in decision making. Therefore, certain information is at a premium: Who votes? What are the voting trends? How have previous elections in the district turned out? What factors influence voter turn out? What have been the hot issues in the past few elections? What are the issues now? What are the emerging issues?

The treasure of information is insightful to strategists. For example, if we look at a candidate's financial report from a previous election, we could learn who provided financial support in previous elections—including individuals, political action committees, or the party structure. When facing an incumbent, we can track patterns of spending as insights into the ways the opposition routinely spends its resources (and when).

Half of the information a campaign needs is readily available to researchers who know how to get it. The problem is that few people know how to retrieve and interpret the data. Thus, campaigns hire the research to be done for them. In the past, retrieving such data required endless trips to the library or some clerk's office where the voting records are stored.

The Internet is slowly changing the information dynamics. Information that was once difficult to obtain is becoming readily available over the Internet. Financial filings of the candidates are being posted in many voting districts. Voting histories are also available (see, e.g., CENSUS—Voting and Registration Data [http://www.census.gov/population/www/socdemo/voting.html]). These examples of information exchange may make it less costly and, therefore, more likely, that those who are willing to put sweat equity into strategy development will be able to access information that is useful in waging an effective campaign.

▶ Campaign Support Industries

Many political campaigns in this country are no longer run by local groups of supporters but by well-oiled businesses whose job is to research and implement strategy on behalf of candidates. Voters may seek out a candidate's web site for any number of reasons. Yet once they connect, persuasion is possible. Design plays an important part here. Can you get voters to the information they need before they decide it isn't worth the effort? Knowing the audience is as important to Internet use as it is to other media.

Having information is not sufficient. Information alone does not ensure that people will know what to do with it or how to use it. Consequently, there are cottage industries springing up on the Web that assist in information processing. For example, one organization, CapitolAdvantage *[http://capitolad vantage.com]* has developed two systems: one to assist organizations during political campaigns and the other to assist political action committees and/or grassroots issue advocates during legislative sessions. The campaign program, called ElectionWiz, provides simple data (names, address, phone, fax, web link, and biographies) on candidates running in both pre- and post-primary races. It permits zip code-to-district searches for mailing applications and zip data analysis. It provides instructions on how voters are registered in each state. The site provides electronic copies of Federal Election Commission PAC reports to track campaign contributions to the candidates. As the company rightly claims, when you combine voter registration details with zip code clustering, you have a "tool to impact the election with grassroots involvement" (CapitolAdvantage, brochure). But they add a proactive design as well. Instead of just receiving information, the site permits web users to transport functions such as screen savers, banners, cartoons, and information links to their own web sites. This enables the less proficient webmaster to integrate designs that make the site an active advocacy tool. These information services are provided at a cost of less than $2,500 per election cycle.

Notably, the information provided by many services is not proprietary. Many people could find and access such information. The problem is that most people lack the organizational and analytical skills to perform the information functions that make the information useful.

Businesses that specialize in such technological and strategy applications are making them available to campaigns at more reasonable costs than the campaigns could manage on their own. Such firms maintain systems that are equipped with the latest technological capabilities but charge the campaigns according to their proportional use. Such firms also have the capability to design campaign interfaces that are truly user friendly, saving campaigns training costs. Finally, the costs are more reasonable because the cost of expensive and powerful data merge programs are centrally housed. The nominal cost charged to campaigns makes such information-organizing agents affordable and available even to start-up campaigns that could not otherwise afford them.

As with so many computer applications, the ability to sell the information packages depends on the packager's ability to make easy use of the program. Many online programs have taken census data from zip clusters in a way that only requires the input of appropriate zip codes. Once the data is pulled, it can be matched against consumer profiles. Importantly, data acquisition and input are not necessary. Neither is it necessary for the campaign to hire a programmer. The challenge is to find someone capable of synthesizing the results and turning that synthesis into effective strategy development.

▶ The Role of the Press

The appeal of the Internet to political reporters is increasingly alluring. Both large media outlets and smaller local news groups are relying more and more on Internet sources. Timely access to information is critical. For most of the nation—and the world, for that matter—getting to the site of an event is difficult. And, of course, getting information accurately and quickly is the competitive benchmark for news teams. The Internet has served well in this capacity, permitting ready access to official information in a timely manner that virtually neutralizes the competitive advantage of all but the more well-financed news organizations.

Political web pages are beginning to cater to press interests. In the past, a campaign's response to a breaking story was usually phoned or faxed to political reporters. The phone was time consuming and unfair since the calls were ordered from most supportive reporters on down. Fax machines provided quicker response times but required reporters to go to the newsroom to retrieve the responses. Using the Internet, campaigns can make information simultaneously available through reporters' e-mail subscriptions to new releases.

Web pages greatly assist campaigns in reaching reporters. Responses can be posted immediately on the web page, often in conjunction with the phone calls and faxes. Reporters, voters, supporters, and opponents can reach the site simultaneously. And, perhaps more importantly, reporters can gain access from remote locations. They do not have to be in the newsroom to get the story.

One of the more important uses of the Internet for political reporters is the ability to get information to the public quickly. Speed places a premium on political information. The distribution of the Starr report against President Clinton serves to illustrate the point. Printed copies of the report took four days to reach the major distribution channels. On the Internet, the public had access as soon as their servers could reach the designated web pages. Providing information when public interest is high is a positive value to news outlets.

Clearly, the press and the public have quicker access to campaigns than ever. At the same time there is a distinct fear concerning the veracity of Internet materials. In some instances, it is difficult to know which Internet sources are reporting facts and which are mirror sites. How do we maintain control over the medium in an age of hackers? How are we to determine which sites present the most valid and reliable information? The news media will find an increasingly important role in answering these questions. First, they will become the trusted sources for linking the public to reliable primary sources. Second, they will become fact filters/synthesizers. Linking the public to relevant web sites requires that facts be boiled down and organized in simple phrases. The logic of such organization will become increasingly important as a different type of sound-bite culture emerges. Third, the Internet will lead to better political reporting. Because facts are often in dispute, reporters will be able to lead readers to sources that disagree with each other. Getting more than just sound bites from opposing sides, readers will be able to explore issues more in depth, should their available time and interest warrant it. Importantly, the sources that will become increasingly important are the primary sources. Media naval gazing—a term I use for the practice of media personalities interviewing other media personalities about the impact of a story—will become less useful and interesting. Fourth, journalists will become increasingly important as the distributors of information. When the Starr report was initially launched on the Internet, the phone lines were tied up with people trying to access it. This is particularly significant since the federal government has quite large server capabilities. We should note that a breaking crisis today—like the Oklahoma City bombing—could overwhelm small government or corporate servers. Journalists would be able to use the model they created during the Starr report release to mirror the findings on their web sites. Thus, news agencies would bear the distribution burden for the news, a factor that would increase public reliance on them as news sources.

Critical to the argument here, the material released during these crises on relevant official Internet sites is information-based. That is a barrier to news groups wishing to perform their infotainment news segments based on the drama of an event. On official sites, we do not find weeping victims, blood and guts, or teasers for the next newsbreak—at least not yet.

National and Global Implications

In a political context, national and international implications for the Internet boil down to a nation's internal and external policies. The boundary-less domain of the Internet is forcing nations to consider who among its internal public will be permitted access to information and the privilege of speech. Simultaneously, nations must consider information as a form of international warfare.

U.S. Internal Policy

Perhaps the most driving force in U.S. policy on the Internet is business. This is not a profound revelation for a capitalistic society, but it is an important element when considering the implications for national and international audiences. As a world leader in Internet development, the influence of U.S. government, U.S. citizens, and U.S. businesses is substantive. According to McChesney (1996), there are "two oppositional and epoch-defining trends" dominating U.S. and global communication. First is the rapid corporate centralization and commercialization of media industries. The second is the "newly developed computer and digital communication technologies" that permit individual control outside the traditional hierarchy.

Internally, commercialization of the Internet has profound implications for policy making regarding elections. Commercial communication firms not only control a sizable amount of money that can aid in candidates' election bids; they also control access to the media through which messages are conveyed to a broader public. Finding support from communication moguls for political agendas is becoming increasingly important. Auletta (1995) found that both the Democratic and Republican parties are closely linked with the large communication firms. Such affiliations should not be dismissed since those who set policy will ultimately affect the governance of the Internet. A 1995 story in the *New York Times* contends that communication lobbies are anxious to influence legislative directives over the $700 billion data highway being constructed by media forces (Andrews, 1995). Just as political parties struggle for dominance in public opinion and political power, corporations struggle for dominance of the Net and economic power. These dominance battles for access and resources permeate both government and free enterprise. The merging of these interests and the subsequent fusion of capitalistic values with political ideologies is notable.

Commercialization has implications for public access as well. The growing schism between the haves and the have-nots is a significant political issue for the nation. Few people might have anticipated the public's desire to access and interact via the Internet. A 1995 report estimated that Internet traffic that year exceeded 30 terabytes of data each month. That is the equivalent of "30 million 700-page novels" (John, 1995). Each year since this report, Internet traffic has grown, often outpacing the ability of servers to handle the load. Minimally, the result is longer retrieval times for information. The strain on capacity has lead some groups to advocate a two-tiered system that would allow paying customers greater, faster access while free users would have to slug it out in a virtual line for openings (see, e.g., Meeks, 1995). Mirabito (1997) argues that the effect of the two-tiered system is a three-tiered system. The third tier is comprised of those who will not or cannot afford to pay for the necessary equipment and/or access fees.

The schism between the haves and the have-nots led President Clinton to advocate the development of a national computer network that would make web access available to everyone. "As the Internet becomes our new town square, a computer in every home—a teacher of all subjects, a connection to all cultures—this will no longer be a dream, but a necessity" (Clinton, 1996). At least in theory, anyone with Internet connections would be able to participate in this virtual national discussion. One may certainly expect that Muir (1994) is correct that "as electronic media further develop, so does the capacity to reach many more people, and in turn, to increase public participation"

(p. 343). Herbeck (1999) suggests that such a rush to participation could create a "hyperactive democracy" (p. 60) that has much activity but little deliberation. Participation without power, voice without audience provides only the illusion of participation and will eventually result in the public's further alienation from the political process (Whillock, 1999). The have-and-have-not issue has profound political implications. Those who have access have the ability to define political reality for the masses.

▶ U.S. External Policy

Nations around the world are attempting to come to terms with the increasing influence of the Internet. The most profound aspect of this struggle is a nation's ability to define itself and control its own destiny.

Those words at first may seem trite. However, in an uncontrolled media environment, those who control the image control the outcome. These are not new revelations. In 1931, publicist Harry Reicheback (1931) noted, "...a thought can be flashed around the world the instant it is conceived. And through this same highly sensitive, swift and efficient mechanism, it is possible for fifty people in a metropolis like New York to dictate the customs, trends, thoughts, fads and opinions of an entire nation of a hundred and twenty million people" (p. 165). Today, it does not require 50 people, nor does it require that they operate in unison. "In the virtual world, power does not depend on how big you are physically; it depends on how much notice people take of you, and how much attention you can force them to pay" (Arthur, 1999).

Two aspects of international relations in this vein merit discussion. The first is the use of mirror sites to influence web content, the use of the Internet to transmit (mis)leading information to a broad public, or outright tampering with government-controlled web sites. The second is the use of information as a weapon of war.

Many mirror sites are developed to ridicule or satirize other sites. In the 1996 U.S. Presidential election, for example, a site that mirrored the official Bob Dole site contained a parody of the campaign through a fictional Dole who owned a banana company. Unsophisticated readers could spend some time on the site before realizing that the information was erroneous. The other manipulation that can occur is the deliberate tampering with a candidate's home page. This was the case in the last British election, where both the Tory and the Labour parties had content changed by hackers (Arthur, 1999). One of the great fears of political strategists is tampering by hackers, including those sponsored by the opposing candidate and foreign interests.

Unlike controls placed on traditional broadcast media, there is no truth-in-advertising law to regulate political content in the United States. Publishing false and misleading information about publicly traded companies could violate Security and Exchange Commission regulations, leaving the disseminators of such information in legal jeopardy—assuming that they could be caught. There are no such penalties for cyber journalists (or pseudo-journalists) writing about politics. The Internet has only compounded the problem. For years, the factors governing journalistic organizations related to that organization's credibility with a watching public. No such controls are currently applicable to the Internet, even among those traditional news agencies who post their papers via the Internet. Misleading stories abound on the Internet among traditional and nontraditional journal venues. Recent stories picked up by notable sources like the *New York Times* have originated with relatively obscure on-line rags. Once these images have found their way into the public psyche, the "pictures in our heads" have been manipulated.

Nations and their relations with others can be intentionally altered by cyberterrorists. For example, images and information can be directly manipulated, or removed from the public domain entirely, by removing a nation's site from the public domain. Consider this actual example. In 1997, Connect-Ireland (an Internet service provider) and Nobel laureates Jose Ramos-Hort and Bishop Carlos Belo created a virtual nation. This Internet site was constructed to protest and support the freedom movement of East Timor, the eastern half of a South Pacific island under Indonesian control. This was not merely a web presence or an interest-group chat site. The founders were able to secure a "top-level" national domain (see, e.g., *http://www.freedom.tp*). (The United Kingdom, for example, is assigned uk at the end of web addresses to denote location.) This meant that the group effectively established an "official" government site. Since Indonesia does not recognized East Timor as a sovereign country but rather as a part of its territory, questions of control were widely discussed. Such actions have interesting implications for other rebel groups residing inside another nation's territory. But the story gets more interesting. In perhaps the most severe attack by virtual terrorists to date, the national site of East Timor had its presence literally erased from the Internet in January 1999 (Arthur, 1999). Anyone attempting to access the East Timor address would only find a blank screen. Imagine, a whole "nation" cut off! Clearly, the best way to sabotage a nation is to interfere with its basic lines of communication. The terrorists not only shut off communication with the East Timor site, but also caused the Internet service provider to shut down its entire operation until the system could be restored. Rumors attributed the attack to Indonesian terrorists.

This is not the first time nations have been accused of interfering with another group's Internet site. The Spanish government was accused of supporting an e-mail bombing of a web site based in San Francisco that supported Basque separatists. So severe is such a threat that FBI Director Louis Freeh asked a Congressional committee for increased funding specifically to cover costs for counterterrorism measures relating to cybercrime (Arthur, 1999). Similarly, U.S. Attorney General Janet Reno noted, "Our systems are more vulnerable than ever to attack because of our unprecedented reliance on technology" (Arthur, 1999).

Already, nations are facing problems with information warfare (IW). The thousands of unauthorized intrusions into government and industrial web sites are staggering. Some attempts are just vandalism, but others have been defined as "industrial espionage and reconnaissance for possible future attacks" (Brogan, 1999). Most Western nations are taking specific steps to combat those who are interested in economically destabilizing Western powers (Brogan, 1999). Top on the list of international terrorists are groups in China and Iraq. Although CIA director John Serabian would neither confirm nor deny which nations were planning such attacks, he has confirmed that the CIA has identified several nations who have "information warfare in their military doctrine as well as their war college curricula" (Threat Assessment, 1998). In response to such threats, governments have begun to set up new initiatives to deal with the threat. In the United States, for example, Clinton established a new post, the National Coordinator of Security, Infrastructure Protection and Counterterrorism (see Presidential Decision Directives (PDD) 62 and 63).

These dangers to the national security constitute direct threats to the will of the people, the power of nations to define and determine their own destinies, and a general sense of well-being.

Conclusion

The real questions for scholars watching the development of the Internet are these: Will the medium form the message or will the message transform the medium? Will some hybrid version evolve? Today, the official sites are quite information based. But there are also news sources online that continue to use the Internet to stream their news over the Internet just as they do the televised "news" produced by their entertainment divisions. Yet today's uses may be quickly overturned by new, innovative, or inventive uses of the media.

Several factors will influence the use and direction of this medium. First, today the Internet is an elite venue. To log on requires computer equipment, means to afford the costs of access (AOL, CompuServe, etc.), and at least minimal intellectual skills to find, sort, and synthesize information. If information processing and financing continue to be factors, the information-load of the medium will become increasingly important. If the medium is transformed into television-style entertainment, users will become increasingly passive and less active. Mass media outlets have traditionally targeted programming to the least common denominator, dumbed down so that a larger audience can understand it. Of course, some people maintain that the Internet can serve both entertainment and information-seeking users. Indeed, the market may show a schism for a while, exploring the various natures of both. Chances are, however, that one form will eventually dominate, as has occurred with other media.

A second factor is the expectations of the user. Today, users are looking for quick access to information. But there are other issues to be considered. Will information remain accessible for free? If not, what kinds of information are people willing to pay for? People with good ideas are not necessarily those with money. Further, people who resist the dominant coalition are often discouraged from public participation. The cost factors are one way to restrict such participation.

A third factor is the control exercised by various nations. How much challenge to authority can nations permit to exist? How serious is the threat for cyberterrorism? Learning to permit free expression, engage in discourse where compromised solutions permit everyone to have a stake in the outcome, and develop a respect for the ideas of oppositional others have rarely been the hallmarks of government. These issues are serious challenges to the development of the Internet.

Politics and the use of the Internet are closely entwined. Years from now we can look back and assess the choices we made at critical junctures. Only then will we know with any certainty the effects of this media upon the political process.

References

http://www.census.gov/population/www/socdemo/voting.html

http://www.freedom.tp

Andrews, E. 1995, June 14. On $700 Billion Data Highway, Persuasion Has a Polite Frenzy. *New York Times,* pp. C1, C4.

Arthur, C. 1999, January 29. The Day East Timor Was Deleted. *The Independent* (London), p. 8.

Auletta, K. 1995, June 5. Pay Per Views. *The New Yorker,* 52–56.

Barrett, T., and Wallace, C. 1994, November/December. Virtual Encounters. *Internet Magazine,* 5 (8): 45–48.

Brogan, B. 1999, January 27. Action Urged to Combat Hackers Threat. *The Herald* (Glasgow), p. 9.

Brookhiser, R. 1996. *Founding Father: Rediscovering George Washington.* New York: The Free Press.

Capital Advantage. [Online]. Retrieval from the World Wide Web: *http://www/capitoladvantage.com*

Citizens Internet Empowerment Coalition. 1999. Complaint. [Online] Retrieved from the World Wide Web: *http://www.pfaw.org/alert/complain.txt*

Clinton, W.J. 1996. State of the Union Address. [Online] Retrieved from the World Wide Web: *http://www2.whitehouse.gov/WH/News/other/stateunion-top.html*

Davis, C.N. 1999. Rethinking Harmful Words: The Demise of the Critical Education Model and Discourse in the Schoolhouse. In D. Slayden and R. Whillock, eds., *Soundbite Culture: The Death of Discourse in a Wired World,* 203–24. Thousand Oaks, CA: Sage.

Dead Woman in Oklahoma Senate Runoff. 1998, September 12. *Dallas Morning News,* p. A9.

Engelman, R. 1997. *Public Radio and Television in America: A Political History.* Thousand Oaks, CA: Sage.

Escobar, A. 1994, June. Welcome to Cyberia. *Journal of Current Anthropology,* 35(.3): 211–31.

Gitlin, T. (1995). *The Twilight of Common Dreams: Why America Is Wracked by Culture Wars.* New York: Metropolitan Books.

Gumpert, G. 1987. *Talking Tombstones and Other Tales of the Media Age.* New York: Oxford University Press.

Herbeck, D. 1999. Democratic Delusions: The Town Meeting in an Electronic Age. In D. Slayden and R.K. Whillock, eds., *Soundbite Culture: The Death of Discourse in a Wired World,* 43–63). Thousand Oaks, CA: Sage.

Janda, R. 1999. Benchmarking a Chinese Offer on Telecommunications: Context and Comparisons. *International Journal of Communication Law & Policy.* [Online] Retrieved from the World Wide Web: *http://www.digital-law.net/IJCLP/2_1999/pdf/ijclp_web doc_6_2_1999.pdf*

John, M. 1995, August. Cybergridlock Feared. *Communications Industry Report,* 12:9.

McChesney, R.W. 1996. The Internet and U.S. Communication Policy Making in Historical and Critical Perspective. [Online] Retrieved from the World Wide Web: *http://www.acusc.org/jcmc/vol11/issue4/mcchesney.html*

Meeks, B. 1995, July 31. Commerce Department Study Highlights Unequal Access. *Inter@ctive Week,* 2:12.

Mirabito, M.M.A. 1997. *The New Communications Technologies,* 3rd ed. Newton, MA: Focal Press.

Muir, J. K. 1994. Clinton Goes to Town Hall. In S.A. Smith, ed., *Bill Clinton on Stump, State and Stage: The Rhetorical Road to the White House*, 341–64. Fayetteville, AR: University of Arkansas Press.

Rheingold, H. 1993. *The Virtual Community.* Addison-Wesley: New York.

Richenback, H. 1931. *Phantom Fame.* New York: Simon and Schuster.

Richter, A. 1999. Local Media Legislation in Russian Provinces: An Old and Winding Road. *International Journal of Communication Law & Policy.* [Online] Retrieved from the World Wide Web: *http://www.digital-law.net/IJCLP/2_1999/pdf/ijclp_webdoc_10_2_1999.pdf*

Serpentelli, J. 1993. Conversational Structure and Personality Correlates of Electronic Communication. Via anonymous FTP: Xerox.Parc.com/pub/papers.

Speier, H. 1980. The Rise of Public Opinion. In Robert Jackall, ed., *Propaganda*, 26–46. New York: NYU Press.

Threat Assessment Section. 1998, December 31. U.S. Mounts Wider Defense. *Intelligence Newsletter.* No. 349.

de Touqueville, A. 1948. *Democracy in America*, Volume 2. New York: The Free Press.

Whillock, R.K. 1997, August. Cyber-politics: The Online Strategies of '96. *American Behavioral Scientist*, 40:1208–25.

Whillock, R.K. 1999. Giant Sucking Sounds: Politics as Illusion. In D. Slayden and R. Whillock, eds., *Soundbite Culture: The Death of Discourse in a Wired World*, 5–28. Thousand Oaks, CA: Sage.

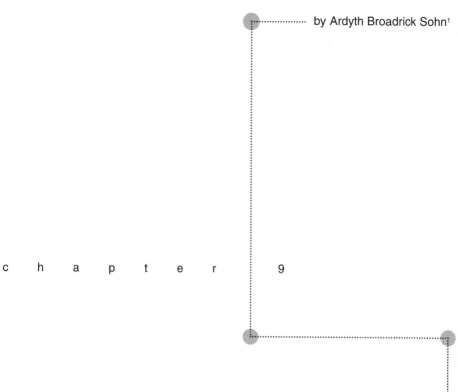

by Ardyth Broadrick Sohn[1]

c   h   a   p   t   e   r   9

Issues of Web Content

In many respects, The Internet demonstrates the best—and the worst—characteristics of an emerging culture. While the Internet shares a "wild west" image with the American frontier, this geographic metaphor becomes almost irrelevant in a territory without traditional boundaries. Like the old American West, the online world is an unrestricted and unmapped space open for settlement by those brave enough and opportunistic enough to venture into a climate of uncertainty. As such, it is a cultural milieu that has fostered the development and widespread dissemination of content that raises significant

[1] The author, who is a professor of journalism, wrote this chapter while on leave from Butler University. She gratefully acknowledges the help of Lewis Miller, dean of libraries at Butler University, for his advice, source suggestions, and constant support via e-mail throughout the writing of this chapter. She also is grateful to her nephew, Matthew McKinney, a law student at the Walter F. George School of Law at Mercer University, for his research suggestions, insights, and copies of important court cases related to this chapter.

concerns for parents, educators, industries, and governments. On the Internet sites offering pornography, obscene or indecent content, deceptive information, hate, and prejudice coexist with all other content forms. This chapter examines the availability of such sites; the difficult social, political, and economic issues raised by questionable Internet content; and efforts to control it.

Online content develops out of the cultural or social expectations of Internet users. Some seek rich personalized exchanges, while others operate on the fringes behind masks of anonymity. Community membership is the goal for some, while others seek separate and individualistic experiences. And these social and behavioral contexts are not permanent but rather dynamic for each user who may choose in one instance to be separate or exclusionary and in the next moment join a collective. For instance, a friend seeking information about his unexplained medical problems did an extensive content-based search of medical journals, libraries, and experts available on the World Wide Web. However, he also relied on the Internet's Usenet service to seek out chat groups, fellow sufferers, and sympathetic medical researchers willing to discuss and analyze aspects of his disease and treatment. He moved easily from singular reader/researcher to group member in his Internet interactions, which eventually resulted in a typical finale to Internet activity—a personal meeting with some of his most promising informants.

This experience demonstrates how easily observer and participant roles are interchanged, depending on the goals, subjects, or presentation formats offered by the Internet. Unlike prior mass media, which delivered content primarily intended for passive consumption, Internet content can be altered, skewed, scanned, and repackaged by the consumer, who may use it privately or interactively. While the Internet can be as effective as the telephone in supporting interpersonal and intimate interactions, it also is capable of reaching the same sort of generic masses that are the targets of newspapers, television, and radio. Therefore, it is appropriate to consider the Internet in comparison with other forms of mediated communication.

By combining text with the graphics, photographic images, animation, music, and video of the Web and with the interactive possibilities offered by e-mail and Usenet, Internet content retains elements of existing media while establishing its potential for revolutionary design. Gates et al. (1996) suggests that the Internet will not reach its full potential until it has moved out of the shadows of prior media, and web communicators develop its unique capabilities for content authoring, dissemination, and retrieval. However, there is considerable confusion about how to achieve "original" content forms for this unique medium. Prior media developed content in response to the needs and preferences of particular target communities that desired useful and entertaining content. The rapid evolution of the Internet requires constant reassessment of our definitions of content, particularly on the World Wide Web, where content has been continually redefined in terms of format, purpose, and delivery, and where content can function within both interpersonal and mass communication contexts (Gates et al., 1996).

Freedom of Expression and Traditional Media in the United States

The regulatory history of U.S. communication channels (including the Internet) stems from the First Amendment to the Constitution, which includes free speech and free press clauses stating that "Congress shall make no law ... abridging the freedom of speech, or of the press," (DeFleur and Dennis, 1998, p. 496). The First Amendment assumes that humans are analytical beings who wish to exercise their ability to choose for themselves what they wish to see, hear, or know. Although the language of the First Amendment may seem unambiguous and straightforward, the U.S. Supreme Court has determined that the Constitution does not protect all forms of content.

Content deemed obscene is illegal to distribute under U.S. criminal law and is therefore not protected by the First Amendment. In *Roth v. United States* (1957), the Court defined content as obscene when the "average person, applying contemporary community standards, would find that the work, taken as a whole, appeals to the prurient interest." The Supreme Court further ruled in *Miller v. California* (1973) that beyond meeting the *Roth* definition a work "must describe, in a patently offensive way, sexual conduct as defined by an applicable state law," and that "the work must lack serious literary, artistic, political, scientific value" (Smith, Meeske, and Wright, 1995, p. 359). Additionally, the First Amendment does not protect child pornography, content in which children (under age 18) are depicted engaging in sexual activity. Child pornography is also illegal, and both the possession and distribution of such material is considered a felony punishable by imprisonment and fines (Esposito, 1998).

While law prohibits these forms of content, other problematic content forms are not illegal in every situation. Content considered indecent includes a wide range of material ranging from profanity to depictions of nudity (sometimes labeled as "soft porn") to graphic and sometimes degrading depictions of sexual activity. The dividing line between so-called hard-core pornography and obscene content relies upon the definition from the *Roth* and *Miller* decisions.

Access to indecent material may be restricted in a manner that is consistent with the First Amendment. For this to happen, government must have a compelling state interest in regulating communication and must carefully structure regulation to address that compelling interest. For example, most pornographic material can be possessed legally by adults. But government, acting in the best interest of young people, is considered to have a compelling state interest in protecting minors from exposure to pornography and other forms of indecent material.

While the First Amendment provides substantial and consistent protections for traditional print media, false and defamatory content that injures reputations or professional livelihoods may result in a legal challenge under civil law. Content is also vulnerable to challenge when it subjects people to hatred or public ridicule. While truth is a universal and unconditional defense for almost any published content, there are qualifications that require that the content not be published with malice (see for instance *New York Times v. Sullivan*, 1964). In addition, content about people who have been elected or thrust into the public arena is considered more protected than content about individuals who are private citizens (see, for instance, *Gertz v. Robert Welch, Inc.*, 1974).

Content from official judicial, legislative, or public proceedings as well as most public records (even if they contain potentially offensive content like the 1998–99 testimony from the impeachment hearings of President Clinton) may be published. In general, print media have a great deal of freedom to publish content that is related to current news or is of immediate public interest.

Free expression of opinions including art, cartoons, and satire about current public affairs is also allowable content for publication.

Broadcast radio and television have always been subject to federal regulation based on the scarcity of broadcast frequencies, a publicly owned resource. For example, during most of the history of broadcasting in the United States, licensees of radio and television stations were required to "balance" expressions of opinion and the exposure of candidates for political office. The ubiquity and "intrusive" nature of radio and television in the home were also used to justify efforts to delineate what kinds of content would be appropriate for audiences tuning in during certain times of the day. Since 1948 the U.S. Criminal Code has prohibited the broadcast of "obscene, indecent, or profane language" (Smith et al., 1995, p. 357). In efforts to apply this law, the Federal Communications Commission defined as indecent in 1970 content which is "patently offensive by contemporary community standards" and "utterly without social value" (Smith et al., 1995, p. 360). This definition was modified in 1987 when the Commission redefined indecency as the "description or depiction of sexual or excretory activities or organs in a manner patently offensive by contemporary community standards for the broadcast media" (Smith et al., 1995, p. 363).

More recently, growing concerns over acts of violence, depictions of sexual situations, and inappropriate language in broadcast television programs led to the development of a voluntary system of rating television programs. In addition, a provision of the Telecommunications Act of 1996 will require television manufacturers to provide a v-chip device to enable parents to block access to content considered inappropriate for younger viewers.

The Internet and the Challenge of Free Expression

The Internet is global, decentralized, and unregulated. The Internet shares with the telegraph and telephone the ability to negate the limitations of physical presence because distant and absent content suppliers can be accessed with all three technologies. But unlike the telephone and telegraph the Internet provides individuals access to a larger content base than any single user could possibly assemble with any other medium. The Internet poses unique challenges to long-held concepts of freedom of expression.

Some believe that the Internet requires less stringent controls than traditional electronic media because accessing problematic online material requires several affirmative steps, often accompanied by warnings. In addition, regulation and oversight of the Internet is contrary to the very core of its expansion, which was founded upon its independence from traditional control sources. If reliance on a community standard is to be used as guidance for appropriate Internet content, then a definition of *community* is critical to the process. The expansive and broad base of the Internet community makes it nearly impossible to imagine a definition that is adequate and equitable. Even conceiving of a national standard is impossible, given the Court's decades-old recognition that local standards of acceptable content deviate dramatically from one part of the United States to another. Further, a worldwide standard acceptable to online communities spanning multiple cultural and language boundaries is impractical not only because of the diversity but also because of the technological inability to monitor or regulate such a network. Nonetheless, unlike earlier communication media, "The Internet is the first medium that offers any kind of content on demand to anybody" (Noam, 1998, p. 2). In the next section we will examine dimensions of several content areas of concern.

Content Areas of Concern

▶ Internet Pornography

Online pornography is big business, and with the noted exception of child pornography, it is legal. In late 1998 an estimated 60,000 pornographic web sites were operating in the United States. Forrester Research estimated that the sites generated $1 billion in revenue, representing 20 percent of all electronic commerce in the United States (Tedesco, 1998). These sites represent a great concern to those with responsibility for the welfare of children: parents, teachers, school administrators, librarians, and even employers. Workers spend increasing amounts of time online, and the use of non-work-related web sites is a growing concern. A Nielsen Media Research study in early 1998 revealed that employees at AT&T, IBM, and Apple Computer had devoted the equivalent of 350 workdays in a single month to the Penthouse Magazine web site (Ey, 1998). No one expects that they were just reading the articles.

Usenet is another source of indecent material. Alleged pornography comes in the form of stories, practical guides (including Frequently Asked Questions or FAQs), jokes, and limericks. Digital graphics and discussion groups also describe the typical content appearing on Usenet (Shade, 1996). Reid (1991) revealed that cultural boundaries are vulnerable when technology challenges familiar norms of etiquette and social cues are bypassed. By providing privacy and the safety of anonymity and distance, Usenet gives users license to test sexual and societal codes that would ordinarily forbid the sharing of explicit content. Computer pornography combines aspects of public and private spheres where, "in the privacy of one's home one can participate in a diverse range of bulletin board services and forums within commercial network providers, available to a relatively anonymous public" (Shade, 1996, p. 15). Usenet also provides the option to go private with content. The "chat" is initiated by invitation, and if the invitation is accepted the individuals retire to a private section of the Internet where typed words appear on the screen while each person is typing. "Hot" chats refer to a conversation that includes sexual topics or fantasies with graphic and detailed content (including simulated sexual activity). Social taboos are removed or challenged in such interactive content sharing which provides a seductive alternative to traditional sexual recreation. As Shields (1996) notes, technology provides an opportunity for users to be several steps ahead of public policy frameworks, resulting in illegitimate contents and forms flowing unrestricted. Shade describes Usenet regulars as inhabiting "a raucous realm which respects no boundaries or borders, physical or mental. A diverse community of international users protects fiercely the notion of free and unfettered communication, and can hide anonymously behind a thick veneer of bandwidth" (Shade, 1996, p. 14). Rules for Usenet are community specific, complex, and driven by cultural, social-psychological, and economic determinants.

▶ Obscene Online Content

Even if indecent (e.g. pornographic) content might be protected, the Supreme Court has established that obscene speech does not enjoy First Amendment protection. In *Stanley v. Georgia* (1969), the Court determined that possession of obscene materials was not the same as creation or delivery of obscenity and while the former did not violate any laws the latter did. Robert and Carleen Thomas learned the meaning of this distinction when they attempted the operation of a sexually explicit and obscene computer bulletin board. The court said that federal obscenity statutes are operational on the Internet, and that privacy rights don't extend to receiving, transporting, or distributing obscene content via the Internet (*United States v. Thomas*, 1996).

▶ Hate Speech

Close behind concerns about pornography are worries over Internet content that would expose (most especially) children to bigoted, hateful, or violent speech aimed at particular groups or categories of individuals. The Simon Weisenthal Center estimates there are 1,426 neo-Nazi, racist, anti-Semitic, anti-Catholic, anti-Moslem, anti-abortion, anti-gay hate sites on the Internet (Marriott, 1999). These sites operate openly and are as accessible as web sites established for any other purpose. Jewish leaders note with concern not only the increasing number of anti-Semitic web sites, but also growth in the number of sites denying the Holocaust (Stephen Roth Institute, 1997/8). Although most would acknowledge that adults have a constitutional right to access hate sites on the Internet, the Anti Defamation League says children or minors who are doing legitimate research on the Internet and are deliberately misinformed by authors of such sites need protection. Jewwatch is one such site, which the Jewish Anti Defamation League says not only provides anti-Semitic material but also claims that the Holocaust never happened (Lowe, 1998). In a related concern, some web sites (including racist/hate sites) provide instructions for bomb making and recipes for chemical or biological weapons.

Federal/State/Local Efforts to Control Internet Content

The World Wide Web is a relatively recent phenomenon. Its emergence and rapid growth has been generally welcomed and supported by the U.S. government. However, growing concerns over the appropriateness of some online content coincided with a period of strong congressional interest in the future of telecommunications in the United States. The Telecommunications Act of 1996 was an effort to meld the guarantees of the First Amendment with societal concerns about propriety. The goal was to allow for fair competition and business growth that would provide access and opportunity for the public. While the main thrust of this legislation was the further deregulation of telecommunications industries, it included as a separate section the Communications Decency Act (CDA) of 1996, the first significant effort by the federal government to regulate content on the Internet. The CDA sought to prohibit both obscene and indecent material on Internet sites accessible to young people.

The CDA was protested almost immediately by a coalition of plaintiffs including the American Civil Liberties Union (ACLU), which filed suit in the Eastern District of Pennsylvania, charging that First Amendment speech rights were threatened by the law. In mid-1996 a federal court in Philadelphia ruled the indecency act was unconstitutional and issued an injunction against enforcement of the provisions affecting indecent material (*ACLU v. Reno*, 1996). The ruling ignored the obscenity element of the CDA because obscene material has long been held to be illegal. One year later, the Supreme Court (*Reno v. ACLU*, 1997) concurred, saying that certain provisions of the Communications Decency Act of 1996 were in violation of the First Amendment and that the provisions of the Act were written too broadly.

In its 7–2 decision the Supreme Court cited a number of defects in the CDA related to the nature of the Internet as a medium and its comparability to broadcast media. The Court saw no clear definition of "indecent" and recognized that "patently offensive" material might have redeeming value as literary, artistic, political, or scientific content. A major focus of the decision was the fact that content providers including newsgroups and chat rooms cannot effectively or practically screen for minors. Even if such technology could be implemented, there would be no guarantee that minors would be prohibited from viewing materials.

The court also made a distinction on the basis of medium. It noted that the Internet is not like preexisting communication media in either its intent or its regulatory history. The decision observed that the Internet is not licensed by government and does not share the scarcity of frequencies limitation which has justified regulating indecency over the airwaves. Further, the Court found that the Internet was not as invasive a medium as broadcasting. Despite evidence that young people with even modest computer and Internet experience can access indecent online content, the Court noted that almost all adult web sites warn visitors of the nature of their content and that it usually takes a series of several deliberate steps to access indecent material (Craig, 1998).

In a further effort to protect children from inappropriate web content Congress passed the Child Online Protection Act in October 1998. This law is more narrowly focused than the Communications Decency Act and applies only to commercial web sites which post material considered harmful to minors. However, the Child Online Protection Act is unlikely to survive judicial scrutiny. The Federal Court in Philadelphia issued a preliminary injunction in February 1999, noting that in its effort to protect children the law limits legal adult access to content which may be inappropriate for children (Policing Cyberspace, 1999).

Both the federal judiciary and critics of federal Internet content policy efforts have noted the impracticality of efforts to control the access of some online users to certain types of Internet content. Because there is no central switching station for information, the ability to monitor, restrict, or enforce content-based regulations is severely frustrated. The Internet is seen by many users as a final frontier where regulation and rules destroy the intent of the medium, which has a decentralized, self-regulated culture that easily accepts anonymity among users and unrestricted access to a wide range of content.

▶ Local Level Issues

Libraries have experienced increasing pressure to act as content censors and cybercops. In the fall of 1997, an Internet policy was passed in Loudoun County, Virginia, prohibiting the local library from allowing patrons to access e-mail, chat rooms, or pornography on library computers. To ensure that the policy was followed, the computers were equipped with site-blocking software that filtered out child pornography and obscene material as well as any other materials deemed harmful to juveniles. Library computers were installed near and in full view of the staff who were authorized to monitor the screens of patrons and call the police if patrons violated the rules. (Electronic Frontier Foundation, 1998). The regulations were ruled unconstitutional in a court test because the court said the filtering software prevented adults from accessing a wide array of mainstream and constitutionally protected contents (*Mainstream Loudoun et al. v. Board of Trustees of the Loudoun County Library, 1998*).

School officials have also targeted elementary schools' online computers as potential entrances to indecent web sites. In many schools up through the college level, students who want to use Internet service provided by the school must sign an agreement that indicates they understand and will follow the terms outlined by the provider school network. Failure to stay away from web sites that contain content considered inappropriate (by the school) results in loss of Internet access and privilege. Teachers and school staff are expected to not only control for specific content viewed by students but also inform authorities about any new and questionable content they might discover on their own.

The next section describes how local efforts to make the Internet "safe" for children face many of the same challenges as national initiatives. Ultimately, though, responsibility for the online welfare of minors may fall to parents. Filtering and screening software offer some degree of safety where younger children are involved, but older children are likely to find ways around these obstacles to online freedom. If filtering software proves to be inadequate, parents will have no choice but to become more actively involved in supervising Internet use by children. A 1999 study by the Annenberg Public Policy Center revealed that 77 percent of parents polled expressed concern about their children divulging personal information (Turow, 1999). Over three-quarters of the parents surveyed set online rules and monitored their children's online activities (Turow, 1999).

▶ Challenges to Control Efforts

The American Civil Liberties Union is part of a coalition of organizations including the American Library Association and other media groups that is opposed to the use of Internet filtering software in public access areas. Since filtering technology usually cannot discriminate between indecent sites and innocent ones, words like *testicle* can filter both legitimate medical information and lewd references. Opponents of blocking devices claim that crude blocking software has the potential to be used to eliminate material about women's rights, political scandals, and even news about and from religious groups like the Society of Friends and mainstream organizations like the American Association of University Women (Harper, 1998).

In addition, the ACLU claims that about 40 percent of the indecent material on the Internet is located outside the United States, so filtering devices focused on national producers of filth would miss a major portion of the material (Harmon, 1997). A blocking device is expected to prevent access to dangerous, indecent, obscene, or pornographic sites; monitor the use of search engines for acceptable information; and block the typing of offensive words, content, or e-mail. However because definitions of offensive content are qualitative, ambiguous, and interpretive, the best chance for implementation rests with programs that are designed for individual rather than collective standards.

International Regulatory Efforts

Nations vary widely in terms of their perceptions of indecent or pornographic materials and their willingness to control such content on the Internet. However, aspects of child pornography are illegal in much of the world. Spain and Sweden are among the most liberal nations, and in both countries possession of child pornography is legal. While other European countries allow its possession, distribution of child pornography is illegal. In Germany and the United Kingdom, governments can force online services and Internet service providers to remove or bar access to sites offering child pornography. The European Union and the United Nations (UNESCO) are working to achieve regional and worldwide consistency in attacking the problem of child pornography, especially online forms (Esposito, 1998).

Problems of Online Content: An Assessment

The Internet is truly an enigma. It is the latest frontier to be hailed as both a danger and an opportunity for civilization. Direct access to unrestricted content supports the development of a new discourse that will affect not only the content but also the design of future literature and language. "Technologies oriented to maximum speed and unchecked flow make it difficult to control the content of that flow," says one observer (Shields, 1996, p. 3). The lack of control means that content is available without social, political, or economic oversight. However, that does not mean context is missing. Maintaining perspective requires users to recognize the differences between content shared face to face and that shared in face to space interactions. Unmonitored debate, free flow fantasies, perpetual dialogue, and irreverent parody threaten, "the old seats of knowledge and power," because no single force dominates or controls the logic or source of the content, says Shields (1996, p. 7). The author further suggests that Internet users both benefit and subject themselves to the limits of the medium because they act as producers as well as consumers of Net content. These dual roles allow users to mediate and adjust content in dynamic ways not possible with other channels of communication.

Many support the maintenance of a totally free and unfettered Internet, while others see a serious need for protecting certain classes of users ranging from minors in some countries to all the inhabitants of more restrictive nations. The strongest advocates for unlimited Internet freedom see almost limitless value in an expansive marketplace of ideas. While the First Amendment provides some general social contours for this emerging and converging medium, it is inadequate to describe, direct, or guide a medium that is outside the control of any one constitution or policing effort. Even countries which have developed ways to enforce other social and political standards realize the futility of trying to control cyber content.

While growth in the number of Internet sites and users has been extraordinary, the public phase of this new medium is still in its infancy. Conflict over issues of problematic Internet content may be resolved in a manner not anticipated by many participants in the debate. The phenomenal growth of the Internet has precipitated a drive toward commercialization of this new form of communication that continues to gain momentum. Chin (1997) has observed that "First, speech power on the Web is already largely dominated by corporations, primarily computer companies and broadcasters. Second, to the extent that speech power is available to individuals, it is dominated by pornography and content derived from corporate providers, rather than self-expression and public discourse" (p. 6). For all its appearance of being a democracy and a free marketplace of ideas, the Web "amplifies the voices of the powerful and silences the powerless" (Chin, 1997, p. 1).

The very real potential exists for the "wild west" of the Internet to be tamed by an alliance of political and commercial interests, as was the old American west.

Obviously this scenario is speculative. The issues of Internet content discussed in this chapter will remain for the foreseeable future. Therefore, it is appropriate to examine the significance of these issues at the individual, group, national, and global levels of analysis.

▶ Individual Level

Individual freedom is one of the most cherished characteristics of the Internet and the online world. Opportunities to find and share broadly those thoughts and ideas that engage and express our uniqueness are more widely available on the Internet than in any other form of communication. These opportunities include the ability to find like-minded people who share both conventional and unconventional ideas. In addition to access to a wide range of content and ideas, the Internet routinely and easily affords the individual complete privacy and anonymity in communication activities. Quite simply, efforts to control Internet content have the strong potential to diminish the value of the Internet to the individual while seeking to protect members of certain groups.

▶ Group Level

Internet content issues impact a wide range of groups with different motivations and needs. The first group that usually comes to mind consists of children, typically defined as anyone under the age of 18. The belief that this group deserves and requires a degree of protection from indecent material has a long history in the United States and is shared by other nations. Generally speaking, parents constitute the group with the most direct concern for the protection of children from inappropriate content. However, not all parents are well informed about these issues. Some have direct experience with the Internet and may possess a high level of awareness of the problematic content that their children might access. Other parents with limited experience may rely on news coverage of these issues as well as information from trusted sources like educators, Net-savvy friends, civic organizations, and their churches. Still others will either ignore or discount the problem.

Schools and libraries represent one of the primary battlegrounds over which issues of Internet content will be fought. These institutions find themselves caught between administrators, politicians, and others advocating control over Internet use and the individuals and organizations that support free and open access. In an environment in which policies require scrutinized or filtered access, educators and librarians may find themselves subject to legal sanctions and litigation.

Other parties to the debate over Internet content include the commercial adult web site operators and the businesses that advertise on these sites. As noted, business has been good, and it is ironic that online pornography has been the most consistently successful and profitable form of online commerce. While these groups have a strong economic motive for retaining the freedom to offer adult content on the Internet, other groups have a more civil libertarian motive. Participants who sustain Usenet groups seek personal gratification through their online activities.

Controlling access to Internet sites that convey hatred, bigotry, and untruthful information also involves children and those responsible for their well-being. However, the social, cultural, and political beliefs experienced at these Internet addresses evoke a wider range of responses (including agreement) from members of a diverse society than do the more numerous pornographic sites. Because these sites often express viewpoints that can be construed, at least in part, as political, they may enjoy strong First Amendment protection.

▶ National Level

The United States has been struggling since 1997 to develop a national policy with respect to indecent material on the Internet. To date, no single effort has survived a Constitutional test. The Supreme Court has recognized not only the differences between the Internet and other media, but also the near futility of attempting to regulate this unique form of communication. Federal law linking a determination of what constitutes indecent content to local community standards did not anticipate a form of communication used by communities that do not exist within political or geographic boundaries. Further, it is unlikely that any reasonable means of restricting access to indecent content could protect minors without hindering the activities of those over the age of 18.

Adding to the dilemma is the fact that nations have different ideas about the kinds of content or materials that are inappropriate or even illegal. Some countries in the Middle East and Asia seek to protect their citizens from a wide range of ideas that might conflict with religion, culture, or political philosophy. Among the nations of the world, the highest level of agreement about online content has been achieved regarding the issue of child pornography. Because this area of content is tied to the exploitation and abuse of children, even nations with liberal policies toward other forms of obscene materials recognize the need to ban child pornography.

In many nations governments have the power to shut down web sites which advocate intolerance or racism, but often the same powers can be used to muzzle dissent. This trade-off between freedom of expression and tolerating unpopular ideas is a hallmark of the U.S. Constitution, but has little or no currency in many other countries. For the most part, issues of Internet content will be framed at the national level.

▶ Global Level

While many nations are in agreement that child pornography must be eradicated in all forms including online versions, coordinated activity on the global or even regional levels is still limited. It is very unlikely that any form of global agreement about obscene, let alone indecent, material will ever develop. Broadly shared content concerns at the global level are far more likely to involve the clash of content with national norms and values.

References

Chin, A. 1997, Winter. Making the World Wide Web Safe for Democracy: A Medium-Specific First Amendment Analysis. *Hastings Communications and Entertainment Law Journal,* 19. [19 pages] [Online] Retreived March 31, 1999, from the World Wide Web: *http://www. democracyweb.com.htm.*

Craig, R. 1998, June. *Reno v. ACLU:* The First Amendment, Electronic Media, and the Internet Indecency Issue. *Communications & the Law,* 20(2): 1–14. [Online] Retrieved March 31, 1999, from online database *Academic Search FullTEXT Elite* [EBSCO Industries, Inc.].

DeFleur, M.L., and Dennis, E.E. 1998. *Understanding Mass Communication: A Liberal Arts Perspective,* 6th ed. Boston: Houghton Mifflin Co.

Electronic Frontier Foundation Statement on Loudoun Ruling. 1998, November 23. [Online] Retrieved from the World Wide Web: *http://www.eff.org/pub/legal/&cases/Loudoun_library/html/1998//23_eff_statement.html.*

Esposito, L.C. 1998. Regulating the Internet: The New Battle against Child Pornography. *Case Western Reserve Journal of International Law,* 30. [20 pages] [Online] Retrieved March 31, 1999, from online database *Academic Search FullTEXT Elite* [EBSCO Industries, Inc.].

Ey, C.S. 1998, February 16. Workers Run Amok on Web. *Baltimore Business Journal.* [3 pages] [Online] Retrieved March 31, 1999, from the World Wide Web: *http://www.amcity.com/baltimore/stories/filtering\Software\Raises\privacy\Concerns.*

Gates, B. (with Myhrvold, N. and Rinearson, P.) 1996. *The Road Ahead.* New York: Penguin Books.

Gertz v. Robert Welch, Inc., 418 U.S. 323 (1974).

Harmon, A. 1997, March 19. Internet Tests Boundaries of Decency—and Nations. *Los Angeles Times,* [5 pages] [Online] Retrieved April 2, 1999, from the World Wide Web: *http://www.latimes.com/archives/doc/rArchive/temp/temp.18366.*

Harper, C. 1998. Bad Law, Tough Issues: The Internet, Free Speech and the CDA. *Interactive.* [4 pages] [Online] Retrieved April 2, 1998, from the World Wide Web: *http://www.mediainfo.com/b=@Hebb94e3807cb55b00487822efade6332:b=w&tid=ea18d9e2e90511d29ed5b46101f04786&domain=Interactive1068&ip=208.148.202.96&fmt=int&it=92306229&expire=925654277&kid=400003.38&ss=env/plweb-cgi/fastweb?getdoc+single+Interactive+1068+0++Bad%20Law,Tough%20Issues.*

Lowe, P. 1998, November 27. Software Filters Out Internet Hate. *The Denver Post,* pp. 31A, 36B.

Marriott, M. 1999, March 18. Rising Tide: Sites Born of Hate. *The New York Times,* p. E 1.

Noam, E. 1998, Summer. Content on Demand. Managing Information, Communication and Media Resources. [18 pages] [Online] Retrieved March 31, 1999, from the World Wide Web: *http://www.columbia.edu~av134/papnoam.htm.*

Policing Cyberspace. 1999, March 1. Nation, 268(8). [2 pages] [Online] Retrieved March 31, 1999, from online database *Academic Search FullTEXT Elite* [EBSCO Industries, Inc.].

Reid, E.M. 1991. *Electropolis: Communication and Community on Internet Relay Chat.* Unpublished honors thesis, University of Melbourne, Department of History.

Shade, L.R. 1996. Is There Free Speech on the Net? Censorship in the Global Information Infrastructure. In R. Shields, ed., *Cultures of Internet: Virtual Spaces, Real Histories, Living Bodies,* 11–32. Thousand Oaks, CA: Sage.

Shields, R., ed. 1996. *Cultures of Internet: Virtual Spaces, Real Histories, Living Bodies.*Thousand Oaks, CA: Sage.

Smith, F.L.; Meeske, M.; and Wright, J.W. 1995. *Electronic Media and Government: the Regulation of Wireless and Wired Mass Communication in the United States.* White Plains, NY: Longman.

Stephen Roth Institute for the Study of Contemporary Anti-Semitism and Racism. 1997/8. Anti-Semitism Worldwide 1997/8: Introduction. [3 pages] [Online] Retrieved April 2, 1999, from the World Wide Web: *http://www.tau.ac.il/Anti-Semitism/asw97-8/ introduction.html.*

Tedesco, R. 1998, October 26. Porn Sites Make Hay. *Broadcasting and Cable,* 128: 64–65.

Turow, J. 1999. The Internet and the Family: The View from Parents, The View from the Press. Philadelphia, PA: Annenberg Public Policy Center, p. 14–20.

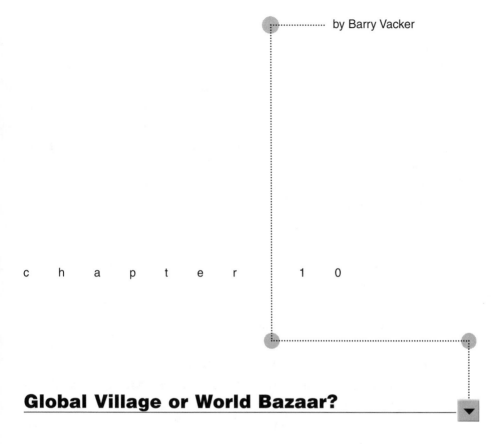

by Barry Vacker

c   h   a   p   t   e   r   1   0

Global Village or World Bazaar?

"Time" has ceased, "space" has vanished. We now live in a global
village ... a simultaneous happening.
                    –Marshall McLuhan

We live in a Cairo bazaar of competing models. In this psychological phantasmagoria we search for a new style,
a new way of ordering our existence.
                    –Alvin Toffler

Introduction ▬

In the classic book *The Medium is the Massage*, Marshall McLuhan (1996) observed that the electronic mass media were collapsing the space-time barriers of traditional human communication, thus creating a "global village" in which events are known and/or experienced simultaneously around the world. For McLuhan, this global village signified a mass tribalism produced by the electronic media, unlike the linear and mechanistic individualism that flourished in the cultural galaxy created by the printing press of Gutenberg (McLuhan, 1962). With the explosion of the Internet and World Wide Web during the last decade, the term *global village* is often used to metaphorically describe the worldwide cultural impact of new media technologies. Not surprisingly, as an expression of the spirit of the World's Fairs of this century, 1996 saw the construction of the Internet World Exposition, which was billed as a "world's fair for the global village," to showcase the cultural and artistic benefits of the Internet and the Web (Malamud, 1997).

In *Future Shock*, Alvin Toffler (1970) observed that advanced industrial technology was accelerating the velocity of cultural change, thus creating a chaotic "Cairo bazaar" in which many cultural styles compete and coexist as models for human living. In this vision, production and media technologies have created and made us aware of many different possible lifestyles from around the world, each of which simultaneously exists in a chaotic cultural landscape that resists industrial "massification" or political unification. There is a subtle, but profound distinction in these two cultural visions. McLuhan's global village suggests a deterministic technological and cultural convergence, whereas Toffler's Cairo bazaar suggests an evolutionary technological and cultural emergence. The question for this chapter is to understand how the Web will culturally impact the individual and the group, the nation and the world: will the Web contribute to a convergent global village or an emergent world bazaar?

While a single chapter cannot fully cover a complex issue such as the cultural impact of the Web, some patterns of cultural change are becoming evident. Without doubt, there is a broad pattern of technological convergence underway in the media. The traditional print and electronic media are converging around the computer and connecting with each other via global telecommunications networks, resulting in what is often described as an information revolution (Levinson, 1997) from which is emerging a new postindustrial economy (Tapscott, 1996). The World Wide Web does signal that an information revolution is certainly underway, but it is not the first innovation to generate a cultural revolution. Since the hypertext of the Web combines both textual and visual media, we should explore the effects of the "textual" revolution generated by the printing press and the "visual" revolution begun by the camera and electronic image. If we want to estimate the cultural impact of the Web, we should examine the effects of past media revolutions upon the individual, group, nation, and world. These past revolutions suggest cultural patterns that will be amplified and mutated by the World Wide Web.

History suggests that a media convergence occurred with Gutenberg's invention of the printing press, which generated the information revolution that ushered in modernity and industrial society. Closer analysis of both the printing press and the Web suggests that a near-complete convergence in media technology amplifies the collective informational power of the previously separate media, effecting a media revolution that subsequently generates an information revolution. The distinction is not trivial, for when media technologies converge to create a new medium, they transform the function and content of the information they were originally designed to communicate. A technological convergence that produces a new form of media does not necessarily mean the disappearance or obsolescence of the previous media. The new media technology usually incorporates, mutates, and exponentially amplifies the information or communication power of the old technologies. The printing press did not make the alphabet obsolete; it transformed and amplified its power. The Web will not make the printing press or television obsolete, but will likely transform and amplify their power. A media revolution occurs when the new style of technology exponentially amplifies the power and information of the previous technologies, which then produces the substance of an information revolution that challenges the prevailing worldviews and forms of the existing culture. To paraphrase McLuhan (1996), convergent media create a new message.

The World Wide Web promises to be at the heart of the emerging media and information revolutions, for it is the product of the technological innovation of hypertext and a dual convergence involving the computer and the global telecommunications networks. Such media and information revolutions necessitate use of a broad, macro perspective in exploring the likely transformations of information and culture suggested by the Web. Information thus includes any kind of communication or expression that uses aural, written, printed, or visual symbols to represent things such as ideas, facts, feelings, knowledge, stories, theories, worldviews, or any other item that can be communicated. Rather than information in a strict narrow sense, information here includes the forms and content of both art and science, as well as all realms of human knowledge and communication. Information and culture exist in a complex reciprocal relation. Culture is the complex tapestry that includes not only the arts and sciences, but also that which is expressed in the overall style and structure of society, from ritual to religion, production to politics, education to entertainment. As indicated by the rise of agricultural and industrial societies, culture can transcend any particular individual, group, or nation as it spreads around the globe.

The printing press served as the revolutionary media technology for the information revolution that fueled the transition from agrarian to industrial society. Similarly, the hypermedia technologies of the Web are emerging from the modern computer and telecommunications networks of industrial society, thus serving as the revolutionary media technologies for an information revolution that signals a transition to postindustrial society. Since information and culture both involve virtually every aspect of society, they exist in a complex reciprocal relation in which information and cultural revolutions shape each other. Culture can be transformed by new forms of information and transmitted by new forms of media, yet information and media themselves are the reciprocal products of culture. How the Web will impact individuals, groups, nations, and the world cannot be understood outside the reciprocal relations between culture and the revolutions of media and information, both visual and textual. (Broadly speaking, *group* is meant to include any economic or social organization.)

This chapter is divided into three basic sections, each accompanied by tabular material that illustrate the main points. The first two sections briefly review the impact of the printing press and the electronic image upon information and culture, illustrating how each transformed the individual, group, nation, and world. Section Three will then outline the impact of the Web on the production of information and the structure of the media, illustrating how it amplifies the past textual and visual revolutions. It will then discuss the impact of the Web on the production of culture and suggest how it may impact the individual, group, nation, and global levels of analysis. In conclusion, this chapter will suggest that the culture of the Web will retain elements of the Global Village as it comes to resemble a chaotic world bazaar.

The Gutenburg Culture

When Gutenberg invented the printing press around 1450, he could not have imagined the future cultural revolutions around the world made possible by his technological innovation. The printing press brought together into a single machine that era's five most advanced media for producing, disseminating, and storing information—alphabetic language, paper, ink, the press process, and movable type. Since the printing press was the first true machine of media convergence and mass production, it represented a media revolution that was to have a significant effect on the production and dissemination of information. The printing press amplified not only the amount of information that could be created and stored, but also the velocity at which such information could be produced and disseminated over both space and time. The modularity of movable type provided the printing press with the production power of standardization and economy-of-scale, both of which reduced the cost (per unit) of information while exponentially increasing the diversity of output. At the time of the invention of the printing press, approximately 50,000 books existed in the world, most of which were under the control of the Church. By 1500, there were an estimated 10 million books and an information revolution was born which was to have enormous individual, group, national, and global consequences (see Table 10.1). We can expect these kinds of consequences to be amplified by the hypertext powers of the Web.

This amplified production power reduced the cost of information, thus making possible less expensive books and periodicals, both of which served to increase individual literacy over the following centuries. Education came to be

Table 10.1. The printing press: patterns of information and cultural revolution.

A Media and Information Revolution	The Reciprocal Cultural Revolution
Media Convergence • Brought together alphabet, paper, ink, movable type, and the press process, creating a media convergence and revolution. *Information Amplification* • Increased dissemination of information across space and time, amplifying the spread of more diverse information around the world and to future eras. • Textual revolution emphasizing the printed word and written communication. • Standardized information increased information efficiency, amplifying (a) the amount and diversity of information which can be created and stored and (b) the velocity at which information can be disseminated. *Overall Media Structure* • Reduced cost of information through standardization and economies of scale. • A linear, one-to-many media system, sending information in one direction from one producer to many consumers.	*Overall Global Impact* • The first machine of mass production, serving as the information technology in the emergence of modern industrial society. • Worked toward decentralizing information and spreading it throughout the world. • Spread modern science, philosophy, literature, and art around the world, generating an intellectual and cultural revolution. *The Individual* • Gave birth to the modern notions of individualism and the rights to free speech and expression. • Broke knowledge monopolies of religious and aristocratic authorities, making individual literacy and mass education possible throughout the world. • Individual had significantly more access to information. *Economic-social Groups* • Publishing was one of the first capitalist enterprises that sought to reach anticipated mass markets. • Prototype for the linear mass production system of the industrial factory and mass labor. *Nation-state* • The standardization of language and the rise of industrialism helped create the modern nation-state.

Note: While the cultural impact is broken down according to the individual, group, nation, and world, there exists a complex relationship between individual effects and group, nation, and global effects. Since society is a complex tapestry, the effects upon one segment impact other segments.

associated with literacy, which was to be produced through the reciprocal systems of the mass media and mass education (the primary, secondary, and university systems that were reliant upon the printed books and periodicals produced by the mass media). Eventually, a citizenry of literate and informed individuals became a modern utopian ideal, shaping the intellectual foundations of modern democratic and socialist nation-states. Despite their differences, democracy and socialism were national or international political systems which both claimed to reconcile the liberation of the literate individual with the needs of educated society (the group) through the legitimate political representation of the people.

From the beginning, with increased literacy came increased individual criticism and dissent. While some members of the Church supported the development of the printing press, its power to mass produce information broke the Church's monopoly on knowledge and helped fuel Martin Luther's Protestant Reformation. Naturally, the prevailing religious and aristocratic authorities saw unrestricted liberty for the printing press as a threat, further increasing the need for a cultural inquisition. The media revolution of the printing press produced chaotic cultural and social (group) effects by partially decentralizing information and intellectual authority, thus fragmenting centuries-old intellectual and social monopolies. The printing press was the media technology that spread both Newtonian science and Enlightenment philosophy, which were fundamental to the emergence of modernity. Eventually, individuals such as writers, journalists, philosophers, scientists, and intellectuals all became workers creating and spreading printed information across space and time. Publishing was an early form of capitalism, for some of the first capitalist entrepreneurs were printers. Often defying social and cultural authorities, printers assumed both monetary and physical risk in publishing books for anticipated markets of readers.

As the standardized and modularized style of the printing press helped spread literacy, it was accompanied by the reciprocal rise of individualism. Prior to the printing press, the group dissemination of knowledge to the populace was done primarily in the town or church via poets and theologians. The structural style of the alphabetic sentence was inherently linear, and the mass production of books helped idealize and increase the individual use of linear deductive logic that came to be seen as an expression of modern reason. While printing permitted the mass production of books for groups or markets of readers, these books were almost exclusively authored singularly by individuals, fostering the ideal of reflective and autonomous individuals employing reason and judgment about the empirical world. Reciprocally, books were read singularly by individuals, further nourishing the ideal of individual reflection.

Over the centuries, the vision of the reflective sovereign individual was to have huge social and cultural consequences in shaping the debate over the control of art, information, and the media. While the printing press was invented in 1450, there was no general theory of freedom of speech and press until the 1700s, a full three centuries later. When John Milton published *Areopagitica* in 1644, it was but a first defense against licensing of the press by the King. Eventually, a free press became synonymous with public liberty and the individual rights to criticize authority, spread knowledge, and exercise intellectual autonomy. Over the latter half of the 18th century, this view became generally accepted in the United States, contributing to the ratification of the First Amendment in 1791 (Powe, 1991). However imperfectly it has been interpreted, the First Amendment expressed a generally individualist view of the media, where individual freedom and social needs are to be reconciled through increased intellectualism and the spread of information (Levy, 1985). The United Nations now recognizes freedom of the press and access to information as universal human rights that should be upheld in every country.

The linear production style of the printing press helped spread the cognitive and social ideal of linearity, which later would be consistent with the universal Newtonianism that permeated modern culture. Employing a mass production process, the printing press became the prototype for the industrial factory and assembly line that was central to both capitalist and socialist production systems. With the spread of industrialism and mass production in the 19th and 20th centuries, the individual became a member of a new group, the industrial labor force employed in the factory. The printing press was also the prototype for the mass media, employing a one-to-many production system, where information flowed from a single producer to many consumers. Whereas the ability of the printing press to standardize information gave it power to diversify and increase knowledge, it also worked to subsume regional dialectical differences through linguistic standardization, producing one of the unifying foundations in the formation of the modern nation-state.

In sum, for the individual, the printing press initiated an information revolution that increased literacy and education, while making possible freedom of press and expression under a representative government. For social and economic groups, the printing press fragmented religious and aristocratic cultural monopolies, ushering in the science, art, and philosophy of modern industrial society. For the nation-state, the printing press spread industrial visions of production standardization, social massification, and territorial unification. For the world, this media revolution did not produce an "information age," but it did contribute to the information revolution that ushered in the new industrial culture. As McLuhan aptly observed, the modern world emerged from the cultural space-time coordinates of Newton's scientific solar system and Gutenberg's informational media galaxy.

The Electronic Image

When Daguerre invented the photograph (1839) and Morse invented the telegraph (1844), they could not have imagined the future cultural revolutions set in motion by their innovations. The electronic media essentially function as extensions of the sense organs, permitting the individual or group to record, send, and receive representations of information across space and time. The initial power of the printing press resided in the prolific production and dissemination of information to readers, whereas the initial power of the electronic media (such as television) resided in the capture and retrieval of images for viewers. The electronic media were to effect a collapse of the traditional space-time barriers that had limited more traditional forms of human communication while also amplifying the quantity of information and the speed of dissemination. For 400 years the printing press had been the sole mass media technology. However, with the birth of the camera and electronic communications, the media landscape was to begin a transformation culminating in the hypermedia systems of the Web.

During the 100 years between 1839 and 1939, six new electronic mass media had begun to spread around the globe—the telegraph, telephone, radio, still and motion pictures, sound recordings, and television. The development of these media represented incremental and partial technological convergences, which are likely to be fulfilled by the cyberspace and virtual reality of the Web. While the telephone was a nonlinear interactive medium, television and radio followed the pattern set by the printing press, in that both expressed a linear, one-to-many model of mass media in which information and entertainment flowed in one direction from broadcasters to millions of viewers. When radio and TV were combined with the technology of Sputnik and Telstar, the result was the possibility for global communication virtually in real time. Paperless media could now pour across borders of the industrial nation-state, as if they were nonexistent, spreading a new culture around the world. While television also combined with the wired phone systems to create cable television and improve picture quality, it also began to fragment the homogenous viewing audience by offering greater programming variety.

The visual power of the camera is central to understanding the cultural impact of the electronic image. Photography recorded highly realistic representations of the empirical world, capturing reality with much greater accuracy and in more detail than any work of art. The power of the camera increased the amount of information that could be disseminated by the mass media, especially since "a picture is a worth a thousand words." Culturally treated as if they were exact copies of reality, photographs became the key source modeling and envisioning the empirical and cultural world. The mass production of photographs via the printing press and motion pictures amplified the spread of visual communication, much like the art of painting, but with much greater magnitude and velocity across space and time. While the printing press had made possible the mass production of information through textual representation, the camera press made possible the mass production of information through visual representation. Now that the mass media were both textual and visual, art and culture would never be the same (see Table 10.2).

The printing press was paper-reliant, whereas cinema and television were paperless, disseminating pictures around the world for the new canvas of a screen. Prior to the invention of the camera, the sole source for visual representation

Table 10.2.   The electronic image: patterns of visual and cultural
               revolution.

A Visual Revolution	The Reciprocal Cultural Revolution
Partial Medial Convergence • Mass media became both textual and visual, representing a media convergence and revolution.	*Overall Global Impact* • Returned to the media the visuals that had been neglected by the printing press, thus increasing the importance of visual communication across culture. • Suggested the emergence of the mass-mediated world—the global village.
Amplification of Information • Collapsed the traditional space-time limits on human communication, thus (a) increasing the velocity of information transmitted in real time and (b) signaling the emergence of global media networks that spanned borders. • Extension of sense organs, retrieving visual information from around the world. • The photograph increased the amount of "information" in the mass media (a picture is worth a thousand words). • Cameras and screens became the new paintbrushes and canvases of culture. • Immaterial "electronic" information would complement "paper" information.	*The Individual* • The individual offered significantly more access to visual and artistic information. *Economic and Social Groups* • Roles of the traditional artist now assumed by photojournalists and cinematographers. • Shaped cultural and individual ideals through the idealization of narrowly defined archetypes—the massification of society. • Created the new mass media of cinema and television.
Overall Media Structure • While the telephone was interactive and nonlinear, the remainder of the electronic media expressed the linear, one-to-many models of the printing press and factory.	*Nation-state* • Used to disseminate visual advertising to consumers of industrial production. • Used to disseminate visual propaganda to citizens of industrial political systems.

was the individual artist. No longer the sole source for visual representation, the visual artist completed the subjective turn inward by surrendering the surrounding empirical world to the camera and the mass media. Photojournalists took over the production of visual representations that documented and influenced world events through the power of a simultaneous empirical objectivity and individual subjectivity. This mixture of objectivism and subjectivism is what gives the electronic image such emotional and artistic power, for it represents empirical reality through the eyes of the subjective, individual human. Photography used this power to penetrate the realms of fine art and high culture. The emergence of Hollywood signified a new art, one that combined literature and theatre with motion picture technology to create the first truly global entertainment industry.

Unfortunately, the power of the camera was used to express the allegedly scientific management techniques pioneered by Frederick Taylor (1947; Kanigel, 1947). Time-lapse and stop-action photography were used in Taylor's famed time-and-motion studies of the production efficiency of industrial laborers, thus permitting the camera to assist in the increased standardization and the maximization of output. Taylor's vision of scientific managers planning every aspect of production influenced industrial economic and social structures around the world, including not only the New Deal, but also Soviet socialism and the German centralization of industry prior to the rise of National Socialism (Merkle, 1980). While such techniques did improve efficiency, they also created a dehumanizing vision of the mechanistic mass worker vividly portrayed in Fritz Lang's utopian masterpiece *Metropolis* (1927) and William Cameron Menzie's adaptation of H. G. Well's *Things to Come* (1936). From cinema to television to advertising, the cultural ideal of the massified industrial society was spread around the globe by the mass media.

Cinema and television could provide images on screens that could be simultaneously and endlessly reproduced for mass audiences around the world. The required synchronicity between dissemination and audience reception suggested media determinism, especially since the role of the media producers was essentially productive and active and the role of consumers was essentially passive and reactive. This naturally made them desirable to the industrial economic and political leaders of the nation-state, assembling consumers for the advertising of industrial production systems and citizens for the propaganda of industrial political systems.

By the 1950s, mass production and mass media had become the dominant forms of production and information technology for both democratic and socialist nations (Toffler, 1980). Even though the economic structures of capitalism and communism differed with regard to the ownership and control of production and media, they were still two systems geared toward mass production for masses of consumer-citizens living in nation-states. During the Cold War, the visual battle was waged between the "capitalist realism" approved by Madison Avenue and the "socialist realism" approved by Moscow. While industrialism and mass media have provided many economic and cultural benefits, lifting individuals from destitution and illiteracy, they have also been used to create narrow visions of an idealized universal culture that spread around the globe with rise of democratic and socialist nation-states.

In sum, the electronic image returned to the media the visual realm that had been neglected by the printing press, thus replacing many functions of the traditional visual arts. For the individual, they could now see art and pictorial representations from around the world via the new mass media of cinema and television. For economic and social groups, the new electronic mass media mirrored the principles of mass production, linearity, standardization, centralization, and synchronization. This made the electronic image perfect for creating idealized visions of narrow archetypes that reflected the modern massified society. For the nation-state and the world, electronic images poured across borders, transforming the sovereign reflective individuals into a tribal chorus living in a mass-mediated global village.

An Emerging World Bazaar

The last two decades of the 20th century have seen the industrial mass media begin a massive technological transformation and convergence whose global cultural consequences may rival those of the printing press. The transformation of the print and electronic mass media began with the global proliferation of magazines, radio stations, television stations, cable networks, and satellite television, all made possible by improved media technologies. Toffler (1980) believed such a media proliferation signaled the permanent decline of the traditional mass media and the emergence of a demassified media landscape, resulting in a significant increase in information producers relative to consumers and a reciprocal decline in the proportional size of the audiences relative to producers. The interactivity of personal computers suggests that the simultaneous media proliferation and audience fragmentation will only be amplified by the convergence of traditional media around the Web and millions of new information producers of varying size, from Microsoft to Matt Drudge. With its ever-increasing digital power, the Web will likely amplify and mutate the textual power of the printing press and the visual power of electronic image as it globally transforms the structure of the media. In any era of significant change, there will be numerous cultural variations, precisely because culture is a complex tapestry. The following two sections will outline the media revolution of the Web and suggest some broad patterns of cultural change involving the individual, groups, nations, and the world.

The Web: Media Convergence and Revolution

History has suggested that media revolutions occur when there is a nearly complete media convergence to create a new technology that amplifies the collective power of the previously singular media. The printing press signified the first such revolution, setting off the information revolution that ushered in modern industrial society. The electronic image expressed a partial convergence among the new electronic media technologies, thus beginning a visual media revolution that continues today. The reason the Web signifies a media revolution is that virtually all previous textual and visual media are converging to create a new digitized and interactive hypermedia network that will amplify the power of the previously separate media.

Two broad patterns of convergence are being fueled by the two basic media technologies of the Web—the local personal computer and global telecommunications networks. Personal computers are integrating virtually all of the previously separate media into a new interactive multimedia technology which utilizes alphabetic language, telephones, radio, cameras, motion pictures, television, and even Gutenberg's printing press. While the electronic media and telecommunications networks have evolved throughout the 20th century, we should remember that computers and the Web are still essentially embryonic media technologies. While no one knows the specific final forms of this technology, there seems no doubt that the media technologies are being incrementally integrated by the personal computer to produce a new interactive multimedia technology. Eventually, over time, the computer-based medium may deploy a mixture of traditional alphabetic keyboards, voice activation, wall screens, holograms, and retinal display in virtual reality, all made possible by improved computer power. The point here is that a new interactive multimedia technology is emerging from the computer.

Individuals, economic and social groups, and governments are forming information links by connecting computers to each other through the wired and wireless telecommunications technologies. Fueling this double convergence has been spiraling increases in computer power coupled with declines in cost, both afforded by the power of silicon microprocessors. Much like Gutenberg's movable type, silicon chips standardize information into the binary system of *1*s and *0*s, and then compress these bits to the microscopic level. This standardization and miniaturization of information is what gives computers such power, creating the possibility for endless variation, much like the alphabet of movable type and the screens of the electronic image. The power of computing promises to expand exponentially as miniaturization spirals downward to the molecular level with DNA computers (Adleman, 1998) and to the subatomic level with quantum computers (Gershenfeld and Chuang, 1998); both of these will possess power exponentially greater than current state-of-the-art supercomputers. These technological developments are important because they suggest that the computer and web-based information revolutions may have just begun.

Like the printing press 500 years ago, the computer and the Web are dramatically reducing the cost of receiving, creating, manipulating, storing, and disseminating information. These reduced costs are amplifying the production of information and the speed at which it is being retrieved and disseminated through the Web. Much like the electronic image, the Web permits electronic visual information to flow around the world, as if there were no local or national borders. Expanding data banks are making it possible for virtually unlimited customization and specialization, resulting in proliferation of textual and visual information. With millions of computers around the globe connecting to the Web, the very essence of the structure of the mass media is being transformed.

The printing press and the electronic media were essentially linear mass production systems in which information flowed in a single direction from relatively few producers to masses of consumers. While the Web will retain and amplify some of these features, the emerging new media structures suggest the continual erosion of the mass audience, a process that will have significant cultural consequences. The demassified media described by Toffler is transforming into a global network whose structure is nonlinear and "molecular," rather than linear and mechanistic.

Computers and the Web will be central to the postindustrial forms of production, serving as potential production, distribution, and media devices. When linked to the Internet, each computer functions as a production and distribution *node*, existing simultaneously as its own *center* for production and as an *edge* for entry into, and exit from, the information networks of the Web. Hypertext functions like an amplified and nonlinear global footnote system that permits an individual to instantaneously access information from different information sources across the world. As more nodes are created and connected, and the technological power amplifies and diversifies, the Web simultaneously becomes more molecularized and less centralized in overall structure. While each computer is its own node and center, there is no single center among the millions of decentered centers. Computers or organizations that can serve as a network center, such as firms or libraries or museums or online servers or personal computers, also serve as nodes and edges, of varying sizes and importance. In essence, no traditional production or distribution center exists across the Web, only the seeming paradox of decentering nodes that are simultaneously edges and centers. The Web is simultaneously local and global, spatial and immaterial. The molecular structure of nodes and edges is creating a production and distribution system of unparalleled complexity and ever-increasing speed. Computer interactivity and hypertext, when combined with satellites and fiber optics, suggest the emergence of a "chaotic" hypermedia system, much different than the linear systems which typified the industrial mass media. With many millions of information producers using networks comprised of an ever-increasing number of nodes, fiber optics, and satellites, the structure of the Web is beginning to resemble the complex molecular systems found in nature (Kauffman, 1995; Kellert, 1993). This molecularization, however, does not mean the complete disappearance of mass media, for pop culture events such as the World Cup, the Super Bowl, and *The Titanic* will continue to draw audiences in the hundreds of millions. However, such mass events will be the exception, rather than the rule. The industrial mass media will no longer dominate; its power will be incrementally eroded by the waves of mutating molecularization being amplified around the globe throughout the unlimited spectrum of the Web.

Terms such as *information superhighway* and the *Infobahn* are outmoded industrial metaphors that suggest an ignorance of the chaotic molecular structure of the hypertextual Web. Unlike the industrial mass media, the Web permits one-to-one, one-to-many, many-to-one, and many-to-many communications in which information flows in multiple directions, in a more horizontal and nonlinear manner. The Web suggests the emergence of a new hypermedia network likely to be characterized by nonlinearity, interactivity, immersion, virtualization, asynchrony, decentering, fluidity, customization, individualization, spatiality without territory, time without distance. Since the structure of media and production technologies have significantly influenced culture in the past, we can expect the Web to have a reciprocal impact on the production of culture as it undermines the dynamics of a massified global village.

Cultural Turbulence

The double convergence toward the computer and the Web suggests the emergence of a chaotic media system, whereas the electronic realms within the Web suggest the creation of a new realm of informational space-time. Together, the chaotic structure and the new realm will work to transform art, media, science, labor, and capital as it becomes the information backbone in the transition to a postindustrial society centered around biotechnology

(Kelly, 1994), nanotechnology (Drexler, 1986), and media technology (Negroponte, 1995). The cultural effects will be reciprocal and turbulent (see Table 10.3).

Cyberspace and virtual reality are the culmination of the electronic image, representing a new realm of space-time that exists simultaneously in the quantum space of the computer chip and the relative space of the Web (Heim,

Table 10.3. The World Wide Web: Patterns of information and cultural revolution and the different structures of the mass media and hypermedia.

Patterns of Information and Cultural Revolution

A Media and Information Revolution	The Reciprocal Cultural Revolution
Media Convergence • Virtually all previous media are converging around the personal computer and the global telecommunications networks. • Information may be produced in any form—text, visual, motion picture, sound.	*Overall Global Impact* • Undermining the mass society of industrialism. • Creating a chaotic marketplace of cultures that prevents the construction of consensus and social unification. • Global villagers amidst an emerging world bazaar.
Information Amplification • Digitization standardizes (1,0) information and increases efficiency, amplifying (a) the amount and diversity of information that can be created and stored and (b) the velocity at which information can be disseminated and received across space and time. • Information may be infinitely specialized, customized, and encrypted. • Reduced cost of information through standardization, economies of scale, and the lack of need for paper.	*The Individual* • Individuals can receive and disseminate more information than ever before, thus enlarging their role in the marketplace of ideas. • There will be continual explosive and contentious debate among individuals. • The volume of information, and its diversity, will place more responsibility upon individuals to determine what they believe is true and false. • There will be increased individualism and independent thought, which undermine dogma and certainty. *Economic and Social Groups* • Progressive group adaptation will increase social and economic entrepreneurialism.

(Table 10.3. Continued)

A Media and Information Revolution	The Reciprocal Cultural Revolution
• Information is transformed because it is reproduced and circulates in cyberspace.	• Marginalized groups will find new outlets to express their ideas and connect with people of like mind.
Overall Medial Structure	• Regressive groups will seek state control and regulation of information and the new technologies.
• A nonlinear interactive network in which information may flow from one-to-one, one-to-many, many-to-many, and many-to-one.	• Virtual communities and markets will thrive, fueling nonterritorial socialization and digital commerce.
• Information instantaneous, real time, and global, flowing across cultures and borders, simultaneously local and global.	• Backbone of postindustrial production systems.
• The new media are highly mobile and central to postindustrial production system.	*Nation-state*
	• As information becomes more fluid, governments likely to heighten information surveillance and censorship.
	• Potential loss of individual and social privacy.
	• Undermine democratic systems and socialist systems born of industrialism.

The Different Structures of the Mass Media and Hypermedia

	Traditional Mass Media	Web Hypermedia
Basic principle	• Mass production	• Mass customization
Key technology	• Printing press, broadcasting	• Computers, microprocessors
Electronic signal	• Analog	• Digital
Information flow	• Linear, point-to-multipoint	• Nonlinear, point-to-multipoint, multipoint-to-point (or multipoint)
Audience goal	• Maximization, homogeneity	• Individualized, diverse
Media usage	• Passive	• Interactive
Media device	• Dumb/ receive information only	• Smart; transmit, alter information
Location	• Home, office, stationary	• Highly mobile, view anywhere
Information producers	• Relatively few	• Millions
Entry cost for messages system	• Very expensive • Aimed at mass audience • Mechanistic, centralized	• Relatively cheap producers • Very special audiences • Organic, decentralized

1993; 1998). This is an inversion of the normal relations of technology, space-time, and culture. While the technologies and cultures of agrarian and industrial society both exist within the physical realm of traditional space-time, cyberspace exists within the technological infrastructure of computer chips and networks. Space and time, the relative external, now also inhabit the quantum internal. The computer and the Web are producing a functional infrastructure and a formal exostructure for the economic and social groups of the new postindustrial production systems. This does not mean that computers and the Web are separating humans from reality, for it seems the new media are permeating reality and thus blurring the lines between representation and reality. These new realms intensify and amplify information while simultaneously fragmenting consensus by permitting real worldviews to become virtual worlds. While this transformation of information relative to space and time is crucial for a true information revolution, it seems almost as if cyberspace and the Web transform space and time relative to information. This implosion of space and time relative to information will produce an explosion of cultural effects as the Web increases in complexity and spreads around the globe, impacting individuals, groups, and nations.

▶ The Individual

In terms of sheer volume and variety, individuals will have significantly more access to textual and visual information than at any other time in human history. There will be more creators and disseminators of information than ever before, enlarging the role of the individual in the global marketplace of ideas. This process can only generate a renewed sense of individual expression and a reciprocal rise in cultural turbulence as the prevailing structures of industrial society struggle to adapt and maintain control.

Individual interactivity and reduced information costs are already producing an increase in the diversity of artistic, scientific, and political expression disseminated across the Web, from virtual museums to the Human Genome Project to global conspiracy theories. Intellectual and cultural dissent is also flourishing on the Web, with its virtually unlimited space and global distribution. Since there are relatively no paper or distribution costs, we can naturally expect many more newspapers, magazines, and books to be produced and distributed at much lower costs via computers and the Web, perhaps generating a global publishing renaissance unparalleled since the printing press. In effect, the individual can be a global information pamphleteer, publisher, and producer, employing a full range of media. The point here is not whether the content of these publications or productions is accurate, or whether we agree or disagree with any of them. Rather, the cultural significance is that they can be disseminated, mutated, and endlessly replicated globally via the Web, almost instantaneously and at virtually the speed of light. The Web permits information to be created and disseminated generally outside the filtering gatekeepers of the mass media institutions of the capitalist and socialist nations. In what seems paradoxical, the convergence of the Web is producing a radical decentering of information, true and false, both of which the traditional mass media tried to centralize or control through the one-to-many model of information production.

This is culturally healthy, yet turbulent, for it undermines mass media centralization and ultimately requires individuals to increase their personal responsibility for the ideas and information they regard as true and false. Those individuals and groups more comfortable with having their truth disseminated for them via the traditional mass media may feel their worldviews threatened in the face of such information chaos. An information revolution tends to undermine cultural dogma, precisely because it amplifies the content of information. On the other hand, the unlimited storage capacity and ability to customize information will provide fertile ground for the survival of many old dogmas and the emergence of many new truths.

In the realm of cyberspace, individuals can transform their abstract worldviews into virtual worlds. Communities can be constructed to reflect any particular philosophical or ideological perspective, permitting individuals to interact with persons who share their ideas or interests. In such specialized communities, individuals can reinforce their own pre-existing worldviews within a narrow range of dialogue. If they want, they can use these communities to isolate themselves from the people and ideas on the Web with which they disagree. On the other hand, individuals can use the speed and diversity of the Web to broaden their worldviews and worlds. Together, such possibilities will likely increase the variety of individuals and groups across the globe.

While some cyber utopians may dream of global unity or world democracy, the reality is that the tableau of the Web is likely to resemble a contentious and chaotic marketplace of cultures. The vision of a homogenous or universal cultural ideal can no longer dominate the media landscape. Instead of a single national or global unity, there will be many different unities within many different groups connected via the Web. We can imagine the worldwide cultural turbulence as the massified culture, idealized under industrial production, is supplanted by many subcultures populated by many different global villagers.

▶ Economic and Social Groups

Broadly speaking, there are four types of social and economic groups that will emerge with the spread of the Web. There are those that will progressively adapt to the hypermedia technologies, seeing in technological change the opportunity to create new communities and markets. In contrast, there will be groups that regressively adapt to the change by seeking to impose government controls upon information, producers, and technology. Because of the inevitable conflict between progressive and regressive adaptation, two other general types of social groups will emerge—those who want to control others' information and those who want to control their own information. These four overlapping groups and their conflicts will have a significant impact on the economies and social systems of nation-states and the world.

Progressive adapters will be those economic and social entrepreneurs who use the reduced information costs and increased power afforded by the Web to expand their opportunities in postindustrial production systems. The industrial print and electronic mass media required significant amounts of capital, as did their distribution systems of trucks, stations, satellites, bookstores, and theatres. In contrast, newspapers, books, TV sets, and movie tickets were inexpensive in relation to their cost of production. The mass production and distribution technologies generated economies of scale, thus creating a system in which information production and distribution were expensive and information reception was inexpensive. While producing and distributing visual information such as movies is still expensive, the power of computers and the Web suggests that the relative production and distribution costs for information will decline over time. Because of the global nature of the Web and the reduced capital needs, we can expect increased economic entrepreneurship. Firms such as Amazon.com and broadcast.com have become billion dollar companies by using the Web's global distribution and low barriers to entry to sell the content of the traditional mass media (books and the retransmission of local radio stations and video, respectively). The fears of a "Microsoft world" are understandable, though likely unwarranted over time. Even though corporations and governments may try, malleable information flowing over chaotic networks will be impossible to centralize. Fluidic information, chaotic networks, and declining costs suggest heightened competition over time and the blurring of lines across the structure and content of the traditional media and production systems (Tapscott, 1996).

Similarly, social entrepreneurs will progressively adapt to the new media and production structures by creating nonterritorial virtual communities around the world. Previously marginalized groups, ranging from rights activists to political dissidents to digital artists, are connecting with each other through the Web to create meaningful social and political virtual communities (Jones, 1997). Such social possibilities are already yielding economic opportunities. With their portals to the Web, firms such as Yahoo! and Excite are making possible the emergence of thousands of virtual communities focused around special topics, ranging from vegetarianism to single parenting to expatriates from Chile (Napoli, 1998). Yahoo! and Excite are functioning like virtual real estate developers as they provide the nonterritorial proximity for communities of interest to emerge and flourish. As the Web diffuses, we can expect these communities to proliferate. On the other hand, this cultural and technological diversification will threaten the prevailing social groups and political authorities, shattering the illusion that they are the only institutions possessing truth and justice. It seems only a matter of time before these kinds of cultural conflicts begin to significantly impact the cultural and political systems of the industrial nation-state, generating progressive and regressive adaptations.

The Nation-state

The chaotic, molecular, and borderless hypermedia network of the Web will function to undermine the ability of the traditional mass media and nation-state to control the production of information, assemble and manage mass political movements, and generate the consensus that justifies the massified political systems of the industrial nation-states. The doctrines of democracy, socialism, and representative government all presume the existence and moral validity of a political consensus that expresses "majoritarian" or mass opinion. Modern mass politics and representative government emerged simultaneously with the one-to-many models of mass media. Political leaders either controlled the mass media, or used the filter of the compliant corporate mass media to disseminate their social visions or propaganda for mass consumption. We are likely entering an era in which centralization and mass movements may be practically impossible. Symptomatic of this pattern is the perpetual political gridlock emerging in the democratic nation-states, signaling not the failure or corruption of their systems, but more likely the eventual irrelevance or obsolescence of the mass political systems born of the industrial age.

When a cultural or political system is being transformed or rendered obsolete, many groups and organizations will feel threatened and will desire regressive adaptation. Medieval religious authorities performed inquisitions, agrarian Luddites destroyed machines, industrial fascists burned books, and postindustrial democratic majoritarian groups employ clipper chips. In the current democratic nation-states, the political majority is comprised of average citizens that usually have little to fear from censorship and surveillance, precisely because they represent the average. This is why majoritarian, "democratic" government offers little defense against censorship. Freedom of expression has generally survived in the United States because of the First Amendment, and in spite of the democratic government (Emord, 1991). Even government attempts to monopolize information usually fail when faced with the chaotic information processes produced by freedom of expression and amplified technology. The printing press functioned in a chaotic manner in pre-Revolutionary America, eventually working to undermine the authority of King George (Powe, 1991). Even the Soviet Union could not control the informational onslaught presented by the new electronic media technologies. While Beijing may have defeated the student protesters in Tiananmen Square, one suspects it will eventually lose the war with the World Wide Web. To the extent that a nation-state tries to control information flowing across the Web, it will become more stagnant; to the extent it permits open media networks and the free flow of information, it will become less relevant.

Since the increased amount of individual expression undermines the power of the prevailing groups and governments of industrial society, it is generating cultural fear and increased calls for censorship and information surveillance, usually in the name of cultural purity, social order, or national security. While computers and the Web can enhance individual expression, they can also be used to suppress such expression through information surveillance and invasions of individual and social privacy. There will be a battle between two groups—those who want to control others' information and those who want to control their own information. Censorship and surveillance are regressive adaptations, which are now being countered by the progressive adaptation of encryption. The first casualty of censorship is freedom of expression; the first casualty of surveillance is privacy. As Orwell (1949) illustrated, the control of information necessitates the elimination of privacy, precisely because information begins in the privacy of one's own thoughts. Free expression and privacy are reciprocal, and without their protection from centralized control the only result would be a spiraling closure of culture and technology in a surveillance society. While these battles will be ugly and produce some casualties, the war is likely to be won by freedom of expression and privacy. Since religious and aristocratic authorities could not put a few hundred printing presses back in Pandora's box, it seems unlikely that world governments will be able to put a few billion computers back in their packing boxes.

Conclusion: Global Villagers amidst a World Bazaar

The emergence of cyberspace and the World Wide Web suggests we rethink the concerns about the impact of the mass media on global culture. Traditionally, the mass media have been criticized for homogenizing global culture in the creation of mass audiences serving mass markets in mass societies. Marxists saw the mass media as creating a society controlled by the power of corporate capitalism, while conservatives saw the mass media as creating a society dominated by the pursuit of secular materialism. On the other hand, many Marxists and conservatives tended to applaud the mass

media when it served their own dominative visions of socialist or tradition-
alist massification.

Operating under the imperative of mass production and cultural unification, the mass media had similar tendencies. Now, the hypermedia of the Web
are fragmenting society and social discourse, creating a chaotic marketplace of
cultures that prevents the centralized construction of consensus and social
unification. It seems that critics of mass homogenized society should welcome
technology that permits greater individualization and customization across
cultures.

The homogenization of culture is now likely impossible, precisely because
of the infinite realms of cyberspace within the chaotic structure of the Web.
Rather than isolating persons, the Web is expanding human communication
beyond artificial territorial borders as individuals from around the world engage each other in the collapsed space-time of the Web. Rather than globally
unifying persons, the hypermedia make possible a greater range of cultural diversity and individual expression as cultures chaotically cooperate, coexist,
compete, and combine into new forms. The computer and the World Wide
Web represent a new style of media that is transforming the substance of culture; the result is a chaotic landscape populated by industrial global villagers
amidst an emergent postindustrial "world bazaar."

References

Adleman, L.M. 1998, August. Computing with DNA. *Scientific American,* 279: 54–61.

Drexler, K.E. 1986. *Engines of Creation: The Coming Era of Nanotechnology.* New York: Anchor
Press.

Emord, J.W. 1991. *Freedom, Technology, and the First Amendment.* San Francisco: Pacific Research Institute.

Gershenfeld, N. and Chuang, I.L. 1998, June. Quantum Computing with Molecules. *Scientific
American,* 278: 66–71.

Hayashi, A.M. 1999, January. The Net Effect. *Scientific American,* 280: 21–22.

Heim, M. 1993. *The Metaphysics of Virtual Reality.* New York: Oxford University Press.

Heim. M. 1998. *Virtual Realism.* New York: Oxford University Press.

Jones, S.G., ed. 1997. *Virtual Culture.* Thousand Oaks: Ca.: Sage Publications.

Kanigel, R. 1997. *The One Best Way: Frederick Winslow Taylor and the Enigma of Efficiency*. New York: Viking.

Kauffman, S.A. 1995. *At Home in the Universe: The Search for the Laws of Self-organization and Complexity*. New York: Oxford University Press.

Kellert, S.H. 1993. *In the Wake of Chaos*. Chicago: The University of Chicago Press.

Kelly, K. 1994. *Out of Control: The New Biology of Machines, Social Systems, and the Economic World*. Reading, MA: Addison-Wesley Publishing Company, Inc.

Levinson, P. 1997. *The Soft Edge: A Natural History and Future of the Information Revolution*. London: Routledge.

Levy, L. 1985. *Emergence of a Free Press*. New York: Oxford University Press.

Malamud, C. 1997. *A World's Fair for the Global Village*. Cambridge: Mit Press.

McLuhan, M. 1962. *The Gutenberg Galaxy*. New York: New American Library.

McLuhan, M. 1996. *The Medium Is The Massage*. San Francisco: HardWired.

McLuhan, M. 1997. *War and Peace in the Global Village*. San Francisco: HardWired.

Merkle, J.A. 1980. *Management and Ideology: The Legacy of the International Scientific Management Movement*. Berkeley: University of California Press.

Napoli, L. 1998, December 6. The Latest Internet Buzzword: Community. *The New York Times*. p. B10.

Negroponte, N. 1995. *Being Digital*. New York: Alfred A. Knopf.

Orwell, G. (1949). *1984*. New York: Harcourt Brace.

Powe, L.A., Jr. 1991. *The Fourth Estate and the Constitution*. Berkeley: University of California Press.

Tapscott, D. 1996. *The Digital Economy*. New York: McGraw-Hill.

Taylor, F.W. 1947. *Scientific Management*. New York: Harper & Row Publishers.

Toffler, A. 1970. *Future Shock*. New York: Random House.

Toffler, A. 1980. *The Third Wave*. New York: William Morrow and Company, Inc.

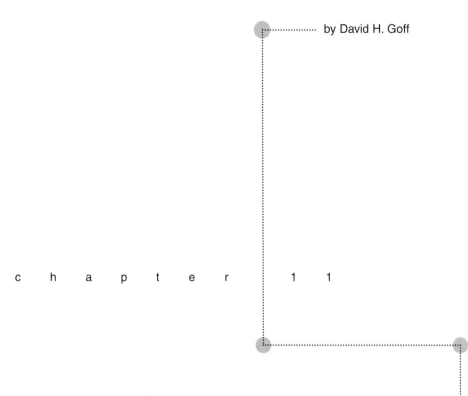

by David H. Goff

c   h   a   p   t   e   r   1   1

Issues of Internet Infrastructure

Introduction

The speed with which the commercial Internet has captured the imagination and interest of the world within in the brief span of years following the introduction of the World Wide Web is astounding. Yet as impressive as the growth in numbers of Internet users and applications has been, its greatest significance is largely invisible to its legions of users. The heart of the Internet phenomenon is its development and refinement of packet switching, a new networking technology (Leiner et al., 1998).

Prior to the Internet, communications networks were dominated by the circuit switching technology of the telephone industry. Circuit switching assigns a separate dedicated circuit for the duration of any communication (like a phone call) between two points or users. By comparison, packet switching subdivides a digital data stream (e.g., text, voice, video, or other digital data) into smaller packets of data that are directed to their destination via the best available path by computers called routers. Packets contain information identifying their destination, source, the order in which they are sent, and size. As they reach their intended destination, computer software extracts data from the packets in the correct order or sequence, reconverting the data into text, pictures, sounds, or even video. If individual packets arrive damaged or corrupted, the receiving computer requests that they be re-sent from the source. Packet switching utilizes network circuits more efficiently because data packets from many different sources can be commingled within the same circuit, and the entire bandwidth (data capacity) of that circuit can be in constant use. Packets can travel through the thousands of independent networks that make up the highly decentralized global Internet, employing a concept called open architecture networking. The Internet's TCP/IP (transmission control protocol/ Internet protocol) enable diverse types of networks, regardless of their original design and purpose, to carry Internet (packet) data (Leiner et al, 1998).

Most Internet users connect by dialing up an online service (like America Online) or a national, local, or regional Internet service provider (ISP). Usually the signal travels from the user's personal computer to the ISP's point of presence (POP) through the public, switched, telephone network (although alternative routes are becoming more commonplace). Internet service providers and other providers of Internet access are at the edge of the Internet's topography. In the center are high-speed, high-capacity (broadband) data pathways, the Internet backbone.

The infrastructure of the Internet, then, is a subset of the communications infrastructure of the world and its nations. Through a remarkable accident of timing, a massive transformation of global information and communication facilities began just prior to the start of the 21st century. Driven by advances in digital technology and by political and economic forces, governments and the leading telecommunications companies of the world accelerated the construction of advanced high-speed, high-capacity communication networks. These developments represent far more than a timely linear extension of the communication technology improvements of the past. The new communications infrastructure which is under construction reflects, enhances, and spreads the most significant communication development of the last years of the 20th century, the Internet.

This chapter examines the efforts and motivations of the builders of the Internet and other components of the developing global information infrastructure (GII), the very unequal global distribution of resources that has resulted from these efforts, and some likely scenarios for future Internet developments. Then the chapter explores the significant social, political, and economic issues associated with the developing Internet infrastructure at the individual, group, national, and global levels of analysis.

Information Infrastructures and the Internet

In the early 1990s, the engaging notion of an information superhighway evolved into a worldwide policy debate about information infrastructures. In the United States, the Clinton administration sought to give substance to the information superhighway metaphor by creating the National Information Infrastructure (NII) Advisory Council in 1994 to recommend policy. The global information infrastructure (GII) was the focus of the first World Telecommunication Development Conference of the International Telecommunications Union in June 1994. In that same month the European Council considered the so-called Bangemann Report of recommendations regarding the role of Europe in the developing global information society (European Union, 1994).

These initiatives all recognized the growing importance of information industries to national economies and of advanced communication systems to competitiveness in the developing global economy. At the same time, policymakers realized that information technologies held tremendous potential for improved delivery of education, health and social services, entertainment, and even (in some countries) the means to increase participation in the political process. The national, regional, and global information policy recommendations drafted between 1992 and 1994 were remarkably similar. Nearly all looked to the private sector for the expertise and funding needed to build new infrastructure. Governments were advised to facilitate innovation and competition, even when that meant ending government-owned or -sanctioned monopolies in telecommunications. The concepts of universal service, open access, privacy, and the need for secure communications were widely embraced. Similarly, the need to protect intellectual property rights was given a high priority.

However, few policy documents of this era actually mentioned the Internet, which had remained largely a communications tool used by research scientists, academics, and selected government officials. However, the development of the World Wide Web and web browser software thrust the Internet into the public limelight, and the newly commercial Internet began a period of explosive growth. In a 1994 report, a study committee of the National Research Council's Computer Science and Telecommunications Board stated,

> ... the NII will be a transformation and extension of today's computing and communications infrastructure (including, for example, the Internet, telephone, cable, cellular, data, and broadcast networks). Trends in each of these component areas are already bringing about a next-generation information infrastructure. Yet the outcome of these trends is far from certain; the nature of the NII that will develop is malleable. Choices will be made in industry and government, beginning with investments in the underlying physical infrastructure (National Research Council, 1994, p.2).

By the end of the decade, the outcome was much clearer. By 1998, the World Wide Web had grown from 3,000 sites in 1994 to more than 2.5 million sites, and the number of Internet users had swelled from 30 million to 134 million worldwide (Steinert-Threlkeld, 1998). Digital technology had erased the boundaries that once divided communication networks and the logic behind deploying separate systems to carry telephone conversations, computer data, cable television, and broadcast television signals. New communications networks today are almost exclusively digital, and existing analog (non-digital) networks are being rebuilt to digital standards as rapidly as possible. More importantly,

> ... the use of Net technologies has removed all doubt as to what basic communications protocols will be used to tie together the

rapidly increasing multitudes of computer systems and networks around the world. The Internet protocols are now the lingua franca of interconnected computing. The only question remains: Will Internet Protocol (IP) become the lingua franca of all electronic communications? (Steinert-Threlkeld, 1998, p. 6)

A 1999 analysis by London-based Ovum, Ltd., asserts that the answer is clear. "By 2005, the argument will be over. Packet-switched carriage will be the basis of most communications networks, both for the telcos and for large enterprises" (Sweet, 1999).

These Networks Are Always under Construction

The United States is home to the most extensive and sophisticated communications infrastructure in the world, and U.S. telecommunications firms are significant players globally. In this country the major owners, operators, and builders of communications infrastructure are the telephone and cable television industries. Once entirely separate, with different business models and different technologies, the wire-line telephone and cable industries are converging into competing information utilities providing telephony, multimedia content, Internet access, and other services. Other significant industries involved in communications/Internet infrastructure are the wireless telephone companies and the Internet backbone network service providers. Smaller scale players likely to become more important in the future include the broadcast television and direct broadcast satellite (DBS) industries and electric utilities. Of course, the hardware and software developments of the computer industry add important components of communications infrastructure.

At present, the next-generation information infrastructure is a mixture of circuit-switched, packet-switched, and hybrid networks. However packet-switched networks are increasing both in number and in share of the world's information infrastructure for two reasons. The Internet has demonstrated the superior efficiency of packet-switched networks, and the growth of the Internet has caused the volume of data traffic to increase 10 times faster than the volume of voice traffic. Circuit switching presently enables greater reliability and higher quality connections for voice. However, the circuit-switched network cannot "scale" or adapt to the explosive growth networks are experiencing (Moore, Johnson, and Kippola, 1999). Firms that build and operate local exchange facilities are expected to see continued strong demand for narrowband services (e.g., e-mail and WWW text/graphics) in the underdeveloped Asia/Pacific markets, the Middle East, and Africa well into the next decade. However, between 2000 and 2005, broadband services will dominate new infrastructure construction in North America, Europe, and Japan (Ovum, Ltd., 1999).

▶ Incumbent Local Exchange Carriers

For the majority of households and businesses, connecting to the communications infrastructure for any purpose means doing business with the local wire-line telephone company. This industry is dominated by the incumbent local exchange carriers (ILECs), particularly the Regional Bell Operating Companies (RBOCs), firms which once enjoyed monopoly status in their markets.[1] Competition, although encouraged by federal policy since the Telecommunications Act of 1996, is limited. The local telephone companies own the "last mile" of the physical connection between customers and communication networks. Unless a would-be competitor has the means to build a duplicate local network, at an estimated cost of $3,000 to $5,000 per home or business, the firm has no choice but to lease lines from the incumbents, usually at unfavorable rates (Ziegler, 1998).

While local telephone companies enjoy the advantage of connecting almost everyone to the public, switched telephone network, most still employ circuit-switched, voice-grade analog technology using twisted-pair copper wire for the physical connection in the local loop. While this technology enables excellent two-way voice communication, it must be upgraded to digital standards in order to provide new information services like high-speed Internet access and video, at a cost of $800 to $1,500 per subscriber line (Takahashi, 1998).

---

[1] In 1984, the local Bell system, operated by AT&T, was separated into seven Regional Bell Operating Companies (RBOCs), which together with GTE, dominated the local exchange market in the United States. Through a series of mergers, including the pending acquisition of GTE by Bell Atlantic and the recently approved combination of Ameritech with SBC Communications, there are now four RBOCs: Bell Atlantic, SBC Communications, Bell South, and US West.

So far, the incentives to upgrade have been limited. The ILECs' public, switched network represents a $250 billion investment. A suite of digital subscriber line (DSL) technologies is available that would enable digital data to flow at high speeds over copper wire for around $60 per month (Steinert-Threlkeld, 1998; Yankee Group, 1998). However, this technology would undercut the revenue the ILECs derive from the more expensive ISDN data service marketed to small businesses, and dedicated T-1 (1.5 Mbs) lines commanding $300 to $400 per month from larger institutions (O'Keefe, 1998b; Steinert-Threlkeld, 1998). In addition, DSL service allows normal phone service while users are connected to the Internet, potentially reducing the demand for second phone lines. While DSL service can utilize copper wire connections, the technology can only be deployed within an approximate three-mile radius of a phone company's local switch. The Yankee Group (1998) estimates that this limits DSL service to 70 percent of U.S. households. As a result, DSL technology has generally been offered to residential customers only in markets where cable modem access (a competing technology) to the Internet is available (O'Keefe, 1998b). Incumbent local exchange carriers (ILECs) face growing challenges from cable television, wireless telephone companies, and a new group of telephone companies called competitive local exchange carriers (CLECs).

Cable Television Companies

Cable television systems connect to 67 percent of U.S. households, and "pass" nearly 97 percent. Unlike local telephone companies which serve large geographic areas, the U.S. cable television marketplace is subdivided among more than 10,000 franchises, each serving widely varying numbers of subscribers (National Cable Television Association, 1998). Cable television systems were designed to provide one-way signals from the franchise head-end to the customer's location. Cable systems are being upgraded to two-way hybrid fiber/coax (HFC) connections to provide telephone service and high-speed Internet access in competition with local telephone companies. The cost of this overhaul is less per household than the comparable expense of upgrading telephone circuits to compete as information utilities (Takahashi, 1998). Cable modem Internet access is faster than DSL technology and slightly less expensive (about $40 per month) after installation. However, at the point where cable networks extend into neighborhoods, online homes "share" access lines. Access speeds can diminish as the number of online households sharing the same line increases.

Early leaders in providing cable telephony include Cox Communications, Time-Warner, and MediaOne. Cable firms have a strong ally in their telephony plans in the form of AT&T, the dominant long distance (or interexchange) carrier. In order to bypass the ILECs' local loops and avoid payment of access fees (compensation to local phone companies for their part in completing long distance calls), AT&T purchased Tele-Communications Inc. (TCI), the nation's largest cable multiple system operator, in 1998. AT&T plans to provide local telephone service in direct competition with the ILECs. At the time of its acquisition, TCI's cables passed nearly one-third of all U.S. households (Schiesel, 1998). AT&T is expected to partner with other cable firms (e.g., TCI and Time-Warner) to increase its ability to capture market share from the ILECs.

▸ Competitive Local Exchange Carriers

Digital technology, deregulation and privatization, and the lure of the $100 billion domestic ($600 billion global) telecommunications market (1998 figures) have attracted new entrants to the local exchange carrier industry. Telecommunications analysts see many long-term benefits for competitive local exchange carriers (CLECs). Their networks rely on state-of-the-art IP technology and optical fiber, technologies the ILECs will be installing for years, perhaps decades (Perrin, 1998).

Competitive local exchange carriers (CLECs) generated revenues of $3.7 billion in 1997, a 60 percent increase over 1996 (Perrin, 1998). The best known firm in this volatile market segment, MCI WorldCom, provides local telephone service in over 100 U.S. markets in addition to its long distance business. Because they are new, the CLECs are free to pursue markets opportunistically, and they typically target businesses (the traditional cash cows of the ILECs) in high-tech markets and larger cities where faster return on investment can be found. While the CLECs enjoy many advantages in the short term, their enormous financial resources, brand identity, and local loop control afford the ILECs a degree of long-term security. No one expects the ILECs to be replaced by CLECs, although a few firms like MCI WorldCom may achieve a degree of parity. But the dominance of data over voice traffic and the dominance of IP technologies, particularly voice-over-IP and further integration of the WWW with telephone services, will drive future developments (The IP Influence, 1999).

▶ Wireless Telephone Companies

Terrestrial wireless telephone services are provided by a mix of cellular telephone companies (providing analog and digital service) and digital PCS (personal communications services) providers. (Personal communications services utilize a technology similar to that of cellular telephony, but operate at a higher frequency.) Markets in the United States are served by up to two cellular providers (one is usually the local ILEC) and up to six PCS competitors. Growth in numbers of subscribers, numbers of competitors, and minutes of use by subscribers has encouraged competition, leading to reductions in cost of service to consumers (O'Keefe, 1998a). Problems of high roaming charges (charges for using a wireless phone outside of a provider's local service area) are being resolved by such major players as Sprint, AT&T, and Bell Atlantic through provision of national wireless service at flat rates for all calls.

Even though wireless telephone service is seen as another way around the local telephone companies' "last mile" bottleneck, market share in the United States trails wire-line telephony by a wide margin. However, wireless has been a great success in the rest of the world (Sandberg, 1998). American firms, including RBOCs, have been major players in building wireless telephone systems in countries with inadequate or antiquated wire-line systems. In such nations wireless technology represents a cost-effective way to bypass or to upgrade the communications infrastructure quickly. As a result, the average European wireless user averages twice as many monthly minutes of use as his American counterpart (Sandberg, 1998). Wireless telephone subscribers are predicted to number 530 million by 2001 (Potter, 1999).

The wireless industry is working to develop cost-effective technologies for connecting wireless devices to the Internet. Wireless phones, handheld palm-top computers, and personal data assistants (PDAs) are being equipped with paging, fax, and e-mail capabilities. In perhaps the boldest, and certainly the most expensive ventures, several firms have launched mobile satellite services (MSS) which rely on low, medium, and geostationary earth-orbiting communications satellites to provide telephone and data services to any spot on the face of the earth. Firms like Iridium and Constellation plan to offer mainly narrowband telephone-related services (Spiegel, 1998). However, Teledesic plans to cover the globe with 288 satellites providing high-speed, broadband services using laser signals (Mack, 1998). Mobile satellite services (MSS) are clearly targeted at business and professional customers with the need for (expensive) communications anywhere on earth. However, the same technology can also be used to provide basic telephony throughout a country or region beset with infrastructure problems. While economics will determine the feasibility of MSS as an infrastructure "solution," politics will affect the viability of MSS as a global service. Mobile satellite services (MSS) operators must acquire a license to operate in each country in which they hope to offer service (Nourouzi, 1998).

▶ Internet Backbone Services

Backbone services provide long-haul broadband circuits that transfer data at speeds ranging from 155 Mbs to 2.4 Gbs (Wayner, 1998). Myriad lower capacity networks connect to the major backbone providers to form the global Internet. For the Internet to work, the large backbone services must exchange data with each other rather than operate independently. The major backbone players (e.g., MCI WorldCom, Sprint, GTE, and PSINet) maintain "peering" agreements whereby they will exchange data with each other ("peers") at no cost. All other (non-peer) networks connecting to the major backbone services pay interconnection fees (How the Internet Works, 1998). The backbone business sector is volatile. Demand for backbone services has been increasing at a rate of 1,000 percent per year, attracting a number of new, smaller backbone service providers and encouraging consolidation within the industry. Worldwide, combined residential bandwidth is expected to increase from 84 billion bits per second to 9 trillion bits per second (Ovum Predicts, 1999).

While the larger Internet backbone services are located in the United States, most are multinational firms. The largest, MCI WorldCom, operates a backbone subsidiary, UUNet, with local operations in Canada and nine European countries in addition to the United States. The UUNet backbone connects to Canada, Europe, and the Asia/Pacific region. Because of the importance of these networks to the Internet, the business relationships between the large backbone service providers and all that wish to connect to their networks are subject to the scrutiny of regulators in the United States and the other nations in which they do business (UUNet, 1999).

The Shape of the Global Internet

If the value of the network increases exponentially with the number of users, then the potential global value of the Internet remains limited by its inaccessibility in many parts of the world. The information infrastructure initiatives of the mid-1990s admonished governments to liberalize and privatize telecommunication industries, opening many markets to competition from domestic and foreign firms. Thus far, the result has been a socially and economically stratified infrastructure that both creates and perpetuates a world of Internet haves and have-nots. In comparison to the rest of the world, the United States is an Internet paradise. Scandinavia, Western Europe, and Japan are well connected, but beyond these areas the availability of the Internet is limited by infrastructure problems; regulatory policies; and the combined effects of low incomes, low levels of literacy, and high cost of access.

For many nations, the scope and scale of infrastructure development require expertise and capital beyond that which domestic resources can provide. The practical solution to this problem has been to open national markets to the transnational North American, European, and Japanese firms which dominate the information technology industries. This strategy seems to work best for better-developed nations, though. Internet infrastructure, like all information technologies, is attracted first to the largest concentrations of potential revenue. Therefore, firms quite sensibly invest in projects that maximize their return on investment.

According to 1996 data from the International Telecommunications Union (ITU), of 220 ITU member nations, only 25 had a teledensity (the number of telephone lines per 100 persons) above 50, while 43 remained below 1.0, and nearly half of the world's households could not afford telephone service. It takes an average of 50 years for a nation's teledensity to increase from a value of 1.0 to 50, although policy initiatives and technology options can speed progress (ITU, 1998). However, even if this time frame is halved (or better), many nations will still have limited access to basic telephone services, let alone the Internet, well into the next century.

One gauge of Internet infrastructure is the worldwide distribution of online users. Table 11.1 shows the dominance of North America, Europe, and the Asia/Pacific region. Worldwide Internet access is projected to quadruple by 2005, with the largest increases in the regions which already have the most people online: North America, Western Europe, and Japan. Until 2000, demand for increased Internet bandwidth will be strongest among business users of the Internet. After 2000, the infrastructure should be in place to meet the pent-up bandwidth demands of the residential market (Bieler and Stevenson, 1998).

▶ Europe

Continued growth in Internet use is expected in Europe, and by 2005 this region will have more residential Internet users than North America (Bieler and Stevenson, 1998). The primary national telecommunications providers remain the dominant source of Internet access in Europe. How-

Table 11.1.   Estimated Internet users worldwide.

World	159.00 million
Africa	1.14 million
Asia/Pacific	26.97 million
Europe	37.15 million
Middle East	0.88 million
North America	88.33 million
South America	4.63 million

Source: NUA, (April 15, 1999).

ever, U.S. firms are acquiring business and consumer ISPs as European Internet use continues to grow (Price, 1998). Although competition is growing, the cost of access varies widely across the region, with the lowest prices in the Scandinavian countries and the highest in the United Kingdom. In addition, most Internet users must also pay for access time by the minute, a condition which caused Internet users in France to boycott France Telecom in December 1998 to protest the high cost of Internet access (Essick, 1999). In France, with 4 million Internet users at the beginning of 1999, over 15 million citizens use Minitel, a text-only service profitably operated by France Telecom for the past 16 years. Improving Internet infrastructure exposes France Telecom not only to the expense of upgrading infrastructure but also to reduced revenues as Minitels' profitable online commerce migrates to the WWW (Jones, 1998).

Under the guidance of the European Union, national initiatives have increased competition in communications industries throughout the region. Major U.S. telecommunications firms are actively involved with European partners in infrastructure projects. Provision of telephony services and Internet access by cable television firms and the widespread availability of wireless services suggest that opportunity exists for increased competition with wireline services for Internet business.

▶ Asia/Pacific

Aside from Japan's well-established infrastructure and a few pockets of modernity like Singapore and Australia, most of the populous Asia/Pacific region represents an enormous growth potential fraught with great expense and political difficulties. Japan is expected to remain the largest Asian Internet user country through 2005 (Bieler and Stevenson, 1998). In terms of potential for infrastructure growth, less than 1 percent of the citizens of China and India, with the largest populations in the world, are online. The Chinese government seems intent on increasing Internet access, particularly to support education, but fears exist that the People's Republic will operate a gigantic Chinese intranet with limited access to the rest of the global Internet (Ramo and Flor-Cruz, 1998). India eliminated the government monopoly on providing Internet service in late 1998, and expects rapid growth in the number of national and regional ISPs, increased PC availability, and an increase in Internet software in local languages (Rao, 1999).

▶ Africa

The African continent remains the least-connected region and faces the most severe infrastructure, political, and economic challenges in joining the rest of the online world. At the end of 1997, Africa averaged less than one Internet user per 5,000 people, compared to one in 40 in Europe and one in six in the United States (Jensen, 1998). Basic telephone service is expensive, with waiting periods of up to two years for installation. Access to the Internet, where available, can cost as much as $10 per hour, and connection speeds are very low. The combined expense of a PC, phone service, and access puts the Internet beyond the reach of the majority of Africans. Because bandwidth is so limited on this continent, e-mail has emerged as the most successful Internet application, and a growing number of e-mail centers in larger towns enable those without personal access to utilize this important Internet function (Spangler, 1998).

Almost 90 percent of Africa's 1.14 million Internet users reside in South Africa, where economic conditions and infrastructure are better. However, South Africans, like their online counterparts in many areas outside the United States, must pay the local telephone service provider an average of $1.60 per hour to connect (Spangler, 1998).

▶ Latin America

Internet access and the number of citizens online is still limited in Latin America, but except for periods of economic uncertainty, it has been one of the fastest growing regions (Ellison, 1996). The largest population of Internet users is found in Brazil, the country with the most competitive ISP sector (Barrett, 1998b). Throughout Central and South America 90 percent of those online are from upper-middle- to high-income households. These population strata follow U.S. and European consumption trends (including Internet commerce) very closely. However, high access costs limit the online time of Latin American Internet users, further increasing consumer interest in alternatives to wire-line services (Ellison, 1996).

The Future Internet: What Will It Be; What Will We Call It?

Globally, demand for increased bandwidth is a major factor in Internet growth. Even in the bandwidth-rich United States, new Internet applications (like streaming media) continue to increase bandwidth demand. Forrester Research expects 15.6 million U.S. households will acquire broadband access by 2002 (MacKenzie, Clemmer, and Morrisette, 1998). As the rest of the world closes the "Internet gap" with the United States, worldwide need for increased bandwidth and speed will become critical. Transoceanic optical fiber and satellite links can meet some of these needs, but further improvements in the technology of the Internet itself are needed. In addition to alleviating Internet congestion, other needs identified for the Internet include improvements in end-to-end security, quality of service, and intellectual property protection (National Research Council, 1996).

The commercial Internet emerged from the collaboration of U.S. universities and the National Science Foundation (NFS) between 1986 and 1994. In 1995, after the Internet had entered the public arena, the NSF funded a very-high-speed backbone network service (vBNS) linking university research centers. The vBNS connects 46 universities and is operated by MCI WorldCom at 622 Mbs. In 1996 a project called Internet 2 was initiated by the University Corporation for Advanced Internet Development (UCAID), a corporate and university consortium established to develop new networked applications for distance learning, multimedia, and collaborative research (Barrett, 1998a). The 10 billion bps Abilene network of Internet 2 was built by Qwest Communications International, Inc.; Cisco Systems, Inc.; and Nortel Telecom, Ltd. and began operating in February 1999. Like the vBNS, Internet 2 will operate apart from the larger Internet, as an experimental system. While private sector Internet backbone engineers are skeptical of Internet 2's potential, others expect that Internet 2 research will foster valuable developments that will transfer to the Internet at large (Barrett, 1998a). One expectation is that Internet 2 research will lead to technologies that facilitate provision of different classes of service based on time critical need (e.g., urgent medical data) and different rate structures (Itoi, 1998).

Certainly the infrastructure will become more complex and widely distributed. Both television and telephone devices are predicted to blend their capabilities with those of the Internet. Digital broadcast television is yet another network technology expected to add or shift to IP technology. At the same time, a host of new devices are being integrated with the Internet. Palmtop computers and handheld PDAs, vehicles, traffic control signals, heating and air conditioning systems, security systems, and even household appliances are being linked to the Internet by researchers and firms eager to find new applications with commercial potential.

Considering the extensive and widespread investment in an improved global information infrastructure, of which the Internet is only a part, it is difficult to predict the future of the Internet beyond a handful of years. Dizard (1997) calls the Internet "a paradigm" for the "Meganet," his term for the developing global network infrastructure (p. 192). Cairncross (1997) describes the Internet as "a prototype and a testing ground for the future of communications" (p. 12). The National Research Council (1996) concluded that an evolved national information infrastructure must include "high data rates to the end point, adequate bandwidth in both directions, multiple session capability, continuous availability of service, real-time and multimedia access, nomadicity, and security" (p. 55). But no one knows if the services will be provided by an evolved public Internet or by some other group of networks. The safest protection of the future is that all forms of digital data, from voice to video, will travel over a set of IP networks at different speeds and levels of reliability. Cost of service will vary with its quality, requiring users to make price/value judgments about the services they will use.

> Today all Internet traffic is equal. There are no Ferraris or banged-up old Fords; every data packet travels at the same unpredictable speed. The next generation of networking equipment promises priority speedways for those willing to pay for premium services (Heading for the Speedway, 1998, paragraph 5).

Analysis

Several broad themes related to the issues of Internet infrastructure have emerged. The most significant social issue is that of access to the Internet. Access remains unequally divided among the nations of the world and among socio-economic strata within nations. This seems unlikely to change in the near future as marketplace forces dictate the provision of basic infrastructure in underdeveloped nations, as well as the availability of modern enhancements in the United States and other developed regions. While most of the world's population has no viable access to the Internet, conditions in places like the United States approach that of "networked lives." Work is increasingly done online (where it is monitored), wireless information devices keep people connected to the workplace and to others, and household devices monitor everything from utility use to the consumption of food, household, and personal products. In many parts of the world serious concerns exist regarding Internet content: the ideas and forms of expression that access enables users to reach. This is an issue with both social and political dimensions.

In terms of political issues, governments and world organizations are active collaborators with the private sector (particularly from developed nations) in the development of Internet infrastructure. While governments claim to act on behalf of the quality of life improvements that infrastructure offers their citizens, a higher priority motivation invariably seems to be a nation's stake in the global economy, the benefits of which are often shared unequally. A communications infrastructure capable of supporting the Internet is the cost of entering the electronic global economy sweepstakes. In the interest of advanced communications, countries have abandoned long-standing national communications policies to liberalize their markets, increase domestic and foreign investment in communications infrastructure, and foster the eventual benefits of competition.

The driving force behind Internet/communications infrastructure development is economics. Nations and firms seek to better (or secure) their positions in the global economy. On a smaller scale, the same electronic connections that power global business energize the actions of firms in national economies. There exists a huge potential market for the construction of advanced communications infrastructures of all types, and firms capable of building such facilities compete globally for projects ranging from new systems in developing nations to infrastructure rebuilding and deployment of new technologies in developed nations. In the most highly developed markets, firms are developing multiple network structures designed to provide perceived value to different classes of customers at variable rates. As communication markets grow they usually become more dynamic. The competition in the United States for providing integrated (telephone, video, Internet access) services to business and residential customers is an example. The ILECs seek to protect their dominant position, but are forced to compete when other firms encroach on their decades-old "turf." Consumers benefit in competitive markets, but market growth and competitive pressures often lead to consolidation, which shifts economic power from consumers to firms as fewer players in an industry can more effectively create economic barriers to entry by potential new competitors.

Against this broad overview of the social, political, and economic dimensions of issues associated with Internet infrastructure, the following analysis examines these issues at the individual, group, national, and global levels.

▶ The Individual Level

Access to the Internet depends on who you are and where you live. Most of the world's inhabitants have no access at all, and where the Internet is available, the quality of access varies. Socioeconomic status is a strong determinant of access, especially in developing nations. Until simpler access devices proliferate, one must have the economic means to afford and the education or training needed to operate a personal computer as well as the ability to pay for Internet access. Efforts by governments to accelerate the provision of widespread Internet access to their citizens are consistently tempered by two economic realities. First, it is usually prudent to provide access to urban areas first (the greatest good for the greatest number). In addition, connecting businesses and government agencies before citizens is viewed as a way to stimulate the economic growth that may be necessary to fund the provision of access to other citizens, especially in remote areas. In many parts of the developing world individuals may not have personal Internet access in their homes for many years. Until that time, individuals will have to rely upon access in the workplace and in centrally located public (e.g., libraries and schools) and private facilities (e.g., Internet cafes).

Regardless of location, once basic access is established, individuals tend to increase their reliance upon the Internet as their experience with the technology increases and the infrastructure itself improves. In the United States, a higher level of Internet use is related to an increased desire for faster access speeds; faster access speeds enable users to stay connected for longer periods of time. As a result, the reliance upon the Internet in the home begins to emulate that found in the workplace where many employees are connected all the time. As more and more work is done online, individual performance is increasingly subject to monitoring, and Internet technology enables worker access from almost any place at any hour of the day. Improved Internet access, then, provides employers valuable tools for maximizing the productivity of human resources, but at the expense of personal independence and individual privacy. The same perceived loss of privacy may be a factor in the ultimate success of online technologies intended to monitor our homes and certain aspects of our at-home behaviors.

Another important set of issues to consider relates to how increased amounts of time spent online will affect interpersonal interaction among individuals.

The Group Level

When considering issues of Internet infrastructure, three sets of interacting groups are relevant: consumers, institutional Internet users, and infrastructure providers. The activities and motives of the infrastructure providers have been examined earlier in this chapter. Therefore, this analysis will concentrate on user groups. Groups can be examined on the basis of how they use the Internet and how their usage patterns will change with the acquisition of advanced infrastructure. It is also important to consider the interaction and interrelationships among groups, particularly in terms of political and economic power.

Consumer groups can be defined along a number of overlapping dimensions (e.g., by their demographic characteristics, as markets or market segments, and by the range of interests they pursue online. For consumers, the same issues of access discussed in the preceding section apply. Compared to individuals, however, groups of Internet users have more influence in the online world. For example, groups of concerned citizens play a role in the ongoing efforts to develop policies designed to protect children from inappropriate web content. In addition to influencing policy-makers, the same groups represent a market for computer software designed to screen or filter web sites. Consumers also have a role to play in shaping their countries' telecommunications policies and infrastructure. While the boycott by French Internet users may seem extreme, it made the point that governments should consider the needs and desires of their online citizenry. As a group, Internet users who desire enhanced access technologies represent more than a market. The expectations of this group will speed the deployment of high-speed access technologies as competing infrastructure providers race to build their market shares.

While there are many institutional uses of the Internet, the major institutional groups considered here are businesses, educational institutions (including libraries), and governments. As noted, the infrastructure needs of the business community (worldwide) constitute the major driving force in the delivery of basic and enhanced Internet infrastructure. In addition, infrastructure innovations developed for the business community eventually become available at the consumer level. Firms use the Internet for every conceivable form of internal and external business communication and, increasingly, as a means to exchange information and conduct retail transactions with consumers. Perhaps as the importance of electronic commerce grows, businesses should become more concerned about the quality of Internet infrastructure available at the consumer level.

Going back to the earliest pronouncements about the information superhighway, the Internet has been touted for its educational potential. Governments at the national, state, and local levels have made extensive efforts, often with private sector support, to make Internet access commonplace in educational institutions. Some colleges and universities require entering students to own personal computers and make Internet use an integral part of most courses. Similar programs can even be found at the elementary school level, but it is more common for schools (and for public and private libraries) to provide shared Internet access in labs equipped with multiple PCs. With some prodding from federal and state governments, ISPs often provide free or low-cost access to schools and libraries. As new Internet access technologies (e.g., cable modems or DSL) are introduced, competitors can both demonstrate their services and gain public relations value by connecting local schools.

Because public educational institutions are operated by governmental entities, the online needs of schools and libraries likely benefit from the early recognition by governments at all levels of the Internet's value as an information resource. As Aikat has demonstrated in Chapter 2 of this book, governments make extensive use of the Internet as a means of disseminating information to the public. Lofty Internet-inspired political rhetoric aside, the marketplace economics that increasingly drive web developments could work to the disadvantage of financially strapped educational institutions.

▶ The National Level

This chapter has identified a number of important issues of Internet infrastructure that the nations of the world are addressing. Belief in the importance of the Internet as a link to the global economy and as a means of delivering educational and social benefits to citizens is almost universal. But in many countries achieving Internet-related goals is complicated by factors of economics, education, politics, religion, and culture.

In order to gain a foothold in the global electronic economy, some developing nations have established corridors or centers of advanced information technologies and have provided many incentives for transnational corporations (TNCs) to locate within these centers. Sussman and Lent (1998) provide a critical analysis of these practices.

> Pursuing the logic of a singular, integrated, and telecommunications-linked world economic system, TNC's and their state allies have mobilized workers into a low-wage, segmented, and flexible global production force, made up of men and women who for the most part will never have the purchasing power to enjoy the goods and services created with their own labor (p. 2).

In order for the benefits of Internet (or any communications) infrastructure to extend to the people of a country, citizens must first be educated in the use of the technology. In many countries the "field of dreams" approach ("If you build it, they will come.") to infrastructure building common in the United States and Europe is inappropriate. While infrastructure providers actively seek access to markets in developed nations and in selected developing nations like India and China, they are not attracted to educationally and economically disadvantaged developing nations. Nations striving to improve low levels of education and literacy through the use of the Internet will have to rely upon available national resources and international aid to develop Internet infrastructure and education simultaneously. At some point, a critical mass of Internet infrastructure and educators trained in its use must be achieved before these countries can begin to achieve a degree of parity with the rest of the online world.

Governments have been convinced to liberalize and privatize their telecommunications systems in the belief that the competition such actions stimulate will be beneficial to both the national economy and the citizenry. It is reasonable to assume that those countries with the most advanced communications systems are most likely to have an experienced communications policy-making apparatus and well-developed policies that are consistent with other concerns. However, some nations may be as lacking in communications policy-making experience as they are in communications infrastructure. Governments in developing countries that are attractive to foreign Internet infrastructure providers must evaluate carefully the plans of these firms and the economic concessions they seek in the context of carefully developed national policies.

The content of the Internet represents another major area of national concern. Because the Internet developed in the United States, English is the standard language of the World Wide Web. At present, 56.3 percent of the online population are native speakers of the English language (Euro-Marketing Associates, 1998). While other languages are expected to become more common on the Internet, the dominance of the English language remains a concern. While a common language facilitates global communication, use of one language as a standard changes other languages and their uses. Quite possibly language translation software may lessen the dominance of the English language online, but many observers expect that most Internet users will need basic English language literacy in addition to their native tongue (The Coming Global Tongue, 1996).

For many nations the diversity of ideas and forms of expressions found on the Web represent a threat to national cultures and to religious and political philosophies. Nations as different as the People's Republic of China and Saudi Arabia have attempted to filter or screen citizens' access to the World Wide

Web (Ramo and FlorCruz, 1998; A Fly in the Web, 1998). Conservative Muslim clerics and the military in Sudan campaigned to disconnect the country from the corrupting influences of the Internet (Bald, 1998). Even in the United States, efforts continue to find reasonable ways to protect children from inappropriate web content and to mitigate the effects of sites that promote hate or intolerance. The organization Human Rights Watch claimed that Internet censorship increased in 1998 (Mendels, 1998). However, the massive size of the Internet makes the screening of all web sites nearly impossible. In addition the Internet's decentralized structure and open architecture provide many means of access to those determined to go online.

The Global Level

In reality, the global information infrastructure (GII) is nothing more than the sum of the world's national information infrastructures. Hence, it is exceptionally uneven in its physical distribution and in the availability of its benefits. The information technology that supports the global economy circumnavigates the earth, but it bypasses some nations that will have to solve infrastructure-related problems at the national level before they will be able to become global players. Organizations like the International Telecommunications Union and the World Trade Organization play an important role in representing the interests of Information Age have-nots in a world dominated by the information haves.

Cairncross (1997) projects an optimistic view of a not-distant future world in which communications infrastructure is more evenly distributed.

> Where countries and their citizens communicate freely, they will surely be less likely to fight one another. Individuals everywhere will know more about the ideas and aspirations of human beings in every other part of the world, thus strengthening the ties that bind us all together (p. 26).

While history suggests otherwise, if this outcome of the Internet and other communications technologies does come to pass, it will be the greatest achievement of the Information Age.

References

Bald, M. 1998, May. Internet Pollution. *World Press Review*, 45(5): 22. Retrieved December 28, 1998, from the online database *Academic Search FullTEXT Elite* [EBSCO Industries, Inc.].

Barrett, R. 1998a, May 4. Internet 2: Can the Commercial Net Benefit? *Inter@ctive Week*. [6 pages].[Online] Retrieved from *http://www.zdnet.com/intweek/stories/news/ 0,4164,313683,00.html*

Barrett, R. 1998b, November 30. Off the Beaten Track: Unexpected Net Hot Spots. *Inter@ctive Week*. 5:44.

Bieler, D., and Stevenson, I. 1998, November. White Paper – Internet Market Forecasts Global Internet Growth 1998–2005. Ovum. [6 pages].[Online] Retrieved February 28, 1999, from *http://www.ovum.com/Ovum/news/net3wp.htm*

Cairncross, F. 1997. *The Death of Distance: How the Communications Revolution Will Change Our Lives*. Boston: Harvard Business School Press.

The Coming Global Tongue. 1996, December 21. *Economist*, 341(7997): 75–8. Retrieved December 28, 1996, from the online database *Academic Search FullTEXT Elite* [EBSCO Industries, Inc.].

Dizard, W.P. 1997. *Meganet: How the Global Communications Network Will Connect Everyone on Earth*. Boulder, CO: Westview Press.

Ellison, K. 1996, December 2. Love Affair with the Internet. *Miami Herald*. [4 pages]. [Online] Retrieved from *http://www.herald.com/business/archive/tech/docs/internet.htm#TOP*

Essick, K. 1999, January 13. French Netizens Plan Second Web Boycott. *The Industry Standard*. [15 paragraphs]. [Online] Retrieved from *http://www.thestandard.com/articles/display/ 0,1449,3129,00.html?home.bf*

Euro-Marketing Associates. 1998, December 24. Global Internet Statistics (by Language). [4 pages] [Online] Retrieved from *http://www.euromktg.com/globstats/index.html*

European Union. 1994. *Europe and Global Information Society: Recommendations to the European Council*. Brussels: European Union.

A Fly in the Web. 1998, October 17. *Economist*, 349(8090): 50–51. Retrieved December 28, 1998, from the online database *Academic Search FullTEXT Elite* [EBSCO Industries, Inc.].

Heading for the Speedway: Internet Traffic Will Soon Be Able to Travel at Different Speeds. 1998, June 3. *Financial Times* [20 paragraphs]. [Online] Retrieved December 30, 1998, from online database *FT.Com Global Archive* [Financial Times, Ltd.].

How the Internet Works. 1998, July 20. *Business Week*, pp. 58–61. Retrieved February 25, 1999, from online database *Academic Search FullTEXT Elite* [EBSCO Industries, Inc.].

International Telecommunications Union. 1998, March. World Telecommunication Development Report 1998: Universal Access Executive Summary. Geneva: ITU.

The IP Influence. 1999, January–April. *Ovum Update*, 5:6–7.

Itoi, N.G. 1998, June 22. An Express Lane? *Industry Week*, 247:48–51.

Jensen, M. 1998, December. Africa Internet Status. *Association for Progressive Communications*. [No pagination] [Online] Retrieved from *http://www3.sn.apc.org/africa/afstat.htm*

Jones, K. 1998, November 30. The French Evolution Comes to the Web—Slowly. *Inter@ctive Week*, 5:25.

Leiner, B.M.; Cerf, V.G.; Clark, D.D.; Kahn, R.E.; Klienrock, L.; Lynch, D.C.; Postel, J.; Roberts, L.G.; and Wolff, S. 1998. A Brief History of the Internet. [17 pages] [Online] Retrieved February 20, 1999, from *http://www.isoc.org/Internet-history/brief.html*

Mack, T. 1998, November 30. The Skies Get Crowded. *Forbes*, 162 (12) 152–53.

MacKenzie, M.; Clemmer, K.; and Morrisette, S. 1998, September 16. Forrester Research Brief: Consumers Are Ready for Broadband Technologies. [4 pages] [Online] Retrieved from *http://www.forrester.com/ER/Research/Brief/0,1317,3858,FF.html*

Mendels, P. 1998, December 18. Governments Expand Restrictions on Internet, Report Says. *New York Times On the Web*. [20 paragraphs] [Online] Retrieved from *http://www. nytimes.com/library/tech/98/12/cyber/cyberlaw/18law.html*

Moore, G.; Johnson, P.; and Kippola, T. 1999, February 22. The Next Network. *Forbes ASAP*, 163 (4) 93.

National Cable Television Association. 1998. Cable Industry Facts-at-a-Glance 1998. [1 page] [Online] Retrieved March 3, 1999 from *http://www.ncta.com/yearend98_6.html*

National Research Council. 1994. *Realizing the Information Future: The Internet and Beyond.* Washington DC: National Academy Press.

National Research Council. 1996. *The Unpredictable Certainty: Information Infrastructure through 2000.* Washington D.C.: National Academy Press.

Nourouzi, A. 1998. Mobile Satellite Services: The Global Mobile Telecoms Service. Ovum, Ltd. [6 pages] [Online] Retrieved February 28, 1999, from *http://www.ovum.com/ovum/news/ le2wp.htm*

NUA. 1999. How Many Online? NUA Internet Surveys. [No pagination] [Online] Retrieved April 15, 1999, from *http://www.nua.net/surveys/how_many_online/index.html*

O'Keefe, S. 1998a, November. The Wireless Boom. *Telecommunications,* [7 pages] [Online] Retrieved February 22, 1999, from *http://www.telecoms-mag.com/issues/199811/tcs/ okeefe.html*

O'Keefe, S. 1998b, December. While RBOCs Drag Their Heels, CLECs, ISP's Mean Business. *Telecommunications,* [3 pages] [Online] Retrieved February 22, 1999, from *http://www. telecoms-mag.com/issues/199812/tcs/okeefe.html*

Ovum, Ltd. 1999. The Future of the Local Loop—Markets and Strategies. [9 pages] [Online] Retrieved February 28, 1999, from *http://www.ovum.com/ovum/news/llewp.htm*

Ovum Predicts. 1999, January–April. *Ovum Update,* 5:3.

Perrin, T. 1998, September. The Market: Prospects, Problems, and Opportunities. *Telecommunications,* [5 pages] [Online] Retrieved February 22, 1999, from *http://www.telecoms-mag.com/issues/199809/tcs/perin.html*

Potter, R. 1999, February. Squeezing the Cellular Network. *Telecommunications,* [28 paragraphs] Retrieved from *http://www.telecoms-mag.com/issues/199902/tci/potter.html*

Price, C. 1998, November 18. U.S. Predators Target ISPs with a "Wall of Money." *Financial Times*. [21 paragraphs] [Online] Retrieved December 30, 1998, from the online database *FT.Com Global Archive* [Financial Times. Ltd.].

Ramo, J.C. and FlorCruz, J.A. 1998, May 11. China Gets Wired. *Time*, 151:52. Retrieved December 28, 1998, from online database *Academic Search FullTEXT in Elite* [EBSCO Industries, Inc.].

Rao, M. 1999, February 23. 72 ISP licenses Issued in India. *InternetNews.com*. [15 paragraphs] [Online] Retrieved from *http://www.internetnews.com/intl-news/article/0,1087,6_72521,00.html*

Sandberg, J. 1998, September 21. Quiet, Please. *The Wall Street Journal Interactive Edition*, [3 pages] [Online] Retrieved from *http://www.wsj.com/articles/SB905788181138060000.htm*

Schiesel, S. 1998, June 25. With Cable Deal, AT&T Makes Move to Regain Empire. *The New York Times*, p. A1

Spangler, T. 1998, November 30. Africa's Net Challenge: Overcoming Regulation, Poor Telecom Infrastructure. *Inter@ctive Week.*, 5:46.

Spiegel, P. 1998, October 19. Let the Big Boys Go First. *Forbes*, 162:68–69.

Steinert-Threlkeld, T. (1998, August 31). The Net: Not Just Data Anymore. *Inter@ctive Week*, 5:6–8.

Sussman, G. and Lent, J. A. 1998. Global Productions. In G.. Sussman and J.A. Lent, (eds., *Global Productions: Labor in the Making of the "Information Society."* Cresskill, NY: Hampton Press.

Sweet, S. 1999. IP: The Impact on Telco Services and Revenues. Ovum Ltd. [12 pages] [Online] Retrieved February 28, 1999, from *http://www.ovum.com/ovum/news/ipt2wp.htm*

Takahashi, D. 1998, September 21. The Cable Edge. *The Wall Street Journal Interactive Edition.* [3 pages] [Online] Retrieved from *http://www.wsj.com/articles/ SB905785870798015000.htm*

UUNet. 1999. Network FAQ. [2 pages] [Online] Retrieved February 21, 1999, from *http://www.uu.net/lang.en/network/faq.html*

Wayner, P. 1998, May 14. Net Metaphors Stretch to Fit the Evolution of Data Flow. *The New York Times,* p. G11.

Yankee Group. 1998, December. The Market and Marketing of Residential Broadband Internet Access. Internet Market Strategies Module, 4. [40 pages] [Online] Retrieved March 2, 1999, from *http://www.yankeegroup.com/imsv4n15/imsv4n15.htm*

Ziegler, B. 1998, September 21. Out of the Loop. *Wall Street Journal Interactive Edition,* [3 pages] [Online] Retrieved from *http://www.wsj.com/articles/SB905786937525126000.htm*

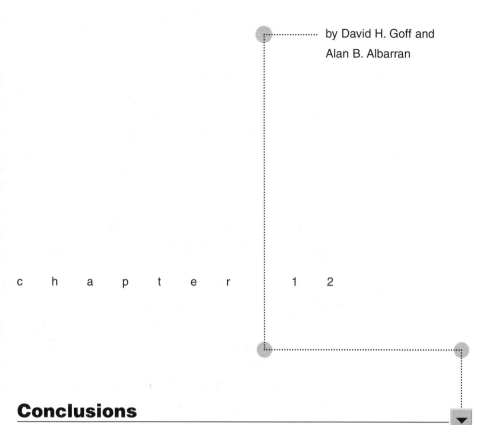

by David H. Goff and
Alan B. Albarran

c   h   a   p   t   e   r   1   2

Conclusions

When we began this project, we set out to provide one of the first comprehensive examinations of the social, political, and economic significance of the
Internet. Many of the early books about the Internet provided equal parts informed speculation and thoughtful analysis of expected developments. We
have enjoyed the advantage of surveying the Internet landscape from a higher
vantage point on the diffusion of innovation curve. During the roughly six
years since the World Wide Web ignited the Internet's explosive growth, a
number of trends have become well established. Clear patterns of online applications and uses, Internet adoption, and infrastructure deployment have
developed. The relationships between governments and the Internet, while
not uniform, can now be categorized in useful ways that foster understanding
and continued inquiry. Although many of the economic models applicable to
the Internet are largely unproven, the major economic applications (like e-
commerce and commercial media services) clearly have emerged.

Loading 267

The preceding 11 chapters have covered a set of topics that we consider to be among the most important to fostering an understanding of the impact of the Internet phenomenon. Our effort in this final chapter is to suggest how to build on the knowledge base assembled thus far. Therefore, we conclude this volume with our thoughts regarding five sets of issues or concerns that we believe warrant both continuing assessment and serious scholarly investigation.

We Need to Understand the Diversity and Interplay of the Needs and Expectations of Internet Users

When considering the Internet, one is reminded of the Indian fable of the blind men and the elephant. Several blind men encountered one of the great beasts and later, having approached and touched the creature, tried to describe it. The man who had touched the elephant's side said the animal was like a wall, but the one who touched the leg described the beast as similar to a tree. One felt the moving trunk and declared the elephant to be snake-like, while the man who grasped the tail disagreed, asserting that the elephant was more like a rope. Each man had experienced, interpreted, and understood the elephant from his own unique but limited perspective. So it is with the Internet.

Understanding the Web requires acquiring an appreciation for how a broad range of individual and institutional users understand and value this means of communication. We need to know a great deal more about what motivations and expectations determine both when and how people choose to participate in the online realm. To fail to attempt to understand the diverse behaviors of Internet users will lead to narrow-minded and myopic thinking, particularly if the most ambitious research efforts are limited to the service of online commercial activities. For example, advertising and media executives see in the Internet both logical extensions of traditional media and exciting new opportunities. But in the end, media businesses are still interested in attracting potential consumers with content and experiences and in being able to determine who has accessed the content and interacted with it. In the online media business, the end result of making a direct sale has also become a significant desired outcome. But the Internet represents far more than a new and improved extension of earlier media.

The majority of information available on the World Wide Web is not packaged as online media content in the traditional sense of the word. Personal web pages, educational materials, anticorporate "gripe sites," and information from government sources comprise major noncommercial elements of the personal and institutional content of the Web. Electronic mail, Internet chat, and the use of newsgroups represent the widely used and highly personal communication capabilities of the Internet. In a very real sense, every type of human activity and interest is represented on the Web, because this form of communication, like no other before it, reflects the diversity of its users.

The study of the Internet and of online behavior affords a tremendous opportunity for scholars from diverse academic fields to build a comprehensive body of knowledge. Academe has a long history of rather rigid compartmentalization of knowledge. The Internet is a powerful tool for discovering and accessing information from a wide variety of sources, allowing users to escape the intellectual confinement that accompanies discipline-specific thinking. Scholars should follow the lead of the Internet and discover the intellectual synergy that can result from truly interdisciplinary study of this communication phenomenon that influences so many areas of the human experience. If instead, the scholarly examination of the Internet proceeds on the parallel tracks of different disciplines, we will, like the ancient blind men, fail to "see" beyond our own experience and interest. As the 19th century American poet John Godfrey Saxe concluded in the moral to his version of "The Blind Men and the Elephant,"

> So oft in theologic wars,
>   The disputants, I ween,
> Rail on in utter ignorance
>   Of what each other mean,
> And prate about an Elephant
>   Not one of them has seen!

(Saxe, 1969)

We Need Continuing and Diverse Efforts to Understand the Culture and the Cultural Significance of the Internet

Internet pioneers and early adopters created a technology and a culture that was decentralized, unregulated, democratic, even "chaotic." The Web has been celebrated for the ability it affords any user not only to communicate with others, but also to post a web site and establish an enduring presence comparable in most regards to that of a major corporation.

However, we must recognize that as the Internet evolves, newcomers continually enter an online world that is different from the one that existed one, two, or five years earlier. Perhaps the unstructured and chaotic nature of the early public Internet that was so engaging to early adopters was a turn-off to others who waited until the Web developed the ability to provide more structured experiences. The distinction between earlier search engines and the recent development of portals provides an illustration.

As one of the first search engines, Alta Vista, established by Digital Equipment Corporation, was embraced by the online community because of the power of its ability to look for search strings in nearly every site on the Web. Alta Vista searches typically return astronomical numbers of "hits," webspeak for the sites that the search engine identified as containing the desired information. These searches usually yielded the information one sought (although not always on the first try) along with a great deal of unexpected, but often useful or interesting, information: an online form of lagniappe that early adopters often valued. The experience gained from just a handful of searches taught one how to separate the informational wheat from the search engine chaff.

The web portal, on the other hand, seems to follow a dictum of multichannel television, the idea that people have to know what's on in order to benefit from having a proliferation of channels. Of course, the Internet multiplies the idea of channels exponentially. Portals are being developed to function as aggregation devices, familiar online "base camps" or gathering places for the online, providing ease-of-use and convenience features that enable people to venture into the Web. At least in theory, a portal's perceived value will cause people to return to its base between missions into uncharted online territory.

As media devices, portals do not serve their corporate masters well if the online public quickly passes through them at the beginning of each web session. The idea is to provide a site so useful and compelling that users will come back to it again and again during each period of online activity. This suggests that portal sites will benefit from being very task oriented, pointing users at specific information and producing fewer serendipitous discoveries. Both portals and the related notion of media brands have their roots in the heyday of 20th-century American mass media.

In Chapter 10, Barry Vacker asked if the Internet represents a global village or a world bazaar. The former is a vision of the Internet as a force that will lead to a kind of shared global culture. While this may imply improved opportunities for world peace and understanding to some, mediated culture has many detractors. Criticism of broadly shared mediated cultural experience, particularly in countries with extensive commercial media systems like the United States, occupies the scholarly agendas of academicians from a number of disciplines. A different approach, cultivation theory, asserts that Americans, especially, live within a "common symbolic environment" created and maintained by television and that the opinions of those who watch the most tend to reflect the medium's distorted view of the world (Gerbner, Gross, Morgan, and Signorielli, 1994). The cultural impact of the worldwide distribution of American television content has been a major issue for nearly 50 years. While the American dominance of the Internet is lessening, the international online world will continue to reflect business models and practices pioneered in the United States for some time to come. The prediction by Cairncross (1997) that the international importance of English language will continue to grow due to the impact of technologies like the Internet is not welcome news in many countries in which their cultural heritage is considered precious, perhaps due to historic repression (The Coming Global Tongue, 1996).

Vacker's other idea, that of the Internet as a world bazaar, is a celebration of personal, national, social, and cultural diversity. Postrel (1999) describes people and their interests in terms of the classic bell curve. While people tend to cluster around the average, most have some ideas and interests that deviate from the norm. "Media gatekeepers," she contends, "yearn for the good old days of a 'common culture,' as defined by three TV networks and near-monopoly newspapers—a culture in which no one could see the out-liers. ... On the Net, the bell curve re-claims its tails. The uncommon is as accessible as the common" (p. 95).

Fortunately, it isn't necessary or inevitable that the Internet will fulfill only one of these visions; it is quite capable of serving both purposes simultane-ously. Those who value the free, unregulated, and decentralized nature of the Internet hope that this important new communication capability will be al-lowed to continue to celebrate its diversity and vitality. However, if we exam-ine carefully the history of media and information technologies we see that time and again we approach the new medium from the perspective of the practices and models of the old. Where the Internet is concerned we should re-member the observation (cleverly illustrated by McLuhan and Fiore, 1967) that we tend to drive into the future with our eyes fixed on the rear view mir-ror. Those who fear the openness and diversity of the Internet argue for its regulation from the perspective of broadcast media. Those who see the op-portunity in the Internet seek to exploit its potential as yet another commer-cial medium.

We Need to Examine Critically and Comprehensively the Commercialization of the Internet

Invoking a phrase popularized by the recent movie, *Jerry McGuire*, we could call this section, "follow the money!" One of the most far-reaching trends since the development of the World Wide Web has been the commercialization of the Internet. In the early era (mid 1990s), Netscape's Navigator web browser and myriad small start-up internet service providers (ISPs) breathed life into the new online industry, while Prodigy, Genie, CompuServe, and AOL pio-neered the online service industry. A small group of web design businesses be-gan creating web sites for larger firms, establishing standard formats for web content in the process. Other developers added new components, like Java ap-plets, frames, and streaming media, but the essential content elements of in-stitutional web sites have been fairly consistent during their short history. As businesses and individuals discovered the Web and the demand for Internet access grew, bigger corporate players muscled their way into the picture, acquiring or replacing many early industry participants. This consolidation has affected all of the most well-developed, successful, and promising commercial applications of the Internet: software, access, infrastructure providers, and online content.

It is quite clear that most forms of mediated communication will ultimately migrate to some form of packet-switched network and that the Web (or one or more Web-like networks) will become the primary entertainment portal to and from the household. While it will take some time to develop a distribution system with enough capacity to make this possible, the future web(s) will not only provide text and graphic information but also offer real-time video and audio. However, the Internet's model of the future of commercial media is dwarfed and will likely be engulfed by the Web's potential for online commerce. Noting the mounting losses incurred by the online ventures of traditional print and electronic media, Lyons (1999) reports that the advertising model of media is beginning to give way to an economic model increasingly based on commissions from direct sales.

Together, electronic commerce and media applications are the driving force behind the development of new infrastructure as well as Internet-related software and hardware (including personal computers). It would be naive to think that corporations are eager to attract newcomers to the ranks of online users simply because the Internet is a strong and empowering tool of personal expression and growth. Like all technologies, the Internet must achieve a critical mass of online users equipped with up-to-date forms of access in order to achieve the enormous commercial potential that has been predicted. This is just another way of saying that the value of the network is related to the number of users connected to it. Cheap computers, free browsers, and low-cost access are calculated efforts to recruit more inhabitants to the increasingly commercial online world.

As Albarran (Chapter 4) has noted, the predicted growth of online electronic commerce is constrained by policy concerns about taxation, the issues of the safety and security of electronic transactions, and the privacy of online shoppers. Technology enables businesses to develop customer databases that can be used to provide valuable services to consumers. Online vendors of books and music like Amazon.com routinely notify regular customers of the availability of new titles based upon recent purchases. Such databases become consumer concerns when the information contained in them is sold to other, unfamiliar businesses. In addition, databases may increasingly come to determine the amount that online consumers will pay for a product or service. Anyone who has shopped aggressively for the lowest air fares knows that ticket prices for any given flight can change daily, if not hourly, based at least in part on the supply of seats on the aircraft and the demand for them. Databases also enable vendors to know who is willing to pay higher prices and who is not. As a result, online bargains may be withheld from shoppers who do not regularly pursue the best buys (Wooley, 1998).

While Internet purists may decry the trend toward commercialization, most would admit that this development is all but unstoppable. The Internet has arrived in an era of limited government control and regulation of business activity in the United States, Europe, and increasingly in other regions of the world. It is quite possible that the Internet is sufficiently diverse and robust in its expandability that it will be able to continue to offer adequate opportunities for personal communication alongside the commercial development. However, we must all realize that spending time on the Internet is a bit like visiting a foreign country. The culture, laws, and regulations of the Web are not those of the nearest shopping mall or corner store, and the ancient admonition, buyer beware, applies.

The Internet Is a Work in Progress and Its Potential Should Be Continually Assessed and Reevaluated

Many observers of the Internet phenomenon continue to label as hype the enthusiastic predictions about the potential of the Net to impact life, work, and society. Our position is that until developed and proven, the Internet's potential is just that, potential. We have presented examples of how the Internet has fostered personal expression, collaboration, and shared experiences. Similarly, we can point to online forms of political expression and entrepreneurship as well as ambitious efforts to harness the teaching and learning potential of the Web. But we must remember that while the Internet continues to grow at a rapid rate throughout the world, we really have very little experience with it. Cairncross (1997) suggests watching for evidence of 30 mostly positive developments that may be fostered by new communications technologies, including global peace. But these developments will not occur overnight. In fact, Cairncross suggests that it will be nearly 50 years before "it will be quite clear what the broadest impacts of new communications have been" (p. 23). In a similar vein, Dizard (1997) has observed that the new communications infrastructure "is being assembled without any clear sense of the overall effect of its parts, including the Internet" (p. 192).

Every new medium has been welcomed with lofty predictions and imbued with great positive potential. Most have disappointed those with the greatest expectations. The same fate may await the Internet, especially if we fail to challenge and to critically evaluate claims about its potential. For all of the excitement about the significance of electronic commerce, it must be disappointing to many of the Internet's strongest advocates that online pornography has been one of this technology's biggest commercial successes. While we recommend that the Internet's potential be continually assessed through ongoing research by a diverse cross section of the scholarly community, we also believe that the Internet's potential will not be realized if the online community at large accepts it as passively as the public accepted television.

A Compelling Need Exists for Internet Literacy

Once issues of Internet access are resolved (and as several contributors have noted, this is no small matter), the value of the Internet will be determined by what people do with it. The Internet is vast, and its capabilities are many and varied. The early Internet adopters and even the early majority (in diffusion of innovation terms) are most likely the kind of people who are comfortable with technologies and bring to them a curiosity and desire for exploration and understanding. Many of these early users learned about the Internet just by going online and spending time there. Other Internet adopters, the curious but timid, needed and found some help in learning their way around the online world from organizations, continuing education efforts of schools, and from other interest groups. Schoolchildren have been introduced to the Internet in large numbers, and many have helped their parents discover the Web.

However, learning how to send e-mail and how to surf the Web represent only the first steps toward Internet literacy. Because the Internet is a place with different cultures as well as minimal and difficult-to-enforce regulations, people must be equipped with a complete and accurate understanding of the online world. Internet literacy should be taught at all levels of formal instruction and should be encouraged in all types of informal instruction. *Understanding the Web* is an effort to provide a thorough examination of the social, political, and economic significance of the Internet as it relates to individuals, groups, nations, and the global community. At a minimum, these topics should form the core of efforts to develop Internet literacy. We hope that advocates of Internet literacy are more successful in the days ahead than were those who promoted general media literacy in the past. It is our wish that our volume will be joined in the marketplace of ideas by many other thoughtful analyses of the Internet phenomenon and that the teaching and learning influenced by our work and that of others to follow will truly foster understanding the Web.

References

Cairncross, F. 1997. *The Death of Distance: How the Communications Revolution Will Change Our Lives*. Boston: Harvard Business School Press.

The Coming Global Tongue. 1996, December 21. *Economist,* pp. 75–78. Retrieved December 28, 1996, from online database *Academic Search FullTEXT Elite* [EBSCO Industries, Inc.].

Dizard, W.P. 1997. *Meganet: How the Global Communications Network Will Connect Everyone on Earth*. Boulder, CO: Westview Press.

Gerbner, G.; Gross, L.; Morgan, M.; and Signorielli, N. 1994. Growing Up with Television: The Cultivation Perspective. In Bryant, J., and Zillman, D., eds. *Media Effects: Advances in Theory and Research*. 17–41. Hillsdale, NJ: Erlbaum.

Lyons, D. 1999, March 22. Desperate.com. *Forbes,* 163(6): 50–51.

McLuhan, M., and Fiore, Q. 1967. *The Medium Is the Massage: An Inventory of Effects*. New York: Bantam.

Postrel, V. 1999, February 22. Alone but Not Lonely. *Forbes ASAP,* 163 (4): 95.

Saxe, J.G. 1963. *The Blind Men and the Elephant.* New York: Whittlesey House.

Wooley, S. 1998, November 2. I Got It Cheaper Than You. *Forbes,* 162(10): 82, 84.

Index